# Capital Offenses

*Victorian Literature and Culture Series*
Jerome J. McGann and Herbert Tucker, Editors

# CAPITAL OFFENSES

Geographies of Class and Crime
in Victorian London

**Simon Joyce**

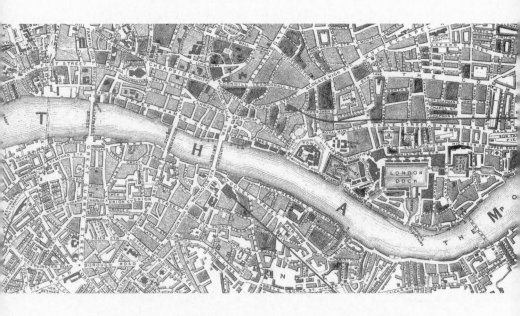

UNIVERSITY OF VIRGINIA PRESS
*Charlottesville and London*

University of Virginia Press
© 2003 by the Rector and Visitors of the University of Virginia
All rights reserved
Printed in the United States of America on acid-free paper
*First published 2003*

9 8 7 6 5 4 3 2 1

LIBRARY OF CONGRESS CATALOGING-IN-PUBLICATION DATA

Joyce, Simon, 1963 –
   Capital offenses : geographies of class and crime in Victorian London /
Simon Joyce.
      p.    cm. — (Victorian literature and culture series)
Includes bibliographical references (p.  ) and index.
   ISBN 0-8139-2180-5 (acid-free paper)
   1. English fiction—19th century—History and criticism.  2. Crime
in literature.  3. English fiction—England—London—History and
criticism.  4. Literature and society—England—London—History—
19th century.  5. Detective and mystery stories, English—History and
criticism.  6. Social Classes—England—London—History—19th century.
7. London (England)—Social conditions—19th century.  8. Crime—
England—London—History—19th century.  9. London (England)—
In literature.  10. Place (Philosophy) in literature.  11. Geography in
literature.  12. Criminals in literature.  I. Title.  II. Series.
   PR878.C74 J69 2003
   823'.80932—dc21

2002154237

# Contents

# Acknowledgments

I MAKE THE POINT early on in *Capital Offenses* that any simple catalog, like those that sought to represent the variety of people who came together in a modern city like London, is inevitably a difficult proposition. This one is no different. Simple amalgamations of people, side by side or in alphabetical order, often impose an abstract sense of equality where none actually exists. Principles of differentiation, though, inevitably impose hierarchies and value judgments. In the list that follows, I have tried to overlap a chronological sequence of debts incurred during the writing of this book with a geographical one, highlighting the spaces in which it was conceived and produced; this seems the best way to organize such a heterogeneous catalog of thanks, even if it sometimes means that colleagues (fellow students and teachers) end up sitting next to committee members and mentors, lifelong friends alongside those who provided more localized and immediate forms of support. I can only hope that everyone listed understands why they are here, and what they have contributed to this project.

In searching for a point of origin, I have to settle on the 1980s, and the memorable intellectual experience of the University of Sussex. Countless times since, and especially while writing this book, I have been reminded of the ways that my thinking was shaped by a remarkable group of teachers and students, in particular Jonathan Dollimore, Stella Fry,

Martin Huseyin and Fiona Morton (later also superb hosts during repeated trips to London), Alan Sinfield, and the late Allon White. Crossing the Atlantic, I found another supportive network of people at the University of Buffalo who helped me in every conceivable way to map out the contours of this particular project: Stephanie Foote, Jim Holstun, Deidre Lynch, Roy Roussel, and Janet Sorensen. Richard Maxwell originally signed on as outside reader for a dissertation, and has volunteered countless kindnesses and acts of support ever since.

During five years in Texas, when this final version was written, my work was sustained in particular by Bonnie Blackwell, Neil Easterbrook, Sharon Harris, Linda Hughes, Jenny Putzi, Alan Shepard, and Gary Tate; I am also very grateful to Lisa Thompson and all of those involved in Texas Christian University's London Centre, for teaching opportunities that allowed me to test and revise some of these arguments. Friends, editors, and colleagues at other institutions form another heterogeneous list: Jim Adams, Amanda Anderson, Martin Danahay, Barry Faulk, Stanley Friedman, Peter Garrett, Jesse Lander, Bill Maxwell, Joanne Slutszky, Joe Valente, and Julia Walker. Cathie Brettschneider at Virginia was patient, tactful, and kept me on track during the final stages.

I am grateful to the following for allowing portions of this book to be reprinted: an early version of chapter 2, "Resisting Arrest/Arresting Resistance: Crime Fiction, Cultural Studies, and the 'Turn to History,'" was published in *Criticism,* and is reprinted with the permission of Wayne State University Press; chapter 3 appeared as "Inspector Bucket versus Tom-all-Alone's: *Bleak House,* Literary Theory, and the Condition-of-England in the 1850s" in *Dickens Studies Annual,* and is reprinted with the permission of AMS Press; part of chapter 4 was first published in *ELH* as "Sexual Politics and the Aesthetics of Crime: Oscar Wilde in the Nineties," and is reprinted with the permission of Johns Hopkins University Press; while a section of chapter 5 appeared as "Castles in the Air: The People's Palace, Cultural Reformism, and the East End Working Class" in *Victorian Studies,* and is reprinted with the permission of Indiana University Press.

Finally, back to the beginning. The Borthwicks and Joyces have given me a measureless inheritance of independent thinking and radical questioning, and a supportive family structure. For all of this, I am very grateful.

May the road rise with you all.

# Capital Offenses

# INTRODUCTION

## A Literary Geography

IN RECENT YEARS, literary studies has begun to speak of a critical engagement with work that has more traditionally been undertaken in departments of geography. Postcolonial criticism has attended to the relationship between the cultural works produced in the former and current imperial centers and those that have emerged from their former dependencies. Urban studies has also had an influence: considering only the literature that relates to nineteenth-century London, we might note recent books by Judith Walkowitz, Deborah Epstein Nord, Julian Wolfreys, and Lynda Nead that have seen the cultural representations of social space as closely tied to the lived experience of the capital, and most notably the experience of an emerging group of "social actors" (including women and immigrants) who gained a new form of access to its streets.[1] Complementing these efforts, Franco Moretti's *Atlas of the European Novel, 1800–1900* has proposed the project of a "literary geography," in which, instead of being relegated to the background of literary analysis, as the mere "setting" for narrative, representations of physical space are seen as actively involved in shaping textual meaning. As Moretti argues, seeing geographical patterns—where Austen's novels begin and end, for example, or the residences of characters in Dickens—can help us to read texts in a new light or give weight to already-suspected meanings: thus, the relative lack of movement on the part of Austen's heroines tells us something about a restricted marriage market, while the grouping of Dickensian figures in the East and West ends of London illustrates the extent to which the center is reserved for work and for lower-middle-class professionals.[2]

Moretti's project intersects in interesting ways with Fredric Jameson's study of "cognitive mapping," a term which he borrows from Kevin Lynch's work in urban geography in order to diagnose the particular insecurities of postmodern living. For Lynch, cities are analyzable in terms of their relative "legibility" or "imageability," with an easily comprehensible environment appearing as "well formed, distinct, remarkable. . . . Such a city would be one that could be apprehended over time as a pattern of high continuity with many distinctive parts clearly interconnected. The perceptive and familiar observer could absorb new sensuous impacts without disruption of his [sic] basic image, and each new impact would touch upon many previous elements."[3] Anxiety increases in city-dwellers when they no longer have a clear map of how the major trajectories, borders, and districts stand in relation to each other, and when their sense of the city as a whole ceases to function as a coherent and organizing frame of reference.

Jameson's major contribution to the theory of "cognitive mapping" has been to align this potential for conflict between the individual and the environment with the history of capital. Writing of twentieth-century multinationalism, he notes how imperialist expansion and the shift to a global form of monopoly capitalism has introduced a growing disjunction between immediate subjective experience and a worldwide economic structure. The sense of a centered subject is increasingly threatened under these circumstances, Jameson argues, since individuals are no longer able to account for their lived experience purely within its own terms.[4] In this context, cultural representations perform a mapping function which is needed in order to bridge between the specificity of individual experience and the totality of geo-social space in which the subject is situated. Such representations are particularly necessary and problematic for the classically modern experiences of urban alienation and self-isolation, which arise directly out of the unmappability of the urban environment. At different points in time, including for Jameson the moment of postmodernism or late capitalism with its tendency to suppress distance and to saturate social space with "a perceptual barrage of immediacy," this inability of the subject to comprehend and delineate a surrounding totality initiates a representational crisis. New ideologies, spatial models, and figures are thus required at the moment when the paradigms of lived experience shift, and the geo-social totality is no longer subsumable beneath older cultural and representational concepts.

As we shall see, this theoretical approach is richly suggestive for the study of nineteenth-century London, and is in many ways an amplifi-cation of tendencies and perceptions that were first registered by visitors like Wordsworth and Engels. The capital experienced a rapid and largely unplanned population expansion of around 20 percent between 1820 and 1840, due largely to an influx of peoples from rural areas of Britain and its colonial territories.[5] The sheer novelty of this agglomeration of peo-ples during the first half of the nineteenth century gave rise to equally new forms of urban journalism and fiction, most obviously associated with Dickens and the urban sketch, and gave impetus to new models of social scientific investigation, such as the cataloging of city populations and trades, first undertaken by Henry Mayhew in the 1840s. As Julian Wolfreys notes, the inverse of these efforts can be glimpsed in the per-sistence of a kind of "citephobia" from the romantics onwards, with the two impulses combining in a characteristic imtermixing of attraction and repulsion. "As the city imposes its images for confused recitation," Wol-freys suggests, "so the subject, compelled by the motion which writes the city as always already a palimpsest of itself barely caught in the act of a constant reinvention, catalogues the urban movements, vanishing in the act of writing the city, caught up in the anxiety over this confronta-tion with the unfolding difference and alterity."[6]

The desire for mapping, cognitive and literal, would seem natural, given this terrifying displacement of self. Since Dickens, at least, it has been a key component of the literature of city life that it provide its read-ers with such maps, often in the form of shorthand metaphors and con-densations that allow the larger totality to appear knowable. Thus, the earlier conjoining of the City of London with Westminster that formed the boundaries of the modern metropolis was rewritten as the uneasy encounter between its polarized West and East ends; this in turn gets par-ticularized in a rhetorical trope linking the slum of St. Giles with the palaces of St. James; later, a center/periphery model emerges with the development of outlying suburbs, which are connected to the city proper via the new system of railways; and so on. In Franco Moretti's reading, the plotting of Dickens's novels reveals these spatial models in quite literal ways: whereas an early novel like *Oliver Twist* tends to cut off the fashionable West End from its poor relation to the east, for instance, *Our Mutual Friend* fills in what Moretti terms "the third London," "a sort of wedge, that holds the two extremes together."[7] Not surprisingly, this is the city that Dickens knew best, and one that his bourgeois readers would also recognize: it is the London of the working middle class (lawyers, bankers, clerks, shopkeepers, journalists) and a space where the antagonisms of mutual misrecognition and suspicion hopefully begin to dissolve. Indeed, as I shall show in chapter 1, the romantic literature and journalism that first sought to anatomize "life in London" was also drawn to this central "third," such as the east-west arteries of the Strand, Fleet Street, and (after its construction in the 1840s) New Oxford Street, as the site for utopian projections of a harmonious and classless city.

London, then, is mapped: in literal ways by surveyors, architects, builders, cartographers; and in more figurative ways by novelists, journalists, sociologists, government investigators. I am primarily concerned here with that latter group of texts, as cultural artifacts that are both distinct from and also an extension of the former. Work in critical geography has recently come to see that maps are in fact texts, and therefore open to interpretation in much the same ways as novels or paintings. As Brian Harley has pointed out, "All maps strive to frame their message in the context of an audience. All maps state an argument about the world, and they are propositional in nature. All maps employ the common devices of rhetoric such as invocations of authority . . . selection, omission, simplification, classification, the creation of hierarchies, and 'symbolization.'"[8] Invoking Foucault, he goes on to argue that maps embody forms of power—to name, define, frame, and color—that seem largely consistent with the ideal of Bentham's Panopticon, where the guiding principle is that authority emanates from a central space that is invisible to those on whom it is exercised, and just possibly empty. If mapmakers have traditionally mimicked such authority, Harley concludes, a critical geography would need to be attuned to the role played by maps "in shaping mental structures, and in imparting a sense of the places of the world" which blocks the circulation of alternative visions and definitions (244–45).

If they seem to originate—like the omniscient narration in classical realist novels—from a point that is everywhere and nowhere, maps explicitly foreground their own use function. While they usually omit the marker "YOU ARE HERE" that would clarify the position of the addressee in relation to the text, they nonetheless allow the user to locate her- or himself in relation to the larger totality of space, as Lynch and Jameson suggest. What weakens the more paranoid sense articulated by Harley that they are only the embodiments of power, then, is the simple fact that maps are *read,* from a variety of subject positions and with an equal variety of interests and motives in play.[9] In an investigation of the visual iconography of late-nineteenth-century London that parallels my own, Lynda Nead usefully summarizes two approaches to the mapping of social space: one is "the panoramic," which "fixes the viewer in a single spot from which the appearance of the city slowly unfolds in a kind of narrative circuit"; the other, a "geometric" approach in which "the city is given in its entirety, simultaneously. . . . There is no specific viewpoint; for the view is everywhere and unmarked."[10] The former is often more "Panoptic" in its effects, as for instance when a city is represented from a hot-air balloon or in satellite footage, while the latter superficially appears more "democratic" in its flattening out of social as well as geographic space. What I term a "fantasy of access" plays out here, with the illusion that any point on the map is as "good" as any other. As I argue in chapter 1, cultural representations that pretend to the second approach—claiming merely to catalog peoples or regions, for instance—in reality have the specific point-of-view of the panoramic approach encoded within them. As we know of narration, discourse always emanates from somewhere, and is equally addressed to specific audiences—again, such readerships are relatively easy to specify for the new urban literature of the romantic period, addressed as it is largely to the bourgeois public that worked and lived in Dickens's "middle third."

Hence a second theoretical distinction I draw from Nead's work (this one ultimately originating with Michel de Certeau): that "the controlling, aerial viewpoint of the city planner" needs to be set against "the point of view of the walker at street level" (75). Whatever political/power interests the former might actually serve, those will not necessarily be registered at the point of reception or actual use; people routinely deface maps, tear them, write over them in ways that derail their intended meaning, in much the same way that readers do with texts. Such a model of reception, identified by Stuart Hall and the Birmingham School of cultural studies as "encoding/decoding," directs us back to practices of reading and the social formations and spaces within which it occurs.[11] A cultural text rarely (if ever) simply advances an ideological agenda, and whatever intentions may have originally animated it are never simply read off by its readers, even if it could somehow manage to precisely identify its target audience. In this sense, Colin Mercer suggests that we abandon the conventional typology by which we seek to differentiate supposedly "progressive" from "reactionary" cultural texts, and focus instead on "the range of techniques [deployed] for configuring the narratives of people, populations, cities, classes, topographies."[12] A simple "political" reading, Mercer notes, cannot allow for the "host of technologies involved in the elaboration of 'occasions of reading'— the range of domestic, public, topographical determinants upon such occasions."[13]

Again, this is not geography as simply the holding in place of the reading subject, as it might be for a Foucauldian criticism,[14] but as one possible function of the text. The extent to which it could successfully perform such a function would depend upon how easily it intersected with those other aspects of the "reading scene": the gender and social class of the reader, the pre-existing beliefs that the reader brings to the text, and so on. As I argue in chapter 2, these other determinants are often unpredictable and might appear unconnected to the text itself: thus, a wide variety of readers (including reviewers, dramatical adapters, and plagiarists) insistently interpreted *Oliver Twist* through the context of the agitation of the Chartists, even when the novel has next to nothing to say about that movement's political aims. If part of Dickens's project was, as Moretti claims, to highlight the increasing polarization of London into East and West Ends, however, then this spatial figure had a clear resonance with the idea that Britain itself was splitting into "two nations," in Disraeli's famous phrase. To the extent that Dickens might have encouraged some sympathy for his criminal characters, that might also shade into support for the Chartists' claims for universal manhood suffrage, and anger at unrepresentative political and legal institutions.[15] I do not mean to place undue emphasis on the example of Dickens's novel here, except to illustrate the ways that *Capital Offenses* attends to questions of reading formations, rather than simply seeking to read off ideological meanings from the content of Victorian crime novels. As is the case with maps, we need to be aware of what uses such texts were put to, as well as the ways that they attempted to reflect, represent, construct, and *re*-construct the social geographies of nineteenth-century London.

Geography has always been a crucial element of crime and detective fiction, but has been largely treated symbolically, to highlight the contrast (for instance) between the rural country houses of an Agatha Christie and the urban "mean streets" of a Dashiell Hammett. When Moretti turns his attention to the Sherlock Holmes stories, which are inseparably linked with London in the cultural imagination, he interestingly discovers that they are largely set in the fashionable West End of the capital or the affluent rural counties of Kent, Surrey, and Sussex. This book sets out to explain why that should be. The literary map of crime which Conan Doyle is sketching in these stories is strikingly at odds, after all, with the social maps of class which were being drawn during the same period, as Moretti's comparative example of Charles Booth's *Life and Labour of the People of London* (1889) makes clear. If an underlying assumption of empirical sociologists like Booth, or Henry Mayhew before him, was that a correlation existed between criminal activity, geographical residence, and social conditions (rates of employment and wages, housing and living conditions, the presence or absence of social amenities, and so on), then it is interesting to see the popular literature of the period trying so strenuously to deny such a link. An environmental causality is assumed in one model, and actively undermined in the other, which prefers to view criminality in terms of an individual pathology. Indeed, as chapters 4 and 5 show, crime was increasingly pathologized in fiction and the emerging social sciences, as a result not only of the dominant beliefs of contemporary medicine and psychology, but also in order to disrupt the habitual associations between class and crime that had grown up in the 1840s and '50s. In the popular fiction of a quarter century later, criminals are likely to emanate not only from outside the city itself, but also from the privileged classes: Professor Moriarty, Dr. Jekyll, Dorian Gray, and (later) E. W. Hornung's aristocratic burglar Raffles.

There is an easy—but ultimately unsatisfactory—explanation for this, which would stress that crime and detective stories are simply escapist fictions, written for the benefit of a privileged readership who did not want to read about the realities of life in the impoverished streets of South or East London; they wanted crime to be something which could be solved, not a problem which is endemic to society and for which they might share some measure of responsibility. There is surely some truth to this, but it only explains half of the story. After all, one consequence of breaking the connection between class and crime is that the criminals need now to be drawn from the comfortable classes themselves, although those in Conan Doyle frequently turn out to impostors, mad, or (even better) foreign. This explanation also fails to account for the existence of studies like Mayhew's or Booth's, which appear periodically throughout the nineteenth century, generally around times of economic recession and crisis. A fascination with lower-class culture and the neighborhoods in which it developed thrived alongside a simultaneous impulse to banish them from thought and sight; indeed, I will be arguing that *forgetting* about the East End was a precondition for subsequent moments of crisis at which it could be rediscovered, reexamined, and remapped. As chapter 5 suggests, the complement to the figure of the privileged offender emerges with the hard-edged naturalist novels of the 1880s and '90s, by which time a criminal pathology can be extended to encompass an entire geographical area, like Arthur Morrison's "the Jago." [16]

This rediscovery of East London, like Freud's return of the repressed, occurs at regular intervals throughout the nineteenth century. Friedrich Engels's *Condition of the Working-Class in England in 1844* quotes an East End clergyman as suggesting that before the bishop of London "called the attention of the public to the state of Bethnal-green, about as little was known at the West-end of the town of this most destitute parish as the wilds of Australia or the islands of the South Seas." [17] Ten years later, Dickens is making much the same point in *Bleak House* with his condemnation of a "telescopic philanthropy" that paid more attention to "the Tockahoopo Indians" than to the fate of a poor London crossing-sweeper under its very nose. I discuss the novel in the pivotal third chapter of *Capital Offenses,* but strikingly similar passages and metaphors can be found later in the book, and later in the century as well: thus, George Sims's *How the Poor Live* directed a renewed attention in the 1880s to East London as "a dark continent that is within easy walking distance of the

Post Office," [18] while William Booth's *In Darkest London, and the Way Out* made explicit the parallels between the East End and Africa in the 1890s, commenting that "[t]he lot of the Negress in the Equatorial Forest is not, perhaps, a very happy one, but is it so very much worse than that of many a pretty orphan girl in our Christian capital?" [19] In this context, "escapism" seems to be a limited option, which would be undermined as soon as economic conditions took a turn for the worse and commentators began to worry (again) about discontent among the London poor. It is no coincidence that these discoveries coincide with larger fears of popular unrest, associated with Chartism in the 1840s and with the New Unionism in the 1880s and '90s.

It seems more accurate, then, to suggest that the principle of escapism embodied in detective fiction developed alongside, and even benefited from, a countervailing desire to learn more about the lives of the urban poor. The history of Victorian London, as I reconstruct it here, gives ample testimony to this fascinating coexistence of antagonistic impulses, attraction and repulsion. Schemes of urban planning, building, transport systems, and policing all testify to the long-standing ambition to separate the rich from the poor, and (as Moretti's mapping of Dickens makes plain) to introduce an intervening buffer zone. Eighteenth-century housing bills and proclamations against new building in the East End revealed what Raymond Williams has termed "a prolonged struggle, by ruling-class interests, to restrain the growth of London, and in particular to prevent the poor settling there," but this was clearly a losing battle. As the population continued to migrate to the capital for work, unsafe and overcrowded buildings to the east increasingly contrasted with the fashionable squares and terraces of the Georgian period which grew up to the north and west of the city's commercial center. [20] In time, overcrowded pockets of poverty also developed in the heart of central London, including the infamous criminal "rookeries" of St. Giles and Seven Dials which both bordered on Bloomsbury and Mayfair.

Such shifts in the "character" (or class composition) of neighborhoods could happen very quickly, as the example of Soho illustrates. Once a respectable residential area, it was rapidly vacated after an outbreak of cholera in the 1850s and rebuilt as a commercial center. It was a haven in the late nineteenth century for successive waves of immigrants, including Marx in the mid-fifties, French radicals following the fall of the Paris Commune in 1871, Swiss patriots, European Jews, Greeks, Italians, and (more recently) Chinese. In the twentieth century it veered in and out of fashion, as the center respectively of the British film industry, "swinging London" during the 1950s and '60s, the sex industry, and British media and advertising.[21] In literature, it is perhaps not surprising that Soho is home to two celebrated split personalities: the evil double in Stevenson's *Dr. Jekyll and Mr. Hyde* (1886), who doubtless saw it as the perfect cover for a life of crime, as well as a convenient distance from Jekyll's West End surgery; and Adolphe Verloc of Conrad's *The Secret Agent* (1907), who juggles careers as an anarchist, police informant, and peddler of pornography. One benefit of a "literary geography" is that it can explain why it is appropriate that the double lives of Verloc or Hyde are located in an equally schizophrenic area like Soho. Like St. Giles and Seven Dials earlier in the century, the area effectively functioned as a kind of double agent in the heart of the city center, harboring the immigrant populations (Verloc, for example, is a European refugee) and criminality—ranging from the sensational murders of Mr. Hyde to the mundane pornography peddled in Verloc's shop—which would preferably be banished to the hinterlands of Whitechapel or Bethnal Green.

Why, Joseph McLaughlin asks, does Conrad choose Soho over the East London dockland locations that would have been familiar to him from his days as a sailor?[22] An attempted bombing of the Greenwich Observatory, like that at the center of *The Secret Agent,* actually occurred in 1894, but Conrad sets the novel almost ten years earlier, when public attention was focused on Whitechapel and the East End. After the Jack the Ripper murders of 1888, as I show in chapter 4, a retroactive reinterpretation of *Dr. Jekyll and Mr. Hyde* focused on the similarities between the killer and Stevenson's protagonist: if, as was widely thought, the Ripper was a "gentleman," then he must have arisen—like Mr. Hyde—from another section of London and a radically different social milieu. (Speculations about the Ripper murders coincided with the literary vogue of the privileged offender, as well as with the immense popularity of Sherlock Holmes.) By the time of Conrad's novel, the idea "of there arising in West London a sort of East London" in the shape of Soho had clearly entered the popular imagination.[23] Ironically, the attack on the observatory is (as Ronald Thomas suggests) an attack on "the authority of geography" itself, as exemplified by the Greenwich meridian;[24] in a novel so saturated with the plotting of geographical locations—from Verloc's Soho shop to the foreign embassies bordering Hyde Park—such an attempt is destined for futility. If there is a net result of the bombing, it is that the authorities might get to rid Britain of the spies and double agents who operate under the cover of the embassies, even if the larger goal of Verloc's embassy paymaster Vladimir, that the country sacrifice civil liberties for a greater feeling of security from crime, fails to materialize.

The more insidious form of surveillance that continues in its place, whereby Inspector Heat can boast of being able to get hold of all of London's anarchists at a moment's notice, might seem to confirm Foucault's thesis that the dispersal of power represents its strength, and not its diminution. Yet we are left with the image of the Professor, free to pass "unsuspected and deadly, like a pest in the street full of men" with his detonator primed and his thoughts "caress[ing] the images of ruin and destruction."[25] Fantasies in which crime is fully contained recur endlessly in nineteenth-century crime fiction, but even Sherlock Holmes has to return time and time again (eventually even out of retirement) to fight new menaces. The nature of the threat is not constant, arising at different times in the East and West Ends, among the destitute poor and the dissolute rich. As the nature of criminality shifts, so too do the presumed and the actual responses of readers, who might be asked at various times to sympathize with criminals, to condemn them, to endorse the tactics of the police, to bemoan their incompetence (especially in contrast to a private detective like Holmes), or to push for legislative change. If such appeals depend upon historical context, they are also articulated through a precise attention to geographical specificities: not just those that are represented in texts, but those of the readers themselves.

# 1  MAPPING THE CAPITAL CITY

ACCOUNTS OF MODERNITY are notoriously varied, depending on when and where it is first thought to emerge and which of its defining features are foregrounded. Modernity might be correlated with stability or with rupture, with a unified or fragmented subject, with a teleological or a discontinuous model of historical development.[1] Often, it is the paradoxical sum of such contrary impulses, born out of an incoherent or internally divided inheritance passed down from the Enlightenment. An early but still influential account, useful here because it focuses on the experience of metropolitan life at the outset of the nineteenth century, is Georg Simmel's. Whereas "[t]he eighteenth century found the individual in oppressive bonds which had become meaningless—bonds of a political, agrarian, guild, and religious character," Enlightenment models of freedom instead promised a liberation that would allow "the noble substance common to all to come to the fore, a substance which nature had deposited in every man and which society and history had only deformed." Such an "ideal of liberation," which animated the emergent republican and workers' organizations in Britain, came in conflict with a countervailing ideology of the nineteenth century, which placed the stress instead on individuation and difference: "Individuals who had been liberated from historical bonds," according to Simmel, "now wished to distinguish themselves from one another."

The conflict between these two modes of thought might be seen as inhering within the ideology of romanticism, but it is Simmel's great insight to see it being played out in a space which seems at first glance entirely alien to romantic sensibilities: the modern metropolis. It was, he argued, the new urban space of the city (and first of all, London) that served as "the arena for this struggle and its reconciliation. For the metropolis presents the peculiar conditions which are revealed to us as the opportunities and the stimuli for the development of both these ways of allocating roles to men [*sic*]."[2] In this chapter, I want to consider in more detail how these twin models of subjective identity, and the larger ideals of collective liberation or differentiated individualism which they articulate, are played out in the accounts of two visitors (William Wordsworth and Friedrich Engels), before going on to suggest some of the key terms and images by which the totality of London was conventionally comprehended in the period: via the opposition between its East and West Ends, in particular; or through the alliterative pairing of the slum of St. Giles with the palaces of St. James; and—as the beginning of the railways opened up new possibilities for commuting—an increasing distinction between the urban and commercial center and its rural or suburban periphery.

In the work of two very different writers like Engels and Wordsworth, what is immediately evident is a combination of excitement and anxiety that is characteristic of urban writing in the first half of the nineteenth century, and indeed will resonate in modified forms through just about all of the texts I will be discussing. Book 7 of the original 1805 text of Wordsworth's *The Prelude* offers an account of his short residence in the capital, which was noticeably muted in later editions of the poem. A sense of youthful enthusiasm is still apparent here as Wordsworth sets out to recapture "the look and aspect of the place,"

> The broad high-way appearance, as it strikes
> On Strangers of all ages, the quick dance
> Of colours, lights and forms, the Babel din
> The endless stream of men, and moving things,
> From hour to hour the illimitable walk
> Still among streets with clouds and sky above.

Already, Wordsworth's experience is marked by speed and confusion, so that sense perception struggles to keep up with the pace, as shapes and sounds blur into each other and "men" seem indistinguishable from "things."

One possible response is simply to go with the flow and attempt as far as possible to merge with the crowds, thereby enabling a collective identification and even a form of liberation—the response, as we shall see, of the urban flâneur. The alternative approach takes up the other side of Simmel's dialectic and insists on differentiation and distance: it seeks out a privileged vantage-point above or away from the crowds in order to catalog the life of the city, and is thus a form of retreat from the mass and into the self. The passage from *The Prelude* continues in this vein, as Wordsworth describes

> The wealth, the bustle and the eagerness,
> The glittering Chariots with their pamper'd Steeds,
> Stalls, Barrows, Porters; . . .
> Here there and everywhere a weary throng
> The Comers and Goers face to face,
> Face after face; the string of dazzling Wares,
> Shop after shop, with Symbols, blazon'd Names,
> And all the Tradesman's honours overhead;
> . . . There, allegoric shapes, female or male;
> Or physiognomies of real men,
> Land-Warriors, Kings, or Admirals of the Sea,
> Boyle, Shakespear, Newton, or the attractive head
> Of some Scotch doctor, famous in his day.[3]

A couple of points need to be made here. The first is that Wordsworth now restores a sense of perspective, in order to distinguish what's "here" from "there": objects are now placed in a landscape, instead of merging into each other as in the previous passage. These catalogs are also endlessly repeatable, since they simply list a set of objects which are made available to the spectating gaze. Later, we are given similar inventories of animals (dogs, dromedaries, monkeys), nationalities (Italians, Jews, Turks . . . ), performers (saw-singers, rope-dancers, giants, dwarfs . . . ), professions (lawyers, judges, senators), and public places (halls, courts, shops, parks) which are also offered up as part of the spectacle of London. Within the terms of the catalog, people and commodities—"faces" and "wares"—are again taken as interchangeable, each reduced to the external appearance of the physiognomical sketch or shop-window advertisement. There would seem to be a process of cultural leveling in operation here, in which Shakespeare and "some Scotch doctor," "real men" and "allegoric shapes," can function as metonymic equals, united by their recognizable use value in helping to promote, endorse, and sell products.

Such a leveling of social or aesthetic status is, however, only apparent in *The Prelude*. This, after all, is the same Wordsworth who had warned four years earlier (in the preface to the *Lyrical Ballads*) that "a multitude of causes, unknown to former times, are now acting with a combined force to blunt the discriminating powers of the mind, and unfitting it for all voluntary exertion to reduce it to a state of almost savage torpor": predominant among such causes, he names "the great national events which are daily taking place, and the increasing accumulation of men in cities, where the uniformity of their occupations produces a craving for extraordinary incident, which the rapid communication of intelligence hourly gratifies."[4] As Dana Brand has argued, Wordsworth is offering an early critique of a modern urban culture here, in which a wide variety of events and information has been flattened out so that each takes on an identical or exchangeable status as an expendable commodity. In an insight usually associated at the end of the nineteenth century with Charles Baudelaire, or in the twentieth with a high modernist like T. S. Eliot, Wordsworth delineates a new form of subjectivity developing out of the spectacular processes of centralization and commodification associated with city life: its defining characteristics, as Brand suggests, are almost entirely passive, and based in new and indiscriminate forms of perception, reception, and consumption that "can only find interest in the way in which each moment differs, grossly and violently, from previous moments . . . in the perpetual liberation from context and continuity that 'extraordinary incident' provides."[5] At the outset of the nineteenth century, then, Wordsworth already identifies the important features by which Simmel would characterize the mental life of the metropolis a hundred years later: the "swift and uninterrupted change of outer and inner stimuli" which registers on consciousness as a simple succession of differences, "the rapid crowding of changing images," the "unexpectedness of onrushing impressions," and so on.[6]

This is a negative experience for Wordsworth, paralleling the process by which (as he argues in the preface) "the works of Shakespeare and

Milton" have been "driven into neglect by frantic novels, sickly and stupid German tragedies, and deluges of idle and extravagant stories in verse." He viewed his cultural project as an attempt to restore such hierarchies of taste and to reimpose divisions among the audience for literature, stressing the processes of differentiation that (for Simmel) countered the democratizing impulse of the Enlightenment. In his "Essay, Supplementary to the Preface" of 1815, Wordsworth speaks of "creating the taste" for his poetry, and indeed part of what defines the ideology of romanticism is its appeal to a narrow minority of readers—Coleridge's clerisy comes to mind, or Shelley's invocation of "the more select classes of poetical readers" for *Prometheus Unbound*—which is deliberately defined against the debased tastes of the masses.[7] By the time of the supplemental essay, then, it is not surprising to find that Wordsworth had abandoned any earlier ambitions of finding favor with "the Public," preferring to invest his hopes in "the People, philosophically characterized": as Martha Woodmansee argues, the shift is away from history and the literary marketplace as well as from the urban masses, in a circular strategy which makes "the measure of literary merit the kind of veneration a (transhistorical) people, or nation, extends to its classics."[8]

In *The Prelude,* after invoking "the Muses' help" to lodge him "Above the press and danger of the Crowd / Upon some Showman's platform" (bk. 7; ll. 658–59), Wordsworth performs a similar act of disengagement from the masses, looking down on a carnival spectacle which is becoming increasingly monstrous:

> —All moveables of wonder from all parts,
> Are here, Albinos, painted Indians, Dwarfs,
> The Horse of Knowledge, and the learned Pig . . .
> The Wax-work, Clock-work, all the marvellous craft
> Of modern Merlins, wild Beasts, Puppet-shows
> All out-o'-th'-way, far-fetch'd, perverted things,
> All freaks of Nature, all Promethean thoughts
> Of man; his dulness, madness, and their feats
> All jumbled up together to make up
> This Parliament of Monsters. (ll. 680–92)

This, we learn, might usefully represent "a type not false / Of what the mighty City itself is" to its inhabitants,

Living amid the same perpetual flow
Of trivial objects, melted and reduced
To one identity, by differences
That have no law, no meaning, and no end. (ll. 696–705)

London, finally, is simply the site of this "blank confusion," which
Wordsworth sees as the defining characteristic of the new urban subjectivity. Earlier, he had distilled what he took to be the "one feeling . . .
which belong'd / To this great City, by exclusive right" (ll. 593–94):
prefiguring the Baudelairean flâneur, who delights in the collective
anonymity and enigma of the city crowds, Wordsworth writes with a
very different emphasis of

How often in the overflowing Streets,
Have I gone forward with the Crowd, and said
Unto myself, the face of every one
That passes by me is a mystery. (ll. 595–98)

In a sense, this is the sensation of mystery that Walter Benjamin argues
arises in and from the city streets, forming a precondition for the emergence of classical detective fiction at midcentury: as a backdrop to the
action of an investigation or pursuit, the anonymous masses function as
"the asylum that shields an asocial person from his persecutors." The task
of the flâneur, as personified by Baudelaire, is to penetrate this indeci-
pherable crowd in order to decipher and represent its mysteries, and it is
in this sense that Benjamin writes of his transformation into "an unwill-
ing detective." Dissolving into the surrounding crowd, the poet "wrests
the poetic booty" of fragmented speech and images from the experience
of city life.[9] Wordsworth's mind, on the other hand, turns elsewhere:
"Thus," he writes,

have I look'd, nor ceas'd to look, oppress'd
By thoughts of what, and whither, when and how,
Until the shapes before my eyes became
A second-sight procession, such as glides
Over still mountains, or appears in dreams. (ll. 599–603)

When faced with a potential dissolution of self, the impulse in romantic poetry is to seek recourse in a redemptive aesthetics of nature, in

ritualistic denunciations of the city, and in the more positive affirmation of a common humanity glimpsed in the figure of a blind beggar on the city streets, whose story might represent for Wordsworth "a type / Or emblem, of the utmost that we know, / Both of ourselves and of the universe" (ll. 618–20). The attempt is both tentative and unconvincing, for reasons which will become apparent later in this chapter. Indeed, if any conclusion can be drawn from the literature of the city in the romantic period, it would be that such transcendent and totalizing figures of an organically interconnected human race are insistently undermined by hierarchical structures of difference, conflict, and exploitation.

We might expect a commentator like Engels to be more attuned to these vectors of social distinction, and to come to radically different conclusions about the spectacle of London life which he observed as a visitor in 1844. Only four years later, he and Marx would confidently declare in *The Communist Manifesto* not only that the bourgeoisie produces its own grave-diggers, but also that the place where it produces them is in the cities. As capitalism sought to increase profits by centralizing production in the great factories, they argued, so it provides an immiserated workforce with the means of combination, collective bargaining, and political agitation. On the one hand, the proletariat is degraded by the move into the cities, and sees its real wages declining through competition from a reserve army of labor ready to accept inferior pay and working conditions: thus, "instead of rising with the progress of industry," the modern worker "sinks deeper and deeper below the conditions of his [sic] own class."[10] On the other hand, industrialism seemed an inevitable and necessary step in the historical movement toward socialism. In a passage which Raymond Williams argues is partly responsible for the Left's lasting fascination for urban technocracy and modernization, the *Manifesto* disparagingly notes that the bourgeoisie "has created enormous cities, has greatly increased the urban population as compared with the rural, and has thus rescued a considerable portion of the population from the idiocy of rural life" (94); as Williams points out, it's a short step from here to Trotsky's summation of the Russian Revolution as the victory of town over country, or to the forced collectivization and modernization at the heart of Stalinist reconstruction.[11] The consolidation of production in the cities forms, in other words, a precondition for the union of workers which is needed to generalize local disputes into a national class struggle: "That union," Marx and Engels add, "to attain which the burghers of the Middle Ages with their miserable highways required centuries, the modern proletarians, thanks to railways, achieve in a few years" (98–99).

According to *The Communist Manifesto,* then, industrialization reveals the devastating consequences of the capitalist system while at the same time creating the means of its destruction.[12] In the opening paragraph of the chapter in *The Condition of the Working-Class in England in 1844* devoted to "The Great Cities," Engels gives a vivid image of this dialectic of the city, describing London first from the perspective of an outside observer: "This enormous agglomeration of people on a single spot," he notes

> has multiplied a hundredfold the economic strength of the two and a half million inhabitants concentrated there. This great population has made London the commercial capital of the world and has created the gigantic docks in which are assembled the thousands of ships which always cover the River Thames. I know nothing more imposing than the view one obtains of the river when sailing from the sea up to London Bridge. Especially above Woolwich the houses and docks are packed masses on both banks of the river. The further one goes up the river the thicker becomes the concentration of ships lying at anchor, so that eventually only a narrow shipping lane is left free in mid-stream. Here hundreds of steamships dart rapidly to and fro. All this is so magnificent and impressive that one is lost in admiration. The traveller has good reason to marvel at England's greatness even before he steps on English soil.[13]

This passage is typical—to the point of appearing almost parodic—of the dominant mode of social observation which was brought to bear on nineteenth-century London: proceeding from the detached position of the visiting stranger, Engels seeks out a panoramic perspective from which to contemplate, comprehend, and contain the totality of the city, while its spectacular wares—its docks, vessels, buildings, wharves—are thought to have been produced only passively, through the efforts of an "enormous agglomeration."

Such a formulation, however, simply rationalizes an economic system, while necessarily eliding the human agency of the workers who—
in an ironic variation on Adam Smith—are the invisible hands that created all of this fabulous wealth. Accordingly, Engels's second paragraph
seeks to redress the blindness of the first: "It is only later," he writes,

> that the traveller appreciates the human suffering which has
> made all this possible. He can only realise the price that has been
> paid for all this magnificence after he has tramped the pavements
> of the main streets of London for some days and has tired him-
> self out by jostling his way through the crowds and by dodging
> the endless stream of coaches and carts which fill the streets. It
> is only when he has visited the slums of this great city that it
> dawns upon him that the inhabitants of modern London have
> had to sacrifice so much that is best in human nature in order to
> create those wonders of civilization with which their city teems.

After a couple of days, then, Engels begins to penetrate the mystification
of the system-as-agency and sees the human productive forces who actually do the work. Not only are they deprived of the wealth which they
help to produce, but their disenfranchisement and alienation seem
causally and proportionately related to the rate of profits and the splendid "wonders of civilization" that the city advertises.[14]

This is not, however, to suggest that he now views London from the
inside, as it were, as opposed to the original, externalized view from a
riverboat on the Thames. As in Wordsworth, the crowd remains at this
point merely an aggregated (and not especially pleasant) mass of bodies,
mirroring the unified but atomized "labour force" abstracted and desired
by capital, and holding self-interest over any concerns for collective solidarity. Thus,

> [t]he restless and noisy activity of the crowded streets is highly
> distasteful, and is surely abhorrent to human nature itself. Hun-
> dreds of thousands of men and women drawn from all classes and
> ranks of society pack the streets of London. Are they not all
> human beings with the same innate characteristics and poten-
> tialities? Are they not equally interested in the pursuit of hap-
> piness? Yet they rush past each other as if they had nothing in

common. They are tacitly agreed on one thing only—that everyone should keep to the right of the pavement so as not to collide with the stream of people moving in the opposite direction. . . . We know well enough that may be aware that the isolation of the individual—this narrow-minded egotism—is everywhere the fundamental principle of modern society. But nowhere is this selfish egotism so blatantly evident as in the frantic bustle of the great city. (30−31)[15]

This passage is consistent with the dominant trend of urban social observation during the nineteenth century, which sought to maintain an absolute distinction between the spectating subject and the contemplated object. The crowd is pictured as both a singular agency and an amalgam of atomized and conflicted individuals, none of whom seems capable of transcending immediate self-interest. Seeking signs of a coherent class consciousness, Engels is disappointed, if quick to ascribe an absence of collectivity to determining economic conditions—a Hobbesian war of all against all in which a strong minority of capitalists control wealth and production, subjecting the majority in the process to conditions of abject poverty. As Williams comments in *The Country and the City,* what underwrites this passage from Engels is ultimately a familiar paradox, "that in the great city itself, the very place and agency—or so it would seem—of collective consciousness, it is an absence of common feeling, an excessive subjectivity, that seems characteristic" (215−16). For Engels, as for earlier observers of nineteenth-century London, what seemed most immediately visible was a sense of isolation embedded in the processes of social integration, as opposed to any potentially transforming combination or collective.

Engels, we might say, looks for the liberatory potential of city life which Simmel wrote about, and which presupposes the ability to imagine a collective consciousness and common political aspirations; but he is constantly pulled back to an initial experience of egoistic isolation which can be read as a debased version of romantic individualism. Wordsworth's belief in the latter is similarly undermined by his own view of the city as one which enforces a homogenization of the population into a kind of lumpen mass, which is in turn a debased version of the collective subject of Marxism. The cultural, aesthetic, and political agendas of *The Prelude* and *The Condition of the Working-Class in England* could hardly be further apart, and yet they are both working through the same dialectic of city life. At this point, I want to specify more precisely why London incited these particular responses in this particular period, before going on to outline a range of rhetorical strategies by which contemporary commentators sought to make sense of the capital city and reorient themselves to its changing configuration.

## Cognitive and Social Mapping

The experience of London in the early nineteenth century represents one of the most important and influential moments of geo-social rupture, at a time when feelings of urban alienation in the crowded streets of the capital were mirrored by an uncertainty among writers and publishers about the size and definition of their preferred readerships. Just as the inhabitants of an expanded city needed new representational models and maps in order to negotiate the experience of London, so the expanding reading public of the same period forced writers to seek out and construct their intended audiences, "creating the taste" in highly specific ways. Meanwhile, those same audiences sought out, in the literature and periodicals of the time, images of their own position within the shifting social hierarchies and networks of the nation. After the success of the *Monthly Magazine,* which first appeared in 1796, a wide variety of journals sought out their potential readerships, addressing in the process audiences who acquired an acute awareness of class differences along with the sense of themselves as readers. Some journals were narrowly identified with political parties—like the Whiggish *Edinburgh Review* (begun in 1802) and the Tory *Quarterly Review* (1809)—or with easily discernible constituencies like the reactionary readers of the *Anti-Jacobin* (1797) or the radical artisans addressed by William Cobbett's *Political Register* (1816). Others like the *London Magazine* (1820), the *Penny Magazine* (1832), and *Bentley's Miscellany* (1837) aimed more broadly, as we shall see, at the new mass audiences of the cities, or addressed themselves to a newly conscious middle class which increasingly saw itself in opposition to both these urban masses and the radical public addressed by Cobbett and others. Suggesting a meaningful intersection with Fredric Jameson's notions of cognitive mapping, Jon Klancher writes of this new middle-class audience that it "learn[ed] to operate those interpretive strategies through which it can 'read' a social world, a symbolic universe, a textual field, and to discover its own purpose within them. Manipulating or fabricating signs, this public both learns and asserts what it means to be 'middle class' in the nineteenth century" (51).

Such readerly and interpretive operations became increasingly vital to life in the modern metropolis, where population density by itself can threaten the subject's understanding of her/his social position. Looking in the faces of passersby, for instance, Wordsworth finds only "mystery," while even an astute reader of social class like Engels initially has trouble deciphering and categorizing the "hundreds and thousands of men and women drawn from all classes and ranks of society" whom he encounters on the mean streets of London. A defining part of the experience was a sense of helpless insecurity, as what Raymond Williams terms the rural or small-town "knowable communities" of friends and neighbors gives way to the teeming city of strangers. In its role as commercial and financial center, London exerted a most extraordinary power of attraction over the rest of the nation, so that it existed simultaneously as both the nation's capital city and also—especially in contrast to a manufacturing city like Manchester—a city of capital. In the early nineteenth century, during which (as Williams writes) "the country was transformed to supply the city," the process was not, he argues, simply a case of "an industrial centre being fed by its rural hinterland," but rather of "a capital city drawing the character of an economy and a society into its extraordinary center" (147).

Describing his first visit to London in 1800, Thomas de Quincey makes the same point, substituting for the term "city" or "capital" the more encompassing title of "The Nation of London": "Often since then," he writes,

> at distances of two and three hundred miles or more from this colossal emporium of men, wealth, arts, and intellectual power, have I felt the sublime expression of her enormous magnitude in one simple form of ordinary occurrence, viz., in the vast droves of cattle, suppose upon the great north roads, all with their heads directed to London, and expounding the size of the attracting body, together with the force of its attractive power, by the never-ending succession of these droves, and the remoteness

from the capital of the lines upon which they were moving. A suction so powerful, felt along radii so vast, and a consciousness, at the same time, that upon other radii still more vast, both by land and by sea, the same suction is operating, night and day, summer and winter, and hurrying forever into one centre the infinite means needed for her infinite purposes, and the endless tributes to the skill or to the luxury of her endless population, crowds the imagination with a pomp to which there is nothing corresponding on this planet, either amongst the things that have been or the things that are.[16]

By extrapolating London as in effect the entire nation, de Quincey provides one example of the spatial figures and metaphors through which the relations between urban center and rural periphery were mapped. Overwhelmingly, such metaphors were drawn from anatomy and natural science, and sought to figure the body of the nation: thus, the capital was repeatedly referred to as the heart or the head, and as either circulating outwards or magnetically drawing in (as with de Quincey's "suction") the life of the country; another version is the image of the city as a spider, sitting in the midst of a web of lines of force projecting centrifugally—like human arteries or de Quincey's "radii"—from an originating terminus.[17] These metaphors were employed, moreover, by both supporters and critics of the industrial cities. Compare, for example, de Quincey's excitement at the extrinsic extension of London into the rural heartlands with the following passage from 1783, in which Josiah Tucker previews the radical critique of the capital normally associated with Cobbett:

London, the Metropolis of Great Britain, has been complained of, for Ages past, as a kind of Monster, with a Head enormously large, and out of all Proportion to its Body. And yet at that Juncture, when this Complaint was first made (about 200 Years ago) The Buildings of London were hardly advanced beyond the City-Bounds: As to Westminster and Southwark (which we now consider as united to the former by their Buildings and Bridges, and making on the whole, a City of a most immense Size) they were then little better than straggling Villages. If therefore the Increase of Building, begun at such an early Period, was looked upon to be no better than a Wen, or Excresence, in the Body Politic, what must we think of those numberless Streets and Squares, which have been added since![18]

In addition to showing the reverse effect of spatial figures of the national/social body, this passage also interestingly prefigures a development I shall examine later in this chapter, in which the expanding city itself becomes unmanageably large, and as such requires the application of metaphor to shrink it back to the size of a knowable totality.

We need to understand the precise function of these spatial concepts, drawn from the diverse disciplines of anatomy, medicine, natural and applied science. They seem designed to operate the way that Kevin Lynch and Fredric Jameson have described cognitive mapping, by providing overarching figures through which to mediate between subjective experience and the social totality; thus, as Steven Marcus writes of the opening paragraphs of "The Great Towns," Engels is there engaged in a search for an organizing or structuring principle that will be able to "intelligibly subordinate the material [of London] that keeps slipping away" (148). In effect, metaphors of the head and body or the spider in the web enable the isolation of the part from the whole, as the capital becomes a representative synecdoche for the nation as a whole. Furthermore, the choice of appropriate spatial metaphors allows a writer to move back and forth between the local particularities of experience and the life of the nation, establishing a continuum within which the former necessarily serves as a condensed but representative example of the latter. If the primary function of cognitive mapping is to help position the subject within a surrounding totality, that position is usually either in the center or (as we saw in the case of Wordsworth) panoramically above the masses on street level, as a kind of free-floating transcendental consciousness able to survey and subsume the social whole.

These two features, centrality and transcendence, define the subjectivity of the urban middle class, which was the privileged addressee of early-nineteenth-century literature and journalism. Together, they aim to ease the threat of subjective dissolution posed by the anonymity, mystery, and self-alienation of city life, as described by Wordsworth and Engels. In "The Nation of London," de Quincey similarly writes of the increasing awareness—on approaching the city for the first time—that "you are no longer noticed: nobody sees you; nobody hears you; nobody regards you; you do not even regard yourself. In fact," he continues, "how should you, at the moment of first ascertaining you own total unimportance in the sum of things?—a poor shivering unit in the aggregate of human life. Now, for the first time, whatever manner of man you were, or seemed to be, at starting, squire or 'squireen,' lord or lordling, and however related to that city, hamlet, or solitary house from which yesterday or to-day you slipped your cable, beyond disguise you find yourself but one wave in a total Atlantic, one plant . . . in a forest of America." In this passage, de Quincey brilliantly conveys the dangers of the annihilation of the subject, while simultaneously providing the appropriate figure of synecdoche—"one wave in a total Atlantic"—through which to restore a sense of a grounded, and only apparently humbled, subjective unity. He goes on to delineate the familiar experience of the city, the sense of loneliness among "hurrying figures of men and women weaving to and fro, with no apparent purposes intelligible to a stranger." And yet, he also suggests a form of consolation reminiscent of Wordsworth's invocation of the blind beggar who could stand in for a common humanity, when he writes that "[n]o man was ever left to himself for the first time in the streets, as yet unknown, of London, but he must have been saddened and mortified, perhaps terrified, by the sense of desertion and utter loneliness which belong to his situation" (208−9). What begins as a leveling of social differences, in which lord and lordlings become temporarily indistinguishable, ends then with a positive affirmation of a common humanity in which feelings of isolation are paradoxically shared by all. This is the transcendental consciousness at work, identifying the writer's own experiences as representative and thereby enabling him to speak for everybody.

This re-centering of the authorial subject is common in prose of the romantic period dealing with the effects and sensations of the modern city. In a letter to Wordsworth refusing an invitation to the Lake District, Charles Lamb—who, like T. S. Eliot, spent his early working years as a clerk in the city—declared in 1801 that "I have passed all my days in London, until I have formed as many and intense local attachments, as any of you mountaineers can have done with dead nature";[19] writing to John and Leigh Hunt's *The Reflector* ten years later, he extends the thought by nominating himself as a "speculative Lord Mayor of London" for having been born in a crowd, and for holding "an almost insurmountable aversion to solitude and rural scenes. Often, when I have felt a weariness or distaste at home, have I rushed out into [London's] crowded Strand, and fed my humour, till tears have wetted my cheek for unutterable sympathies with the multitudinous moving picture, which she never fails to present at all hours, like the scenes of a shifting pantomime."[20] In such passages, we might trace a countertendency within romanticism which consciously championed an urban experience and aesthetics to the pastoral preferences of the Lakeland poets.

Its in-house journal was undoubtedly the *London Magazine,* which first published de Quincey's *Confessions of an English Opium Eater,* Charles Lamb's *Essays of Elia,* and William Hazlitt's *Table-Talk.* It was launched in 1820 with the stated ambition of correcting the capital's underrepresentation in the ranks of fashionable periodicals, the most important of which were still being published from Edinburgh. Its aim, as the introductory Prospectus outlined in an extension of the heart/artery metaphor, was to "convey the very 'image, form, and pressure' of that 'mighty heart' whose vast pulsations circulate life, strength, and spirits throughout this great Empire," and to capture something of the quickening pace of contemporary life: "Opinion," it stated in a sentence which gives positive value to those aspects of modernity earlier derided by Wordsworth, "now busies itself with more venturous themes than of yore; discussion must start fleeter and subtler game; excitements must be stronger; the stakes of all sorts higher; the game more complicated and hazardous."[21] The politics of this new periodical are, moreover, quickly ascertained from the first issue, in which a regular feature surveying "Public Events" comments on the Peterloo massacre, when army troops opened fire on a massive radical demonstration outside Manchester and killed ten. The government's response to a national outcry of protest was to prosecute the organizers of the meeting for treason and introduce the repressive Six Acts against military-style drilling, mass meetings, "unstamped" periodicals, and seditious libel. Adopting a careful stance which neither endorsed the government's actions nor expressed the radical sympathies which Shelley would convey in "The Masque of Anarchy," the *London Magazine* characterized the events of Peterloo as unnecessarily polarizing divisions within the country. By its harsh response, the government had effectively reduced politics to a simple choice between "themselves, the servants, and dependents of the crown, on one side,—and the mob of unemployed manufacturers, and ignorant and malignant anarchists, on the other: in other words, that the stake on the hazard of the die was to be despotism or revolutionary anarchy." But for the journal, as for the ascendant middle class for which it hoped to speak, such options were falsely drawn, and lacked a conciliatory third way which might defuse the dangerous levels of tension incited by these events. Placing blame squarely on both sides, it agreed with the government that the radical rhetoric of the meeting was "incompatible with that confidence of personal security, and of the preservation of the public peace, which it is one of the subject's most sacred rights to enjoy," while allowing that ministers "might have reckoned on the cordial approbation and support of every honest, enlightened, and patriotic member of the community, in proposing measures calculated to repress this new and crying evil," without resorting to an outright military attack which may have lacked a legal foundation.[22]

This is a political intervention which displays many of the characteristic qualities of urban-romantic journalists of the period: the reflex first to see the current state of social discourse as trapped within unproductive binaries; then, the desire to seek out a third position either above or between two poles that they themselves have helped to construct; and finally, a claim to speak for the people, as the neglected repository of common sense and moderation. As Dickens would later in the century, the literati of the period also claimed a sympathetic identification with the urban masses, proceeding from an unquestioned ability to correctly read, interpret, and represent them. In the process, the motives and actions of the populace are reduced to a simple pantomime. John Fisher Murray boasted, for example, of his power of representing "the inexhaustible mime" of London's people so that his readers may "become intimate with other men, without the trouble of making their acquaintance, and without much expenditure of thinking." The thoughts and feelings of these strangers, which Wordsworth found so impenetrably mysterious, are simply given to Murray, who regards all as "my very good friends." The social antagonisms made visible by Peterloo are merely illusory, because London, while "individually discordant, . . .

forms a universal harmony; and although the interests of any one man may appear directly in opposition to the interests of any other man, as regards the whole mass they are really the same."[23]

Such sentiments seem frankly propagandist, but understandably consolatory for the urban middle-class readers who would have recently witnessed a new wave of mass demonstrations in London for the presentation of the first Chartist petition in 1839. Writing about these events some time later in *The Seer,* Leigh Hunt expressed a sense of relief about the absence of violence, as well as a familiar rhetorical appeal to fellow-feeling and common humanity: "We believe," he declared, "that, without any reference to politics whatsoever, no man of reflection or sensibility looked upon the great and moving mass and succession of human beings, which assembled a little while ago in London, without being consciously or unconsciously moved with emotions of this kind." Having established the basis for a bond based in personal sympathy, Hunt goes on to suggest that

> [a] crowd is but the reduplication of ourselves,—of our own faces, hopes, wants, and relations,—our own connections of wives and children,—our own strengths, weaknesses, formidable powers, pitiable tears. We may differ with it, we may be angry with it, fear it, think we scorn it; but we must scorn ourselves first, or have no feeling and imagination. All the hearts beating in those bosoms are palpitations of our own. We feel them somehow or other, and glow, or turn pale. We cannot behold ourselves in that shape of power or mighty want, and not feel that we are men.

Again, conflicts are only apparent, and mask a deeper common interest which stands above politics. The crowd is simply an extension and multiplication of the individual part. All that is required is a form of sympathetic introjection in order to grasp the fundamental humanity that all share. Indeed, Hunt proposes a mental exercise to help his readers attain enlightenment, suggesting that "we have only to fancy ourselves born in any particular class, and to have lived, loved, and suffered in it, in order to feel the mistakes and circumstances of those who belong to it, even when they appear to sympathize least with ourselves." The subjects he takes for these experiments are moreover quite revealing: first, the

aristocrats, democrats, and "popish conspirators" of the French revolution, then a Chartist demonstrator who had been witnessed marching
with a copy of *The Seer,* and who therefore "could hardly be thinking of
burning down half London, even if the government did continue bent
upon not receiving his petition."[24]

These pages condense one version of the political unconscious of the
period, which feared the masses brought together by Chartism as a form
of domestic Jacobinism. Against sure evidence of class division, represented at either end of the political spectrum by French aristocrats and
English radicals, Hunt proposes his own disinterested transcendental
consciousness, which is able to comprehend and explain the positions
of others in part by synecdochically reducing the Chartist millions to a
single representative. From this optimistic perspective, the threat of social transformation which these masses were thought to portend seems
unjustified, even if Hunt betrays this sense of calm a little at the end of
his article. There, he cites a long quotation from Matthew Lewis's *The
Monk* (1795) to demonstrate how "a human being may be seized by his
angry fellow-creatures, and by dint of being pulled hither and thither,
and struck at, even with no direct mortal intentions on their part, be reduced in the course of a few frightful moments to a condition, which,
in the present state of the community, would equally fill with remorse
the parties that regarded it, on either side" (332). The passage, one of the
more sensational in this most sensational of Gothic novels, interestingly
deals with a frenzied mob's attack on an oppressive Catholic abbey, and
so carries strong echoes of the storming of the Bastille six years earlier,
and of the revolutionary upheaval which seems uppermost in Hunt's
thoughts.[25]

This cautionary reference to *The Monk* helps to undermine the com-
placent self-assurance with which Hunt makes the case for a common
and essentially rational humanity in the rest of his article. In fact, the
specter of violence conveyed in the passage from Lewis seems to be a
classic case of the Freudian return of the repressed, in which the forms
of class conflict which the nineteenth-century bourgeoisie had sought
to expel from its fantasies of national unity continually threaten its precarious political hegemony. Thus, for example, Hunt imagines a form of
Chartist mob violence that would ultimately be regarded with remorse
"on either side" of the reform question, thereby projecting himself in a

position of neutrality, symbolically above or between the contending forces. As we have seen, this kind of positioning is typical of the ideological work of early-nineteenth-century periodicals, which aimed not only to give their readers a sense of themselves but also of their relative status in a changing social hierarchy.

The city streets were where the different classes would rub shoulders, and accordingly provided the urbane romantics of contemporary journalism with ample material from which to construct their elaborate maps of social and cultural distinction. In "Life in London" (1824), for example, an anonymous author in the *New Monthly Magazine* expresses a familiar paradox, that London as seen from Regent's Park connotes a form of opulence which is invisible when viewed from the perspective of the slums around London Bridge: "On the one hand, pleasure in all its endless varieties, ease, comfort, order, propriety; one the other, close, filthy, foggy tenements, excluding light and air, and a dense population of dirty and unhealthy wretches, bespeaking a state of existence many degrees below the most abject penury of a country cottage, from which the beauty and the healthfulness of nature cannot be excluded." The pertinent question for Engels was why these latter continue to move to the city, but the writer is reluctant to consider it: like all others, the poor must "flock up to London," he concludes, simply because they are "tormented with the desire to be rich." [26]

In fact, the article seems less interested in the laboring poor than in those who more accurately personify these upwardly mobile ambitions, in particular poor tradesmen whose need to acquire cultural capital causes them to overspend their meager disposable incomes, and clubmen who seem merely "addicted to sensual indulgence, and ambitious of figuring in the gay circles." This attention to the hypocrisies and emptiness of modern metropolitan life finally explodes in a condemnation of "those who in their class and sphere can avail themselves of the superior civilization and concentrated advantages of the capital." It seems that those to whom such benefits appear as entitlements, rather than as distant aspirations, lack the taste and "intellectual resources" to fully appreciate them:

> Nay, the very physical enjoyments of the metropolis are but ill understood; and the sensual pleasures of a London life are often

defeated by the bungling attempts of those who strive to realize them. The upper classes of society, when their secret is penetrated, are for the most part found to exist in a state of appalling distaste for all around them. An apathy, bordering on despair, accompanies them in their most splendid indulgences. Of all the forms of human woe, this is the most sickening.

At this point, the article returns to the original counterexample of the working poor, who are deserving of sympathy even if a necessary by-product of industrialization: "Poverty, disease, and heart-breaking labour, are calamities evidently arising out of the scheme of human nature," we read, "and they form so necessary and inevitable a part of the great whole, that though they excite commiseration for the sufferers, they do not revolt the imagination." How much worse, though, are those "sufferings arising immediately out of the plenitude of indulgence" which the tasteless rich delight in, and which "seem so perverse and so unnatural a dispensation, as to exasperate the spectator against his species."

It is easy to see articles like this as carving out an imaginative space which the magazine's bourgeois readers will come to occupy, as representatives of what Jon Klancher terms the "cultural class." Effortlessly combining the necessary taste, wealth, and intellectual resources, such readers might imagine themselves in stark contrast to both the idle rich and the deserving poor, the empty-headed clubman and the ambitious tradesman. A careful reading of articles like this, however, reveals the evasions and elisions of social tension which form a precondition for the fantasies of this "cultural class," and thus enables a sense of conflict to be seen in accounts which ostensibly set out to show the organic totality of the city and the nation. Another essay titled "Life in London" (this time from the *Mirror of Literature*) nicely illustrates this tension. "A sameness in London! Preposterous!" it opens with characteristic enthusiasm. "Every street, every square, every public walk, and every theatre presents novelty and variety. The very shops," it continues, "with their shopmen and shopwomen, their proprietors and customers, offer a world of information and a wide field for remarks." What follows is a seemingly inexhaustible cataloging of the urban figures that are made available to the active and penetrating mind of one who "finds employment in all classes of life, can draw experience and knowledge from every character and every scene in the eventful drama of existence."

Recalling the panorama of people, commodities and spectacles that Wordsworth found on display in London's streets, the article goes on to imagine a typical stroll in the city. Suppose, for example, that the observing flâneur wanders

> into Bond Street, and pursues his course down the Strand. How many various characters will he see in one linen-draper's shop! The superb dame who is there from idleness, and buys every thing, the fickle, troublesome fashionable, who shops from vacancy of mind and habit, and who turns over every thing without the least intention of purchasing, the boarding-school miss who looks wistfully at a rich aunt, but cannot soften her aunt into the purchase of a lace vale or a French shawl, the arch cyprian who eyes an embroidered gown and the linen-draper, or some male customer in the shop, with equal fondness—and, lastly, the adroit shop-lifter, with Argus eyes on every side, endeavouring to seize the opportunity of taking off some article of value whilst the attention of those serving in the shop is occupied.[27]

Each individual stands in for a social type, yet they are also delineated with sufficient distinctiveness to suggest that an infinite number of similar combinations might be visible to the trained eye, on any day in any London street. Within the microcosm of the draper's shop, however, there is clearly a hierarchical principle of social distinction in operation, which dictates that the narrative descend progressively from the "superb dame," through the fashionable bourgeois and lower middle-class "school miss," to the low-lifes represented by the prostitute and thief. This would seem initially to be another case in which social differences are invoked in order that they might be transcended, as the signs of class distinction come to form the terms through and against which an organic ideal of community can emerge; the presence of dames and thieves together is intended, in other words, to show the underlying humanity which unites them, and which is supposed to outweigh the obvious distinctions of wealth and status. In reality, of course, the classes maintain very specific relations not only to each other, but to the commodities on sale; in the ideology of the city, however, their proximity is read as a sign of the mutual cohabitation among the classes.

But "Life in London" also shows us how such beliefs create a space for exploitation, as gullible travelers unskilled in reading the social signs find themselves the targets for tricksters in disguise. Thus, when the imaginary walker returns to the Strand by way of St. James's Park, he sees a more menacing drama being played out:

> That pretty brunette who trips so nimbly, as if in haste with a band-box in her hand, has been up and down the Strand half a dozen times. The band-box is a lure:—see the alderman taken in by it. . . . Had she been dressed like a west end of the town cyprian, the sugar-baker had not been caught. That fellow disguised as a Quaker, too, is no Quaker at all. He has an oil-skin bundle of samples—this is a blind. Follow him close. He is sticking to the skirts of a countryman, who is gaping and staring into every window. He will follow him to St. Dunstan's church. The clock and the false Quaker strike at the same time. Giles Jolter's pocket-book and watch are no longer in their master's pocket.

Already, the matching of individual to social type seems more complicated than originally conceived, and requires a process of interpretation in order to distinguish the "true" social signs from the falsities of disguise. Such skills take time, experience, and taste to acquire, and are the forte of the cultural class. We have seen how periodicals like the *Mirror of Literature* circulated an enabling fiction of a harmonious—even classless—society in the city, in which these interpretive qualities were prized above all others. The problem, though, is that such fictions cannot wish away class altogether. Indeed, as Jon Klancher notes, "trivializing class order is another way to reveal its necessity," as both the indexical marker designating the signs and symbols of social distinction and as a backdrop against which to organize propagandist narratives of a classless society (87).

In the example given above, it is important that this meeting of opposites is imagined as occurring in the Strand, which forms one of the central horizontal trajectories uniting the different socioeconomic spheres of London. Even today, the Strand marks a kind of ground zero of the capital, the place where Westminster merges with the old City of London. With its origins in the district of WC (West Central) 2 giving way at the other end to Fleet Street, in the shadow of St. Paul's Cathedral in EC (East Central) 4, the Strand still unites the West and East Ends of London, regions that are conventionally considered as separate entities with carefully delimited boundaries and distinctive characteristics. The gap between them grew wider throughout the eighteenth century, and was encouraged by forms of development and urban planning. As F. S. Schwarzbach has noted, this arrangement did not arise by chance, but was rather determined by the geography of the city and the interests of its ruling class. Prior to the implementation of an effective sewage disposal system, the prevailing westerly winds dictated that "the smoke and smell produced in the city normally would be blown down the Thames Valley to the sea," so that the east-west model of residential development helped to ensure that any unhealthy or unpalatable by-products of urban life would be carried "out of harm's way, or, in what amounted to the same thing, toward the eastern part of the city where the poor generally lived."[28] To the north and west from Charing Cross outwards, then, a series of fashionable squares were built to cater to the needs of the aristocracy and upper-middle class for residential town-houses: Soho and Golden Squares below Oxford Street, Bedford and Russell Squares to the north in Bloomsbury, Berkeley and Grosvenor Squares in Mayfair, and so on. Meanwhile, the pursuit of profits encouraged the proliferation of the working-class slums, alleys and tenements to the east and along the Thames, in Clerkenwell, Bethnal Green, Whitechapel, Wapping, and the Isle of Dogs. Efforts—both architectural and ideological—to maintain and strengthen the boundary between East and West were enacted throughout the nineteenth century, with varying results.

### The Proximate Poor

In an important contribution to debates concerning the relations between power and resistance, about which I will be saying more in chapter 2, Jonathan Dollimore has proposed "the proximate" as an available subject position with the potential to destabilize conventional binary oppositions between self and other. In an argument that draws on psychoanalytic and Foucauldian explanations of deviancy, the term "transgressive reinscription" denotes the process classically defined by Freud as the return of the repressed, in which that which has been denied, suppressed, or maintained at arm's length re-emerges as symbolically and constitutively central to normative definitions of the dominant: the outlaw, Dollimore notes paradoxically, is in this sense also always an in-law. There is a perversely dynamic logic within Western culture, he argues, within which the antithetical other "inheres within, and is partly produced by, what it opposes." The hegemonic culture represented by London's West End, in the example I have been using, thus requires a correspondingly demonized East End, against which it is able to validate and consolidate its generalizable, normative, and (supposedly) classless values.

But what most accounts of the binary opposition between the dominant and its deviant Other usually miss, according to Dollimore, is the destabilizing potentialities of a third term, the proximate, which is defined as "that which is (1) adjacent and *there-by* related temporally or spatially, or (2) that which is approaching (again either temporally or spatially), . . . and thus (3) the opposite of *remote* or *ultimate*."[29] His main purpose here is to attempt a reevaluation of the figure of the pervert, who seems at once socially marginal and symbolically central in Western culture, yet this focus on spatiality suggests a useful resonance with my argument about class relations in nineteenth-century London: thus, we might say that while the West End needs the East as authenticating Other, the hierarchical systems of social classification which these terms embody begin to break down when the subversive or revolutionary potentiality of the East End suddenly appears out of place, having moved from its assigned geographical and social margin to the heart of the city. Such a model of the proximate would enable an understanding of why notions of adjacency in particular seem to haunt writing on the city throughout the early nineteenth century, and why it is drawn so insistently to moments of public disturbance—like the meeting in the Strand described a moment ago—when the symbolic and physical separation of the classes is bridged or breached.[30] At moments like this, the transcendental perspective that was so desired by the romantics is forced to acknowledge a very real social difference at ground level.

Evidence of a disruptive proximity between rich and poor is provided by Engels, who wrote of the England he observed in 1844 that poverty is sometimes "to be found hidden away in alleys close to the stately homes of the wealthy." This is not the general case, of course, as the poor are more normally "segregated in separate districts where they struggle through life as best they can out of sight of the more fortunate classes of society." Such is demonstrably not the case, however, with the exemplary slum that Engels proposes to examine in some detail. The "rookery" of St. Giles is, he notes, "situated in the most densely-populated part of London and is surrounded by splendid wide streets which are used by the fashionable world. It is close to Oxford Street, Trafalgar Street, and the Strand." Here and in the more "respectable" area of Long Acre (in the immediate vicinity of Drury Lane's theaters) live some of "the poorest of the poor" in London, according to Engels, in particular the recent Irish immigrants who crowd into the filthy and decaying passages between houses with broken windows, crumbling walls, and rotting door-frames. Additional evidence is provided by the *Journal of the Statistical Society,* which (he noted) in 1843 reported 1,465 families—or about 6,000 people—living in the Inner Ward of "the aristocratic parish of St. George, Hanover Square," off Oxford and Regent Streets.[31]

Such appalling poverty was known, if at all, only as a direct result of its proximity to the city's commercial and residential centers. Indeed, ignorance of such areas might well have seemed preferable to a knowledge that inevitably carried with it a real danger of class conflict, thereby undermining consolatory notions of the city as a site of peaceful coexistence. A *Times* leader concerning incidents of homelessness and prostitution reported in 1843 at Marlborough Street Police Office, in fashionable South Kensington, captures something of the prevailing ambivalence: poverty is "truly horrible," it editorialized, but especially so "within the precincts of wealth, gaiety, and fashion" around St. James's Palace. The paper went on to call, somewhat vaguely, for action, and even to suggest that the blame for this shameless adjacency of opposites lies not with the poor, but the rich: in a telling image, it places responsibility on a personification of "Wealth," which offers up "from its bright saloons . . . an insolently heedless laugh—at the unknown wounds of want! Pleasure, cruelly but unconsciously mocking the pain that moans below!" And yet, that "unconsciously" saves the day for the paper's respectable readers, especially when read alongside an earlier statement that "[p]oor there must be everywhere. Indigence will find its way and set up its hideous state in the heart of a great and luxurious city. Amid the thousand narrow lanes and by-streets of a populous metropolis there must always, we fear, be much suffering—much that offends the eye—much that lurks unseen."[32] Such misery, we can only conclude, would be acceptable if it were kept hidden within the prescribed boundaries of the East End, where it might "lurk unseen" by the Victorian middle class.

The unease that Engels and the *Times* experienced for different reasons at the close proximity of the classes in London is in a direct sense the inverse of the liberal dream of a common humanity, of that commingling of dames, dandies, school teachers, and shoplifters in the stores of the Strand. The tension between these two visions of the city—as either harmonious melting pot or Hobbesian battleground—is moreover one which cuts through Kevin Lynch's analysis of modern urban space. In his view, sharply differentiated neighborhoods form the building blocks out of which inhabitants construct spatial maps of the city as a totality, but they can also produce a sense of uniformity or restriction, in which residents of one area fear to journey into another. On this basis, Lynch calls for a certain "plasticity" in urban design which might allow for a more democratic use of public space, while at the same time warning of the potentially destabilizing effects of a blurring of regional boundaries: "let the mishap of disorientation once occur," he cautions, "and the sense of anxiety and even terror that accompanies it reveals to us how closely it is linked to our sense of balance and well-being. The very word 'lost' in our language means much more than simple geographical uncertainty; it carries overtones of utter disaster."[33] This sense of psychic trauma now reads very much like the familiar complaint of a privileged (and usually white) city-resident who has strayed into an unfamiliar (and usually black) neighborhood. In nineteenth-century London, however, it would more likely be expressed by a West End resident who suddenly finds herself or himself beyond the limits of the City or in the courtyards behind Oxford Street, facing the repressed Other of Whitechapel or Seven Dials. In either case, the point is that this sense of dread only goes in one direction, and is only articulated by those with something to lose—ironically, by those who under different circumstances might advocate the principles of social harmony and posit a common human interest.

As we have seen, new meanings, tensions, and divisions accreted around various sectors of London throughout the early nineteenth century, with the result that the city itself became a sort of battleground to some, and a testing-ground to others engaged in the ideological projection of a more harmonious model of social interaction. My purpose here has been to return a sense of agency to debates about urban life, and to read these struggles over social space as the symptoms and inflections of a more fundamental struggle between the classes in English society—one which was also evident (as we shall see) in contemporary debates about the appropriate policing, treatment, and sentencing of criminals. Like the urban masses with which they were often felt to be synonymous, London's criminal population was generally considered to be a threat to social order which could most profitably be dealt with through strategies of isolation and containment. The problem of social control only really arose as an issue when this population began to circulate outside of the ghettoized slums to the north and east of London's commercial center. Indeed, it is this threatening sense of a lawless East End slum transplanted into the metropolitan center which generated the privileged figure for social relations in mid-nineteenth-century London: the symbolic and alliterative pairing of the palace of St. James with the archetypal slum of St. Giles.

Through the course of the nineteenth century, the structural relation between the diverse populations of London was increasingly expressed as that between a bustling urban center and the peaceful periphery of the suburban Green Belt to which "city gents" retire at evenings and weekends. In the literature and journalism of the romantic period, however, the segregation of the classes was still usually represented schematically by a series of shorthand oppositions condensing the bipolar relations between rich and poor. Recounting his first visit to the capital, for example, de Quincey recalls how a lack of time forced him and his companions to search for a representative London landmark, and thus to choose between the contrasting attractions of Westminster Abbey to the west and St. Paul's Cathedral to the east: "The spectacles were too many by thousands," he writes, and "our very wealth made us poor. . . . But which of them all could be thought general or representative enough to stand for the universe of London? We could not traverse the whole circumference of this mighty orb; that was clear; and therefore, the next best thing was to place ourselves as much as possible in some relation to the spectacles of London, which might answer to the centre. Yet how?" The visitors are finally forced to toss up between the "rival edifices," each roughly equidistant from their unnamed vantage point but "too remote from each other to allow of our seeing both."[34]

The privileged opposition organizing cognitive maps of the city was probably the pairing of St. James in the West End with the sprawling rookery of St. Giles. As early as 1824, for example, the author of "Life in London" could write in the *Mirror of Literature* that the urban flâneur must be equally conversant with "the court end of the town and the city, St. James's and St. Giles's, the puny efforts of the coxcomb's table wit and the broad farce and vulgar cant of the river boatman" (173). Seventeen years later, in the 1841 preface to *Oliver Twist,* Dickens similarly defended himself against objections leveled by Thackeray and others about his presentation of urban poverty by claiming that "I saw no reason, when I wrote this book, why the very dregs of life, so long as their speech did not offend the ear, should not serve the purpose of a moral, at least as well as its froth and cream. Nor did I doubt that there lay festering in St. Giles's, as good materials towards the truth as any to be found in St. James's."[35] A *Punch* illustration from 1850 recalled the *Times's* sense of moral indignation at the presence of the homeless in the landscapes of West London, by depicting "St. James turning St. Giles out of his Parks."[36]

The region of St. Giles was in fact located to the north between Covent Garden and Tottenham Court Road, but was considered a synecdoche—along with the adjacent region of Seven Dials—for all of the slums of the capital. Indeed, it was precisely its central position within the topography of London that enabled St. Giles to function in the bourgeois imaginary like Dollimore's proximate, as a kind of fifth column of poverty or impassable enclave in the heart of the city. Its name served as a shorthand for unmitigated forms of lawlessness and criminal deviancy, which seemingly existed unchecked (and even licensed) under the very noses of fashionable Londoners. Historically, as the *Edinburgh Review* noted in a review of policing in London, St. Giles had presented no organized "impediment" to crime prior to the founding of the Metropolitan Police in 1829. Under the previous system of parish constables and watchmen, areas like this had fallen "'under no particular Act of Parliament': the precise effect of which was, that the constables collected as much money as they could from the inhabitants for police purposes, the inhabitants paid what they pleased, and the constables never accounted for anything they received."[37] Over time, St. Giles in particular took on the aspect of a criminal fortress, in close proximity to the fashionable London of Bloomsbury and Mayfair. Kellow Chesney notes, for example, that nearby St. George's church, in Bloomsbury, was rumored to have been built in the first place because "respectable" families didn't dare venture through the rookery to the church of St. Giles, and something of the danger which it represented can be glimpsed in a report he cites of the 1840 arrest of a gang engaged in manufacturing fake coins. As police reinforcements prepared to do battle with a growing mob of local residents, Chesney notes, "the combined force, with the coiners in the middle, began to struggle out of the rookery, not towards St. Giles Station House which lay a dangerous hundred yards or so to the south, but north towards the nearest open space in Bloomsbury Square."[38]

It was presumably this threat of open class warfare in the center of the capital that helped make St. Giles a convenient candidate for the slum clearance programs of the late 1840s, when construction of the arterial road system of New Oxford Street required the demolition of large residential areas of central London. Some sense of the transformation of the region can be drawn from Henry Mayhew, who noted during the following decade that "[t]he houses we visited in George Street, and the streets adjacent, were formerly part of the rookery of St. Giles-in-the-Fields, celebrated as one of the chief haunts of redoubtable thieves and suspicious characters in London. Deserted as it comparatively is now, except by the labouring poor vagrants and low prostitutes, it was once the resort of all classes, from the proud noble to the beggar picking up a livelihood from door to door." Mayhew relies on the inspector of lodging houses for the district for his accounts of St. Giles in the heyday of "twenty years ago, before a number of these disreputable streets were removed to make way for New Oxford Street," and concludes (somewhat contradictorily) that "[n]ow, however, the district is considerably changed, the inhabitants are rapidly rising in decency, cleanliness, and order, and the rookery of St. Giles will soon be ranked among the memories of the past."[39]

Contemporary writers attempting to understand the poor and criminal classes of London continued to take St. Giles as their localized focus even after its effective demolition, since the alliterative association with the park and palace of St. James enabled a range of commentaries on relations between the classes. A punning street ballad gives us some sense of the oppositions which it helped to solidify within the popular consciousness:

> In St. James's the officers mess at the club,
> In St. Giles's they often have messes for grub;
> In St. James's they feast on the highest of game
> In St. Giles's they live on foul air just the same.[40]

The pairing also found a resonance, though, within the very different registers of State policy and philanthropic concern. It helped, for example, to structure the policing strategy of the Metropolitan Police Force, who—according to the *Edinburgh Review* of 1852—continued to take it as axiomatic that "you guard St. James by watching St. Giles."[41] One year earlier, Dickens had similarly noted the interdependence of the two regions in a speech to the Metropolitan Sanitary Association, insisting "that no man can estimate the amount of mischief grown in dirt,— that no man can say the evil stops here or stops there, either in its moral or physical effects, or can deny that it begins in the cradle and is not at rest in the miserable grave." Picking up on the reference to "foul air" in the rhyme cited above, he went on to remark that such effects of poor sanitation were as certain "as it is that the air from Gin Lane will be carried by an easterly wind into Mayfair, or that the furious pestilence raging in St. Giles's no mortal list of lady patronesses can keep out of Almack's," a fashionable Pall Mall assembly room for gambling and dancing.[42]

Perhaps the most elaborate working out of the relations between these metonymic regions occurs in a popular crime novel from 1845, written by Dickens's friend and fellow-journalist Douglas Jerrold. Following the success of novels like *Oliver Twist* and William Harrison Ainsworth's *Jack Sheppard*, Jerrold attempted in *St. Giles and St. James* to delineate the varied trajectories that were marked out for the children of the rich and poor in contemporary London. In fact, the prototype for Jerrold's parable—as earlier for Ainsworth's—was Hogarth's "Industry and Idleness" (1747), in which two contemporaries end up respectively as Lord Mayor of London and an executed criminal. Unlike Ainsworth, however, Jerrold aimed to decenter the conventional moral opposition of good and evil, and replace it with the alternative binary of rich and poor. St. Giles and St. James in fact refer simultaneously to real geographical locations in the novel and to two boys of the same names born six months apart, in a social commentary which is thus underwritten by an overt environmental determinism. We are given an account of the early life of the child St. Giles, for example, in the wholly negative terms of deprivation. A "dwarfed man," St. Giles experiences "no dallying pause, no middle space for him, to play with life, knowing not his playmate—no bit of green sward, with flowers for toys. Oh, no! he was made with sudden violence to know life." By way of contrast,

> how very differently did young St. James con his lesson, life! In reality, only six months younger than his squalid brother—for in this story St. Giles and St. James must fraternize—he was still the veriest babe. Why, it was gladness to the heart to look at him—to hear his blithe voice—to see him, in that happy freedom of infancy, when children play in the vestibule of life. . . . And what prophecies—with what "sweet breath composed"— were uttered to his glorification! What a man he would make![43]

The didactic purpose of the novel seems clear, then: to show a common humanity blighted in the one instance and encouraged to flourish in the other. Indeed, Bright Jem Aniseed—himself an interesting figure, an honest worker living amid the criminality of St. Giles—makes the point for us on first seeing the young lord from St. James's Palace: "What a beautiful creetur! . . . He's been kept out of the mud of the world, hasn't he? I say; it would be a hard job supposing that blooming little fellow—with rags on his back, matches in his hand, and nothin' in his belly, eh? Quite as hard to think young St. Giles was him, eh? And yet it might ha' been, mightn't it?" (55)

Within this morality tale, though, Jerrold also seeks to comment more directly on public perceptions of class relations, and to do so through the conventional spatial opposition of St. Giles / St. James which I have been discussing up to now. Thus, the terms often migrate from a particularized reference to the two boys to the larger geographical regions for which they stand. Even before our introduction to these characters, we read of Bright Jem's sister-in-law, Kitty Muggs, who works as a kitchen-maid in St. James's Square, and accordingly holds "a due contempt for St. Giles's, and all its dwellers." On the rare occasions of her visits to her poor relations in Short's Gardens, she feels it "impossible for her not to make it known to St. Giles the vast debt of gratitude due from it to St. James." Later, the figure of St. Giles does accrue a debt to his wealthy counterpart, though at this point Jerrold means simply to point to the stylized snobbery of Kitty Muggs, who feels on visits that "the tea was always so coarse, and not a bit like their gunpowder [at St. James]; and the bacon was rusty, not a bit like their hams; and in fact there was nothing, no, not even the flesh and blood of Short's Gardens, like the flesh and blood of the West-End" (11). Later, when St. Giles has seemingly fulfilled his destiny and ended up in the condemned cell of Newgate prison, Jerrold again tries to explain his short criminal career in terms of human potential and environmental deprivation: "Poor wretch!" he writes. "Let the men who guide the world—the large-brained politicians, who tinker the social scheme, making themselves the masters and guardians of their fellow-men—let them look into this Newgate dungeon; let them contemplate this blighted human bud; this child felon, never taught the path of right, and now to be hanged for his most sinful ignorance." As we shall see, Dickens assigns the blame in very similar ways for society's treatment of *Bleak House*'s "poor Jo," a character who exists in a similar state of irreducible ignorance. In *St. Giles and St. James,* his friend Jerrold also moves to a decisive denunciation of Victorian hypocrisy, in which the names of "St. Giles" and "St. James" reattach themselves once again to the wider geo-social constituencies for which they stand: "Oh, politicians! Oh, rulers of the world! Oh, law-making masters and taskers of the common million, may not this cast-off wretch, this human nuisance, be your accuser at the bar of Heaven? Egregious folly! Impossible! What—stars and garters denounced by rags and tatters! St. James denounced by St. Giles! Impudent and ridiculous!" (96–97).

The passage effects a remarkable rhetorical chiasmus by which the slum of St. Giles appears as accuser of the palace of St. James. For in fact, the character St. Giles stands convicted at this moment for having stolen a pony belonging to St. James! Indeed, his criminal career has earlier been shown to have begun with the theft of his counterpart's hat, and he relies on both occasions on the latter's pardon. In the early part of the novel, then, the two most certainly do "fraternize," if on the quite markedly unequal terms of thief and property-owner. Indeed, the opportunity for stealing St. James's pony only occurs because St. Giles had been planning to con a gullible old woman, who turns out to be the young lord's former nurse: seeing a poor man in the room, St. James instantly adopts the position of superior (as later, he becomes his employer) by asking his counterpart to exercise the horse. All of this, and the ensuing pardon which causes St. Giles to be transported to Botany Bay for life, is depicted as an admirable example of *lèse majesté,* brought about by the intervention of Bright Jem and his friend, the misanthropic muffin-maker Mr. Capstick. Jerrold reveals a remarkably naive vision of parliamentary representation in all of this, suggesting that St. James acts on behalf of his constituents: it appears that he has received an electoral challenge for his family seat in the rotten borough of Liquorish, and so grants access to Capstick as "a native of Liquorish, with a vote for the borough." Later, in a sequence of events too complicated to describe here, Capstick is himself elected to Parliament, although the novel's optimistic view of the political process seems tempered at one point by St. Giles's terse statement to one of St. James's agents that "I've never had a vote . . . nothing of the sort. I wish I had" (178).

He nevertheless experiences a form of personal reformation through his various coincidental meetings with the aristocracy, with St. James appearing as "a sort of earthly angel; a being of altogether another kind to the boys St. Giles had ordinarily met with" (64). Some measure of the transformation which this brings can be glimpsed in a long passage after he illegally returns from transportation a reformed man: as he heads for St. James's Square (where his counterpart has unknowingly offered him a job),

> the way before him was a path of pleasure. How changed was London-bridge! To his boyhood it had been a mass of smoked, grimed stone: and now it seemed a shape of grace and beauty. He looked, too, at the thousand ships that, wherever the sea rolled, with mute gigantic power told the strength, the wealth, and enterprise of England. . . . And then St. Giles passed along Cheapside, and stood before St. Paul's church; and then for the first time felt somewhat of its tremendous beauty. It had been to him a mere mountain of stone, with a clock upon it: and now,

he felt himself subdued, refined, as the Cathedral, like some strange harmony, sank into his soul. . . . St. Giles, the returned transport, the ignorant and sinning man; St. Giles, whose innocence of childhood had been offered to the Moloch selfishness of society, even St. Giles felt all this; and with swelling heart and the tears in his throat, passed down Ludgate-Hill with a fervent devotion, thanking his God who had brought him from the land of the cannibals to the land of the Christians. (162–63)

The "land of the cannibals" referred to here is presumably meant to signify Australia, but within the terms of the novel also the area of St. Giles itself, from which its namesake is rescued and delivered to St. James's Square. Religious conversion causes St. Giles to refigure his entire perception of London, in other words, and to see beauty where previously he had seen only buildings of inaccessible wealth and privilege. Not surprisingly, a return to his childhood home produces a sense of revulsion, particularly when he is relieved of his new handkerchief by his own half-brother: "He saw not a face he knew. All he had left were dead; and new tenants, other wretches, fighting against want, and gin, and typhus, were preparing new loam for the churchyard. . . . How sudden, and how great was St. Giles's revulsion at the villain thief! Never had St. Giles felt so virtuous!" (169).

Alongside this transformation of St. Giles, the logic of the novel should presumably suggest an accompanying alteration in the figure of St. James, who might at least acknowledge his complicity in the impoverishment of the less-fortunate of London. In fact, something like this appears to be signaled at the end of the novel, when—having narrowly avoided the gallows himself—St. James makes "noble amends" for his life of vanity through "many a pilgrimage . . . to the Hog-Lanes, that, like hidden ulcers rot the social body." For this lesson in humility, moreover, we read that "he owed its first knowledge to his fitful companionship with St. Giles; to his strange association with a wretched being who, first sinned against by society, became the avenging sinner. . . . Hence, our nobleman proved it by all his after life, how much St. James in his brocade, may profitably learn of St. Giles in his tatters" (392). The problem is that such a conclusion seems patently false for the tale that Jerrold has been telling, in which the only equality before the law that St. Giles and St. James experience consists in riding (at the latter's gracious bidding) in the same prisoners' cart. The presumption of innocence afforded to St. James is for example certainly denied to St. Giles at the end: accused of kidnapping the wife of a local nobleman, and later of murdering the husband who comes to rescue her from captivity, St. James is acquitted through the services of a clever, but expensive, lawyer; his counterpart, however, condemned to death for returning from transportation despite evidence that the original charge of horse-stealing was false, escapes only through the intervention of royal pardon. Throughout the novel, we have witnessed St. James relying with increasing imperiousness on the privileges of rank to exempt him not only from legal constraints but also those of parliamentary procedure; if anything, then, this ending simply effects a reification of class relations, by enshrining a kind of divine right of privilege that is occasionally tempered by voluntary displays of mercy.

Indeed, as Robert Colby notes, the original serialization in *Douglas Jerrold's Shilling Magazine* (which ran from January 1845 to May 1847) ended very differently: in it, St. James fled abroad after the trial, "made the grand tour, returned, married a duke's daughter, and to the end of his days, supported the dignity of his order." Colby suggests that its original readers may have demanded a more mutual enlightenment, since the preface to the book version in 1851 mentions accusations that its author had acted as "a sort of moral Robin Hood, stripping the rich of their virtues that only the veriest poor might strut in the plunder" (iii). Alternately, he argues, the revised ending might have been tailored to a wealthier audience for the book version, in spite of Jerrold's worthy desire in its prospectus to "appeal to the hearts of the Masses of England." [44] At any rate, the new preface from 1851 attempts to disarm charges that the novel displays a "desire to despoil the high for the profit of the low," claiming instead that St. Giles should be read as "the victim of the disregard of the social claims of the poor upon the rich; of the governed millions upon the governing few." The basis of these claims, however, remains occluded within the form of the novel, in which the social relations between St. Giles and St. James seem as unequal at the conclusion as at the start. If, as I have suggested, these characters undergo any kind of reformation through the course of the novel, such changes take place on a strictly personal and voluntary basis. The wider relations between

the geographical regions of St. Giles and St. James are moreover neglected, as Jerrold sets the bulk of his novel outside the bounds of the
capital in the surrounding suburbs and the countryside of Kent. As it increasingly takes on the appearance of a picaresque or Gothic novel, complete with an abducted heroine and her spiteful and miserly husband, the
underlying connections between its central characters and the regions
which they supposedly represent seem increasingly tenuous and difficult
to maintain. If "St. Giles and St. James must fraternize," as we are told at
the beginning, this ultimately seems possible only on the basis of con-
trived meetings between individuals, which take place on an abstracted
terrain at some considerable distance from the antagonistic social space
of the city.

### The Flight to the Suburbs

While St. Giles is away in Australia, the muffin-maker Capstick is said to
have earned sufficient money to enable him to retire from Seven Dials.
He eventually settles on the fictional village of Liquorish, but only after
a struggle with his city-bound wife, who "would never hear of going to
be buried alive from London; and therefore resolved upon nothing more
remote than a suburban whereabout. Hackney, or Pimlico, or Islington,
she might be brought to endure; but no, if she knew herself, nothing
should make her go and live, as she pathetically put it, like an owl in a
bush" (185–86). The boroughs she names seem strange from a modern
perspective, since all have long since been incorporated into the metropolitan limits, but her attraction to the suburbs seems surprisingly familiar, since they stood as now somewhere between the overcrowded delights of the city and the simple comforts of the country. Indeed, the
impulse to combine the two is followed in the novel by the miserly
Mr. Snipeton, who transplants his home and miserable wife to a small
cottage in "a green, sequestered nook, half-way between Hampstead and
Kilburn," conveniently located "within an hour's ride" of his business at
St. Mary's Axe (276). Snipeton is in fact the archetypal modern commuter, shuttling back and forth throughout the closing section of the
novel between his work in the city and the rural pleasures of home.

If these passages produce an unintentionally comic effect among
readers used to modern London, this is only because our understanding
of "the suburbs" or "the commuter" depend so much on a process of

train transportation from later in the century. In fact, the building of London's great railway termini, so memorably described by Dickens in 1848's *Dombey and Son,* had already begun to transform the appearance of the capital when *St. Giles and St. James* was first published: Euston Station had opened seven years earlier in 1838 to service trains between London and Birmingham, for example, while a terminus for the Great Western Railway had just been opened at Paddington in 1844. Suburbanization is, as Jerrold's novel implies, a relative process of separation. In fact, the OED dates the term "suburb" from as early as the fourteenth century, and offers a number of examples which are specific to central London.[45] Like Jerrold's examples of Hackney and Islington, a place like Covent Garden seems an unlikely suburb by modern standards, but the difference is simply one of scale. It was the completion of the New Road in 1757 that consolidated the process by which outlying villages to the north were linked to the commercial life of the city, and helped to spur the growth of more distant areas like Hampstead, Highgate, and Tottenham which were little more than an hour's carriage-ride away.[46] By 1817, Byron even refers to an ill-dressed man in "Beppo" as "vulgar, dowdyish, and suburban," thereby anticipating a modern tradition of anti-suburban sentiment.[47]

As Lewis Mumford has argued, the suburbs of the mid-nineteenth century perfected a lateral segregation between classes as well as their more obvious physical separation. "Except for a small detail of tradesmen and handymen," he notes, "the suburb was a one-class community: it boasts, in fact, of its 'exclusiveness'—which means, sociologically speaking, of the fact that it was not and could not become a city." The suburb also banished the characteristic dialectic of technical progress and urban squalor which we have identified with the romantic city, effecting a total removal of industrial production from the products' primary market: with the notable exception of the iron rails which carried commuter trains into the city stations, Mumford suggests, "there was no visible connecting link . . . between the barbarous industries that manufactured the goods and the romantic suburban homes, remote from the grime and the sweat, where these things were consumed."[48] The flight from industry, and the dirt, noise, and overcrowding which inevitably accompanied it, was accomplished on the basis of a flight from the city itself.

One important consequence of this was to divide the city temporally, along the same class lines which had previously functioned to divide it spatially into the twin halves of East and West. Rather than abandoning the capital for good, the Victorian middle class increasingly separated work from home, using the railways to commute between the private sphere of the suburban household and the commercial public sphere of the city. Such a separation is foregrounded in both the content and means of address employed by the periodical literature of the time, and underlies a classic early literary treatment of urban life, Poe's "The Man of the Crowd" (1840). In the story, a convalescent sits at the window of a coffee house in the center of London, watching the world pass by. Thanks to gas lighting, which had been introduced in the capital during the first decade of the nineteenth century, the narrator is able to continue his observations after nightfall.[49] A couple of points can be made about this story at the outset. First, Poe offers a typical viewpoint on the congestion of the city streets, noting how "two dense and continuous tides of population were rushing past the door":

> By far the greater number of those who went by had a satisfied business-like demeanour, and seemed to be thinking only of making their way through the press. Their brows were knit, and their eyes rolled quickly; when pushed against by fellow-wayfarers they evinced no symptom of impatience, but adjusted their clothes and hurried on. Others, still a numerous class, were restless in their movements, had flushed faces, and talked and gesticulated to themselves, as if feeling in solitude on account of the very denseness of the company around. When impeded in their progress, these people suddenly ceased muttering, but redoubled their gesticulations, and awaited, with an absent and overdone smile upon the lips, the course of the persons impeding them. . . . There was nothing very distinctive about these two large classes beyond what I have noted. Their habiliments belonged to that order which is pointedly termed the decent. They were undoubtedly noblemen, merchants, attorneys, tradesmen, stock-jobbers.[50]

As Benjamin points out, we can see here a crystallization of the techniques of observation and classification which define the urban flâneur: Poe's narrator claims the ability to read details of class, profession, and personality from the outward signs of dress, demeanor, and facial expression.[51] Thus, these men of leisure and business are distinguished from successive classifications of clerks (subdivided into upper and junior varieties), pickpockets, gamblers, pedlars, beggars, invalids, prostitutes, drunkards, "pie-men, porters, coal-heavers, sweeps; organ-grinders, monkey-exhibitors, and ballad-mongers."

In a sense, this performance simply hypostatizes the self-image of the cultural class, which I have already described as one centrally invested in reading the signs of social distinction. Alternatively, it anticipates the extensive researches of Mayhew and others, whose desire was precisely to produce this kind of minute typography of the London poor. As urban reportage, the story follows the conventional organizational strategies of working from high to low so that the account proceeds—in the narrator's words—by "descending in the scale of what is termed gentility." While we have seen such a structuring principle at work before, the strategy usually seems a more or less arbitrary one, which could be as easily inverted by proceeding from bottom to top. In "The Man of the Crowd," we learn why this hierarchical principle should hold, and just where the leisured class is in such a hurry to get to. As the nameless narrator insists upon explaining at some length,

> As the night deepened, so deepened to me the interest of the scene; for not only did the general character of the crowd materially alter (its gentler features retiring in the gradual withdrawal of the more orderly portion of the people, and its harsher ones coming out into bolder relief, as the late hour brought forth every species of infamy from its den), but the rays of the gaslamps, feeble at first in their struggle with the dying day, had now at length gained ascendancy, and threw over everything a fitful and garish lustre. (111)

These lines make clear what has only been implicit up to this point—that the streets of London belong to the poor after nightfall because their wealthy counterparts have now retired. As much as anything else, this demonstration of the temporal divisions of urban life links Poe's story with texts written at the end of the century by Conan Doyle, H. G. Wells, or G. K. Chesterton, which would present an alternative view of London from the perspective of the middle-class commuter.

An even earlier account of this suburban consciousness appeared in 1837, under the editorship of Dickens in *Bentley's Miscellany*. Shortly after reading about Oliver Twist's first encounter with the criminal subcultures of London, the magazine's subscribers were offered a cautionary tale by Edward Mayhew called "Midnight Mishaps," concerning the perils of country retirement: "Oh the rural suburbs of London!" it began, "—the filthy suburbs!—where nothing is green but the water, nothing natural but the dirt,—where the trees are clipt into poles, and the hedges grow behind palings,—where 'no thoroughfare' forbids you to talk in one place, and the dust prevents you from walking in another,—the filthy suburbs!" After this shocking opening, which reverses conventional wisdom about the relative cleanliness of the city's center and periphery, we are introduced to Mr. Jacob Tweasle, who has recently decided to retire from the cigar-shop in Snow Hill where he has worked for forty years to an Italian villa, which is "beautifully situated in a back lane near Hornsey" and consists of twenty square yards of lawn, an ornamental Chinese bridge, low rooms, small windows, and a picturesque view of St. Paul's Cathedral.[52] Tweasle's movement, then, is slightly westward, but mainly upward out of the city and away from the congestion and commerce of Snow Hill, in the vicinity of Fleet Street and Newgate prison. From there to Hornsey is a long way plotted on a map, but the psychic distance is even greater: the journey would have to proceed first through Clerkenwell, where Fagin initially establishes his headquarters; then further north past Pentonville and Camden Town, which would recently have experienced the tremendous transformation brought on by the development of the great railway termini at King's Cross and Euston; and still further north, skirting Hampstead Heath and the archetypal suburbs of Hampstead and Highgate. The joke is presumably that St. Paul's would only have looked picturesque from such a distance; it might have towered over the cigar-shop at the beginning of Tweasle's journey, but would of course have been invisible as a result.

The move brings Tweasle a remarkably modern sense of suburban paranoia, as he immediately sets about securing his country fortress from the criminals he doubtless thought he had left behind. In a characteristically paradoxical split, he divides his time between defensive operations designed to shield the home from invasion and gardening experiments for the small patch of lawn, which are quite clearly designed to advertise its appeal: "He gave his attention to the noble arts of agriculture and self-defence, botanical theories, treatises, and directories. Horticultural implements, instruments, and improvements, swords and pistols, guns and blunderbusses, detonating crackers for the shutters, and alarums for the bedrooms, he spared neither trouble nor expense to procure." In both its miniaturized scale and overdetermined defensive systems, Tweasle's villa seems a prototype for Mr. Wemmick's celebrated South London fortress in *Great Expectations,* which incorporates mock Gothic design with a moat, drawbridge, and mounted gun. The ornamental Chinese bridge suggests a particular combination of vanity and vulnerability, and Tweasle's fate seems assured early in the story, as he declares to his wife that "here's everything a contented mind could desire: the thieves will know better than to come where we are."

In time, of course, they *do* come, following the trail of wealth and ostentatious display by which Tweasle marks his rural retreat. First, he is forced to postpone his journey by some last-minute business in the city, and instructs his wife to go ahead in the carriage and "set the steel-traps" at the villa. Next, Tweasle is observed receiving £300 from a debtor, and pronounces out loud that he is armed, in order to frighten off a nearby beggar. As he finally sets out on foot for Hornsey, he continually touches the pistols in his coat pockets to feel safe, and volubly declares himself to be unafraid, despite venturing through territory which he feels to be "just such a spot as a murder might be committed in." Disturbed near his final destination by the sound of a donkey in the dark, he accidentally fires and loses the pistols, only to be accosted by the same beggar who had earlier witnessed his wealth at first-hand. Tweasle reluctantly hands over the waistcoat inside of which he had pinned his money, and proceeds to his new home, where the wife had earlier told the servants "to be watchful in their sleep for fear of robbers, as she was certain Mr. Tweasle would not be home that night, and did not know what his absence might bring about" (204). The story's ending is inevitable, but nonetheless cruel. Hearing steps on the Chinese bridge as they sit up regaling each other with "tales of midnight assassination," the family and servants "ventured to the upper windows, whence they could plainly see what all agreed was a countryman in a white smock-frock pacing to and fro in front of the house in all the bitterest rage of excessive disappointment." After he knocks and is heard vowing vengeance on the family, they move to the back of the house, where they see him "with a lofty courage that disdained at broken bottles, scale the garden-wall; and to their extreme delight, just as they were certain the back-door would not hold out, beheld him approach the jessamine bower where [a servant] had on the previous evening set one of the man-traps—and there he stayed." Tweasle's son Charles fires a shot from the blunderbuss, then goes out into the garden to find "*his father* writhing and moaning, with one leg fast in a trap, which, according to his own orders, had been set for the protection of the cabbages" (205, emphasis in original).

As I have suggested, this story is a curiously modern parable of suburban life, which neatly captures the tension between the desire for ostentatious display and a countervailing paranoia that manifests itself in elaborate security measures. Part of what this points to is a bifurcation within the ideology of suburbanization itself, which consisted of more than a simple separation of the classes. Indeed, as Donald Olsen has argued, the midcentury redrawing of the map of London involved the application of "two coexistent but incompatible Victorian ideals: individual privacy and public accountability." The acquisition and protection of the former was a hallmark of building plans dating back to the late eighteenth century, when the appearance of enclosed squares and terraces in West London gave testimony to the wealth and power of the Georgian aristocracy. Suburban development seems essentially to be the same plan on a larger scale: as the gap between rich and poor begins to collapse in central and West London, the privileged classes simply built further out in order to reassert a sense of safety and isolation from the dangers represented by the urban poor. As Olsen notes, however, this second wave of development carried with it the scars of the first, in the form of a pressing need to expose and highlight the lives of the poor, and to keep them under a steady surveillance: "The middle classes," he writes, "desired privacy for themselves, but wished the lives of the lower orders to be lived in the full blaze of publicity. Street improvements and slum clearance schemes were designed to bring the poor out into the open, where they could be observed, reproved, and instructed by their superiors."[53] This is the sense in which the suburban ring was intended to function as a *cordon sanitaire* around London, separating an overcrowded inner space, in which life was to be lived in the glare of publicity, from a heavily secured periphery dedicated to privacy, domesticity, and leisure.

Inhabitants of the latter were of course required to cross over into the space of the city to work, but the force of urban policing, horse patrols, and private security systems were all designed so that the traffic only went one way. By this time, as we have seen, the popular northern suburbs like Highgate and Hornsey were relatively safe. Indeed, we might say that Mr. Tweasle is victimized less by the traditional bands of brigands and highway robbers which his imagination conjures up, than by his own siege mentality, which causes him to invest in steel traps, weapons, and household alarms. The joke is not simply that these defenses work against him, but also that he has directly brought the threatening shadows of crime with him from the city, in the modest form of an opportunistic beggar attracted by Tweasle's own suspicious behavior. Ultimately, the story seems to suggest a problem with the entire strategy of suburban isolation, which depended for its success on a containment of the poor within the city walls. The fact that they are able to traverse the psychic boundary between the urban center and its suburban periphery reveals it to be as unstable and permeable as that separating the East End from central and West London. In this context, we can begin to see why Mr. Tweasle's midnight mishaps might constitute a cautionary tale not just about the suburban unconscious, but about the failure of an entire strategy of urban planning and segregation.

In *The Politics and Poetics of Transgression,* Peter Stallybrass and Allon White offer a useful account of why this strategy breaks down. Referring back to the dual tactics of maintaining a privatized bourgeois space in the suburbs over and against a highly public inner city, they show how the distinction constantly threatened to disintegrate: "even as the separation of the suburb from the slum established a certain class difference," they argue, "the development of the city simultaneously threatened the clarity of that segregation."[54] The controlling bourgeois gaze which sought to illuminate the dark spaces of working-class life was itself problematic, caught up within cycles of attraction and repulsion, excitement and disgust, proximity and distance. As a variety of contemporary evidence suggests—from the moral panics about contagion and contamination to the vogue for "slumming" excited by Pierce Egan's *Life in London*—the tropes of East End life continued to fascinate and titillate observers from other parts of London, and to implicate them in a less-distanced sense of urban cohabitation. We must assume that the purpose of visiting the slums of Ratcliff Highway, even when accompanied by police detectives, was precisely for the West End "bloods" inspired by Egan to feel some sense of *frisson* at the apparent collapse of the boundaries which would normally separate them from the sailors, prostitutes, and thieves that they encountered there. But it was also the case, as Stallybrass and White suggest, that this fascinated bourgeois gaze was often returned by a stare which rarely denoted "deference and respect." As we shall see, this stubborn but often ingenious tactic of non-cooperation consistently threatened to exploit the contradictory impulses within bourgeois strategies of containment, and to reveal the submerged class politics which Victorian journalists, philanthropists, novelists, and reformers all preferred to excise from their accounts of city life.

My major focus in chapters 2 and 3 will be on Dickens, who usefully combines many of the most prominent features of this group. As a successful novelist, he was of course an enormous influence on the shape of public representations of London throughout much of the nineteenth century, and continues to be today. As a reformer, engaged in small-scale local projects like the Ragged Schools or Urania Cottage for "fallen women," he shared many of the aspirations, frustrations, and blind spots of a generation of Victorian reformers. And as a journalist and magazine editor, first for *Bentley's Miscellany* and later with his own *Household Words,* he contributed to a new school of urban journalism which aimed both to represent the city and to palliate its more disturbing effects for a rural—and increasingly suburban—readership. As I have tried to suggest throughout this first chapter, the new periodicals of the 1830s and '40s seemed an appropriate place for developing a dual strategy of private isolation and public exposé. Addressed primarily to the ascendant middle class, periodicals like *Bentley's* alternated between reassuring articles promoting a comfortable consumer lifestyle and activist interventions concerning the poor of the capital. Dickens's prologue to the first volume in 1837 codified this oscillation in terms of party politics, while staking out the same "neutral" position that we saw earlier with Leigh Hunt and the *London Magazine.* Just a few years after the upheavals of the First Reform and Poor Law acts, and at the onset of the Chartist agitation, *Bentley's* introduced itself to its readership with the proud claim to "have nothing to do with politics":

> We are so far Conservative as to wish that all things which are good and honourable for our native country should be preserved

with jealous hand. We are so far Reformers as to desire that every
weed which defaces our conservatory should be unsparingly
plucked up and cast away. But is it a matter of absolute necessity
that people's political opinions should be perpetually obtruded
upon public notice? Is there not something more in the world
to be talked about than Whig and Tory?[55]

The image of the conservatory here suggests the comforts of the rural retreat, which is linked in turn (by the consonance of conserva-
tory/Conservative) to the idea of the nation as a whole. The identity of
those defacing "weeds" would have been known to readers in the 1830s:
radicals recently aligned with France, the "undeserving" poor, and the
criminal subcultures which Dickens chose for the subject of *Oliver Twist,*
the featured story in the opening volumes of this new magazine. Spurred
into action, the editor elects himself the guardian of the national heritage while simultaneously promising to "pluck and cast away" the threatening weeds with a crusader's zeal. It is indeed a complex position that
he is staking here, that of the conservative reformer. Readers of Dickens
have wrestled with its inconsistencies ever since; as we shall see from the
reviews, responses, adaptations, and outright plagiarisms that followed
the publication of *Oliver Twist,* the struggle to pin Dickens down, and to
decode the political unconscious of his texts, began immediately. The
novel offers a kind of map of social relations in London, although one
that seems strikingly unbalanced and incomplete. Those struggles over
textual interpretation are also, then, efforts to fill in the gaps and see the
larger picture.

# 2   READING RUN RIOT

Criminal Subcultures in the Newgate Novel

IN CONSIDERING NOVELS like *Oliver Twist* or William Harrison Ainsworth's *Jack Sheppard* (1839–40) after reading Wordsworth and the romantics, we are confronted by a very different urban geography, in which issues of political effect—of how such texts would be read, and by whom—are insistently foregrounded. There is, I will be arguing, a rhetoric of inversion underlying Victorian crime fiction of this period, which seeks to indict lawful society from the perspective and interests of those who were excluded from political representation. In a period that was dominated by Chartism and associated fears of a situation of dual power, it is my larger contention that these texts were received and reproduced in contexts that bore little connection to any straightforward notion of authorial intent.

The reading I am presenting in this chapter aims to sidestep—or at least reframe—the standard critical question about exactly how "subversive" these novels actually were. Answering this question almost inevitably invites a more lengthy discussion of recent critical practice: arguments about expanding the literary canon, for example, which might see the juxtaposition of Ainsworth's "popular" novel with Dickens's "canonical" one as itself a subversive gesture, aimed either at elevating the former to critical attention or exposing a more radical subtext in the latter; or the New Historicist assault on the notion of a purely radical text, and the counterargument that such texts often produce sites and moments of subversion only to neutralize them within a larger narrative of containment and closure. To take an obvious example of this latter argument, and paraphrase an influential version of it from Foucault, forms of criminal or sexual deviancy function to police the boundaries of a sanctioned and normative subjectivity, which is strengthened rather than challenged by contrast with its demonized others. The next stage of the argument is then to suggest that such marginal and ostensibly transgressive subjectivities are in fact produced by the dominant power structure itself, and should be viewed as something like the licensed excesses of Carnival, negative images of power which as a consequence have no independent basis from which to mount a revolutionary challenge.

The argument is a familiar one by now, and especially suited to literary studies which have consistently seen textual closure as a final moment of restabilization that neutralizes any dissenting forces produced by and in the movement of the narrative: in *Oliver Twist* (for the sake of argument), the alternative lifestyle associated with the deviant criminal subculture grouped around Fagin is effectively dismantled—and its representatives either killed, transported, or reformed—as the text moves toward its triumphant affirmation of a reconstituted bourgeois family around Harry and Rose Maylie, Mr. Brownlow, and Oliver.

In this chapter, I outline "subversive" readings of *Oliver Twist* and *Jack Sheppard,* as well as a version of the containment thesis sketched above. On the basis of the limitations of these readings, however, I argue for a more complex interpretation of both texts in the context of their original appearance in *Bentley's Miscellany,* the responses and appropriations they provoked among nineteenth-century readers, and the contemporary genre of the "Newgate novel" with which they were associated. In each case, I attend not only to the texts themselves but also to what Tony Bennett has termed the "reading formation," defined as the "set of intersecting discourses which productively activate a given body of texts and the relations between them in a specific way."[1] In an earlier study of James Bond, Bennett and Janet Woollacott offer a useful instance of such a formation in their exemplary inter-textual analysis of the complex network of novels, films, interviews, serializations, reviews, theme songs, and so on, which collectively constitute the cultural figure of Bond.[2] In the case of *Oliver Twist,* we might define the "inter-text" as including not only Dickens's own text, as published serially from February 1837 to April 1839 and in novel form with a succession of revisions from 1838 onwards, but also concurrent popular plagiarisms like *Oliver Twiss,* published by Lloyd's of Bloomsbury in 1838–39; printed responses to Dickens, including reviews, criticism, and poems inspired by the novel which also appeared in *Bentley's* during its serialized debut; stage and film versions dating back to the 1840s, and including David Lean's 1948 film, Lionel Bart's musical *Oliver!* and *its* screen adaptation from 1968; and so on.[3] In the case of *Jack Sheppard,* the story of a real-life thief and jail-breaker from the 1720s which appeared in novel form during its serialization in 1839–40, we might look at other versions of the Sheppard biography, along with critical responses and the controversial dramatic adaptations which the novel's appearance incited.

I will return to these plays later in this chapter, and to the critical controversy which they ignited concerning the political effectivity of popular crime fiction. For now, though, I want mainly to stress how each of these versions is produced by—and helps to constitute—a discrete scene of reading: just as the version encourages (but cannot exhaustively predict) a range of possible interpretations, it is also a reading of the original novel, and makes conscious choices about what aspects to alter, highlight, or excise. Each puts the story to work in different ways, and in so doing assigns it a functional use value. Some of the determinants of this value have been outlined by Barbara Herrnstein Smith, who argues that any critical judgment involves three aspects: "a) . . . an estimate of how well that work will serve certain implicitly defined functions b) for a specific implicitly defined audience c) who are conceived of as experiencing the work under certain implicitly defined conditions."[4] As such, according to Herrnstein Smith, one measure of the durability of a literary work is whether "under changing conditions and in competition with newly produced and other re-produced works, it continues to perform some desired/able functions particularly well, even if not the same ones for which it was initially valued," in which case "it will continue to be cited and re-cited, continue to be visible and available to succeeding generations of subjects, and thus continue to be culturally reproduced" (49).

Of the two novels under discussion, this description fits *Oliver Twist* rather than *Jack Sheppard*. If the story of Oliver has experienced a pro-longed shelf-life, this is due in large part to its considerable adaptability to changing contexts and interests. To take the twentieth-century adaptations, we might see that the revisionist efforts of David Lean and Lionel Bart effectively rewrite the story to suit local or historical interests. Besides reducing the range of characters in Dickens's original by conflating some and de-emphasizing others, these films and stage versions adapt a specific attitude toward its portrayal of criminality, which can be readily ascribed to the historical contexts in which they were produced. The musical appears, for example, during a decade in which social attitudes toward criminality were more likely to favor the possibility of rehabilitation, and so risks humanizing Fagin by having him consider giving up his life of crime at one point (the song, "I Think I'd Better Think It Out Again"); in place of the death cell ending of the original novel, *Oliver!* concludes on a more upbeat note, as Fagin and the Artful Dodger walk off into the sunset. Even Lean's version, from 1948, seems to suggest a softening on the issue of capital punishment: Fagin is simply led away by police at the end, while Bill Sikes's climactic rooftop hanging—which appears in the novel as the manifestation of a collective will of the people—is instead precipitated by a policeman's bullet.

In making these changes, Bart and Lean were replicating the established practices of Dickens's own time, when theatrical versions had to be closed down for inciting audiences with sensationalized performances of the murder of Nancy. The most successful version by George Almar from 1838 prefigures the Lean film, for instance, in its concern to condense and rearrange the scenes in the last third of the novel, although his decision may have been determined more by practical matters, since the novel had not yet been finished in serial form![5] Even so, his version provides a powerful dramatic ending, as Sikes remained for some time dangling on the London stage in a gruesome—yet presumably cathartic—tableau which closed the performance. John Hollingshead remembered a similar version at the Victoria Theatre, and the audience's reactions to Sikes: "It was," he noted,

> a heavy leaden mass when the play was dull and didactic, but with a fifty-ironclad store of reserved force, which, like a slumbering volcano, could be roused into violent action at any

moment. . . . The "murder of Nancy" was the great scene. . . .
No language ever dreamt in Bedlam could equal the outburst. A
thousand enraged voices, which sounded like ten thousand . . .
filled the theatre, and . . . when the smiling ruffian came forward
and bowed, . . . expressed a fierce determination to tear his sanguinary entrails from his sanguinary body.[6]

His description recalls some of the excitement generated by staged performances of *Jack Sheppard,* of which there were eight versions running
concurrently in London at the height of the novel's popularity. According to Keith Hollingsworth, the fad was "at least the equal of anything in
popular entertainment in the present century," prompting such tie-ins as
the sale of souvenir "Sheppard-bags" in theater lobbies, complete with
tools of the jailbreaker's trade like pick-locks, screwdrivers, and iron
levers, and the spin-off success of a "flash song" from the play, "Nix My
Dolly, Pals, Fake Away."[7] One first-hand account from Sir Theodore
Martin noted that this song "traveled everywhere, and made the patter
of thieves and burglars 'familiar in our mouths as household words.'
It deafened us in the streets, where it was as popular with the organ-
grinders and German bands as Sullivan's brightest melodies were in a later
day. It clanged at midday from the steeple of St. Giles, the Edinburgh
Cathedral . . . ; it was whistled by every dirty guttersnipe, and chanted
in drawing-rooms by fair lips, little knowing the meaning of the words
they sang."[8]

The astonishing portability of the song here—which clearly crossed
demarcated lines of class in moving from the lowest gutters to the lofty
spires of high church—helps to explain the fears which the texts of *Jack
Sheppard* incited among bourgeois audiences. Domestic novelist Mary
Russell Mitford offered an extreme example of this paranoia when she
wrote of having "been struck by the great danger, in these times, of representing authorities so constantly and fearfully in the wrong." The character of the villainous Jonathan Wild struck her in particular as "a representation of power—government or law, call it as you may—the ruling
power," which is thus implicitly indicted for Wild's own treacherous and
self-serving actions. What is especially notable about Mitford's reading is
its independence of traditional considerations of authorial intention: in a
pattern that we shall see repeated in similar considerations of theatrical

adaptation, she explictly notes that "Mr. Ainsworth had no such design, but such is the effect; and as the millions who see it represented at the minor theatres will not distinguish between now and a hundred years back, all the Chartists in the land are less dangerous than this nightmare of a book." Mitford identifies herself as a Radical, yet also denounces "any additional temptations to outbreak" that crime novels and dramas might help to incite among the masses, mindful of the ways that the Chartist movement had helped to form the preconditions for such actions.[9] It might seem strange to worry about the possible effects of a story about a thief from a century earlier, but the anticipated dangers of texts like *Jack Sheppard* hardly seem to have been exaggerated, as I hope to show in the final section of this chapter. For now, we need only note that even a self-identified Radical like Mitford recoiled, interpreting popular sympathies for the hero in light of the Chartist agitation. The whole Sheppard craze, as I hope to show, might be read as a cautionary tale concerning the power which might inhere in or be activated by a commercial popular culture.

We might ask why Jack Sheppard disappears from mass consciousness more quickly than Oliver, especially given that the respective authorial reputations of Dickens and Ainsworth were then more comparable than posterity might suggest; indeed, the two were close friends for a time, forming a self-named Trio with John Forster until the time when Ainsworth replaced Dickens as editor at *Bentley's*.[10] Part of the answer, as we shall see, lies in the different attitudes which critics, reviewers, and journalists adopted toward Ainsworth's novel, which increasingly came to stand in for an entire genre of "Newgate novels" meriting censure: works by authors like Edward Bulwer Lytton or Douglas Jerrold were usually grouped with Ainsworth's, whereas *Oliver Twist* was increasingly exempted, for reasons which may well have to do with Dickens's rising-star status.[11] It is also significant that *Jack Sheppard* found a meaningful context only in relation to the Chartist agitation, which generally dispersed around 1848. As a real-life historical figure, Jack lacks the mobility of literary characters like Oliver or Fagin, who can be successively redrawn in order to adapt to a variety of interests and uses. For these reasons, they have experienced a steady longevity lasting into our own century, whereas the character of Sheppard had a more dramatic but short-lived career in the Victorian cultural imagination.

### Oliver's Subversive Twists

In a poem entitled "The Three Literary Graces," which appeared in *Bentley's Miscellany* a month after the final installment of *Oliver Twist,* a reader offers a quick sketch of how that novel might have been received by its intended audience. Personifying the journal itself by the torturous pun of "Miss Cellany," and his own family as representing a class of country readers who depend on periodicals to provide them with the reflected cultural capital of London, "Buller, Senior" reconstructs the *frisson* of moral outrage which this audience were supposed to feel at the treatment of Oliver:

> She comes once a-month to one's house on a visit;
> And Laura cries out, "Is it Missy? Oh, is it?
> Dear Missy, pray take me the first on your knee;
> Don't talk to mamma, but take notice of me,
> And tell me, oh! tell me the ending, do pray,
> Of the beautiful tale you began t'other day,
> That wicked man Bumble!—and Fagin the Jew!—
> Is it all your own fancy, or actually true?"

The issue of credibility is further raised by the response of her brother, Alfred, who "[l]ooks grave as a lion, and doubles his fist / To thrash the oppressors of Oliver Twist." The belief in the reality of narratives that the poem is mocking here is not confined to young readers, however, since the location of Buller, Senior, indicates that he would be unfamiliar with the urban setting of Dickens's novel and therefore need to take Dickens's descriptions on trust. Indeed, for this particular reader at least, the journal seems to be more specifically addressed to those "in the counties," who might turn to it with interest "when the weather's too rainy / for hunting the fox."

*Bentley's* is simultaneously praised for its appeal to rural readers and for its realistic depiction of a particular locale, the slums of London. This may only seem like a contradiction, however, since it is in fact designed to smooth over a more serious point of tension in the poem, concerning the gap that separates the novel's location from that of its readers. As the poem ends, "my Lord" passes judgment on Miss Cellany's accuracy, noting "[h]ow exactly she traces / The site . . . of these pickpocket places—/ Jacob's Island, to wit, and that horrible Mint! / As if the fair lady had really been in't!"[12] Like the dialectic I traced in chapter 1 between the competing feelings of inter-class proximity and distance established by the cultural representations of London, the journalistic discourse of *Bentley's* maintains a separation between its privileged readers and the urban poor, about whom they nonetheless acknowledge a discomforting fascination. The journal's conscious elaboration of the space separating country and city suggests that any verdict that its rural readers make on the truthfulness of Dickens's writing can have had no experiential basis. Like "Miss Cellany," it is unlikely that they would ever have "really been in't," and yet they feel an immense confidence in the novelist's ability to represent "these pickpocket places." This is, in a sense, what Dickens's novels are famous for: by providing a kind of "reality effect" in his depictions of the urban underworld, Dickens generated a sense of trust among reforming and conservative readers alike, each of whom thereby assented to the iconic reputation of Dickens as the preferred chronicler and interpreter of lower-class London.[13]

These same interlocking concerns with audience and authenticity recur in contemporary reviews of the published novel. The *Monthly Review,* for example, praised its authentic representation of the London underworld, while taking pains to qualify its own ability to make such judgments: according to the reviewer, *Oliver Twist* was best read not as "a cunningly conceived plot, or a progressively arresting tale," but as a collection of sketches "of character, scenes, and events *as they are supposed, with much seeming of truth,* to exist among London paupers, pauper officers, the relatives and friends of paupers, receivers of stolen goods, thieves, etc."[14] A similar hesitation can be found in the *Quarterly Review,* which praised the London settings while contrasting them with rural episodes in the novel, which seemed unconvincing in part because they were populated by characters who lacked the requisite geo-social specificity: "his descriptions of rural felicity and country scenes, of which he clearly knows much less than of London . . . are," the reviewer noted, "except when comical, over-laboured and out of nature. His 'gentle and genteel folks' are unendurable; they are devoid of grace, repose, and ease of good society; a something between Cheltenham and New York." London scenes, by contrast, are felt to have been presented with a precision comparable to that of the *camera obscura:* "Fagin, Sikes, and the dog especially, are always in their proper and natural places, always speaking, barking, and acting exactly as they ought to have done, and, as far as we are able to judge, with every appearance of truth." [15] The hesitation of "as far as we are able" here—like the *Monthly's* "much seeming of truth"—enacts the same double move of praising Dickens for accurately representing a way of life which it needs at the same time to keep at arm's length, as if giving the novelist *carte blanche* to explore this alien underworld on behalf of its willfully ignorant readers.

Conferring this kind of absolute authority on Dickens carried with it certain risks for the critics, who thereby undercut the potential ground for negative commentary: to reproach the novelist for inaccuracy or a romantic investment in his criminal characters would in effect mean confessing to a closer and more intimate knowledge of the underworld than that of Dickens. We can see some of these problems in the critical writings of Thackeray, who consistently attacked the "Newgate novelists" for their authorial irresponsibility. In an unsigned article on Ainsworth from 1840, for example, he compares their urban landscapes with Byron's pirate adventures to make the point that in the "Cockney realms" of London, "exploits of priggery done there upon sundry butchers, and bakers, and candlestick-makers, cannot be so grand-sounding to the ear as the adventures upon the nameless shore of the Pirate's isle. . . . We must insist upon it that our thieves are nothing more than thieves, whom it is hopeless to attempt gilding over with the graces and glories of chivalry." [16] By this point, Thackeray had been consistently campaigning against crime novels for over a year, accusing them of romantic exaggeration and lack of moral rectitude. As early as April 1839, when *Oliver Twist* was still being published in serial form, he produced "Horae Catnachianae" for *Fraser's Magazine,* complaining of how such novels "mislead the public" with their crime novels: "Depend upon it," Thackeray notes with an air of confidence,

> that Shire Lane does not in the least resemble Mr. Dickens's description of that locality; that the robber's den in *Pelham,* or the Bath rendezvous of the thieves in *Paul Clifford,* are but creations of the fancy of the honourable baronet [Bulwer Lytton] who wrote those popular novels, and who knows as much about low

life as he does of German metaphysics. As, indeed, how should he know? He never had half an hour's conversation with the thieves, cut-throats, old-clothesmen, prostitutes, or pickpockets, described; nor can the admirable Boz be expected to have had any such experience.

But this assault on the realism of these novels is hard to sustain, and Thackeray quickly shifts to the more familiar territory of moral criticism, suggesting that criminal characters are dangerous precisely on account of their romanticized representation: "We could 'hug the rogues and love them,' and do—*in private*. In public it is, however, quite wrong to avow such likings, and to be seen in such company." [17] These comments need to be seen as part of a wider campaign on Thackeray's part against the fashion for crime themes in popular fiction. In a review of a new edition of Fielding's works from 1840, for example, he returned to the issue of moral responsibility in an attempt to exempt the author of *Tom Jones* and *Jonathan Wild* from these censures, claiming that "vice is never to be mistaken for virtue in Fielding's honest downright books; it goes by its name, and invariably gets its punishment." By this point, however, issues of realism had become hopelessly confused with moralism, and Thackeray could only defend his own counter-canon of earlier crime texts—which included John Gay and Hogarth, as well as Fielding—by arguing that social standards have changed for the worse: thus, these earlier artists could afford to be both truthful and morally responsible because eighteenth-century society permitted it. Forced into a corner, he could only conclude that such a luxury could no longer be endorsed under Victorian codes of conduct, which required a crippling double standard of public and private behavior:

> The world does not tolerate now such satire as that of Hogarth and Fielding, and the world no doubt is right in a great part of its squeamishness; for it is good to pretend to the virtue of chastity even though we do not possess it; nay, the very restraint which the hypocrisy lays on a man is not unapt, in some instances, to profit him. . . . It is wise that the public modesty should be as prudish as it is; that writers should be forced to chasten their humour, and when it would play with points of life

and character which are essentially immoral, that they should be compelled, by the general outcry, to be silent altogether.[18]

His solutions are perhaps extreme, but symptomatic of the prevailing response to these new crime novels, which registered a palpable sense of unease at their possible influence.

If Dickens himself was commonly exempted from criticism, both reviews I have cited also expressed concerns about possible imitators, raising the specter (as the *Monthly* put it) of "a less skillful and considerate performer [who might] adventure after him." These concerns were very real, as we shall see, but cannot be divorced from a more substantial fear of audiences who might read the novel according to different criteria and interests. In effect, Dickens became a victim of his own success, as "a truly national author" belonging to Britain as a whole. As the *Quarterly Review* went on to elaborate, a text like *Oliver Twist* in fact appealed much more to "the numerical majority of the young, and of the lower orders—(for whom books in shilling Numbers have the *appearance* of being mainly designed)," so that Dickens might be seen as playing to their degraded or underdeveloped tastes "in spite of honest intentions." Interestingly, this reviewer seems most concerned about the issue of language, which helps to crystallize the kind of critical double bind I have been outlining here. Dickens is initially praised for his detailed knowledge of the rhythms and terminology of subcultural speech, as "the regius professor of slang, that expression of the mother-wit, the low humour of the lower classes, their Sanscrit, their hitherto unknown tongue," but an undertone of concern is registered as the reviewer notes that such speech "in the present phasis of society and politics, seems likely to become the idiom of England." In doing so, I would argue, the review highlights the larger political context in which these discussions of crime literature occurred, in a time that was dominated by political reform and the Chartist threat. It also registers the weak position of the middle-class readership, who once again have to depend on Dickens to translate for them. According to the standards of realism by which the novel was measured, the underworld characters must of course speak in their own language; "In order to fully enjoy their force," though, genteel readers "must know the conventional value of these symbols of ideas, [even] though we do not understand the lingo like Boz, who has it at his finger-ends."[19]

This review betrays what I am reading as a kind of repressed context for the reception of these crime texts, which were adopted as a forum through which to address and debate current issues of class politics. This thesis is determined in part by simple chronology: the original publications of novels like *Oliver Twist* and *Jack Sheppard,* as well as Dickens's subsequent account of the Gordon riots in *Barnaby Rudge* (1841) are bracketed by the abortive national holiday and Newport Rising following the first Chartist Convention of 1839, and by the more serious waves of rioting and strikes that occurred in 1842, a year when, as Dorothy Thompson notes, "more people were arrested and sentenced for offences concerned with speaking, agitating, rioting and demonstrating" than in any other year of the nineteenth century.[20] After the failed Newport Rising, its leaders received death sentences for treason, which were commuted to transportation for life, in January of 1840, amid fears that the hangings might succeed where the original uprising failed in generalizing discrete local protests into a significant national agitation; one month later, the final installment of *Jack Sheppard,* including a failed attempt to rescue Jack from the gallows, appeared in *Bentley's.*

To a remarkable degree, Chartism came to permeate English political and cultural discourse during this period, which also produced the genre of the industrial novel specifically focused on issues of social justice and the disparity between the classes. The title of one such novel by future Prime Minister Disraeli, *Sybil; or, the Two Nations* (1845), neatly foregrounds how the depth of popular support for Chartism caused various sectors of Victorian society to imagine a situation of dual political power, in a scenario which became a more real possibility three years later, when the Chartist convention of 1848 unsuccessfully tried to constitute itself as an alternative locus of government. *Blackwood's Edinburgh Magazine* recognized the danger as early as 1839, when it editorialized against the first London convention in the aftermath of the Newport uprising:

> the very idea of a National Convention—that is, an Assembly of Delegates elected by the people by Universal Suffrage, without either the authority of the Crown or the sanction of the Legislature, and issuing proclamations and orders which they expect to be obeyed by millions in the community, and certainly are

acted upon by hundreds and thousands of the people—is itself an usurpation of the royal prerogative, the establishment of an *imperium in imperio,* utterly inconsistent with the existence of order or the security of property in the realm.[21]

Subsequent events suggest that this may have taken the Chartists too literally at their word, but the sense it conveys of a legislative body existing within the larger parliamentary framework usefully captures how the Chartist threat was viewed. By establishing the national convention, the movement provided a literal image to exemplify its status as a potential fifth column, an enemy which sought to erode and supplant legal authority from within.[22]

I do not mean to suggest that these novels directly intersected with or advanced the explicit demands of the Charter, the famous "Six Points" arguing for universal manhood suffrage, voting by ballot, equal electoral districts, annual Parliaments, abolition of property qualifications for candidates, and payment of M.P.s. As Patrick Brantlinger has suggested, Dickens was particularly unsettled by the Chartist campaign, and addressed it only obliquely in his novels, in a manner which separated its political goals from their basis in the experiences of labor in a newly industrial society.[23] I will look, however, at how some versions of the story of *Oliver Twist* resituated it in more overtly political contexts, by placing speeches about the justice system, property rights, and police brutality in the mouths of characters as varied as Mr. Brownlow and Fagin. My thesis is that each of these texts participated in a larger public forum about what Carlyle famously termed "the condition of England," in which a radical discourse forcefully articulated a distinctive vision of popular rights and interests in ways which seemed to give support to the Chartist cause. As Gareth Stedman Jones has argued, this language of rights was founded upon a populist-democratic analysis of society, in which the fact of the poor's exclusion from the political process could explain all of their problems. Without universal suffrage, the system of parliamentary representation by itself supported and legitimated an unjust rule of law, in which the privileged sought to promote their exclusive interests, so that Chartist rhetoric aimed to expose the basis on which the products and profits of labor were denied, "by unjust *exchanges* . . . supported by force or fraud, whether by direct operation of the law, or by indirect operation of unjust social arrangements." Within such a framework, the new police were condemned as "in effect another standing army—to make people submit to all the insults and oppressions which government contemplates forcing upon them," and the ruling class held responsible for numerous crimes against humanity, including the expropriation of labor power, profiteering, corruption, and murder.[24]

Given this rhetorical dimension, and the structuring framework of the two nations into which it played, the depictions of a linguistic diversity in texts like *Oliver Twist* and *Jack Sheppard* can come to be seen as highly provocative and incendiary gestures. The use of underworld slang emerged as a key issue for critics of popular crime novels, in other words, because it quite explicitly interpellated a mass audience while underscoring the firm distinctions which existed between various classes of readers—hence, Mary Russell Mitford's reference to the theater-going masses as continuous with, and even more dangerous than, the organized Chartist movement. For the *Quarterly Review,* the craze for underworld "flash" incited by these novels constituted a doubled threat, of controversial ideas themselves and also a new mode of expression by which they were able to circulate: "We object to familiarising our ingenious youth with 'slang,'" it proclaimed, since

> it is based in travestie of better things. Nobler and generous ideas, when expressed in low and mean terms, become ludicrous from the contrast and incongruity. . . . But the base vehicle conveys too frequently opinions and sentiments which could thus alone gain admission. . . . They corrupt pure taste and pervert morality, for vice loses shame when treated as a fool-born joke, and those who are not ashamed to talk of a thing will not be long ashamed to put it into practice. These Dodgers and Sikes break into our Johnson, rob the queen's lawful current English.

As if to clarify the real danger here, spreading outward from grammatical usage to the struggles for political representation, the author concludes the passage by characterizing such "slangers" as speaking in "the energetic tone of this era of popular outbreaks."[25]

It is hardly surprising that language became a politically charged issue in debates about popular theatrical adaptations, one hallmark of which was a heightened use of slang. George Almar's version from 1838 seems typical, especially in its concern to maximize the on-stage time of the popular Artful Dodger at the expense of others in Fagin's gang like Charley Bates, Toby Crackit, and Noah Claypole. In Dickens's novel, the Dodger is sentenced to transportation for stealing "a common two-penny halfpenny sneezebox," causing his admirer Charley to wonder how his illustrious criminal career will finally appear in the annals of *The Newgate Calendar* (390). Perhaps sensing that such a fate truly was inadequate for such a popular figure, Almar has Charley transported in his place.[26] The Dodger's popularity is further attested to by the increased use of "flash" in the stage version: on first meeting Oliver, for example, he obscurely tells him "Oh, yes, over the bender; so tip your rags a gallop, and dare up at both ends, my covey"; later, he refers to a £5 note as a "fi'-pun flimsy," to gin as "max," and to Charley's fate as being "lagged for life for a silver sneezer." All of this flash language remains impenetrable to Oliver, of course, as perhaps to segments of the London theater audience, and Almar jokes at Oliver's naiveté in the following scene, where he first goes out in the company of Charley and the Dodger:

> DODGER: You hear what Fagin says, you're to do exactly what two nice gentlemen tell you.
>
> OLIVER: I know I am.
>
> D: Well, then, mizzle.
>
> O: I don't know how to mizzle.
>
> D: Cut your stick.
>
> O: I haven't got a knife.
>
> D: My eyes! how jolly green he is.[27]

Scenes like this also appear in Dickens, of course, but the difference is that the narrative voice performs a mediating function there, as a translator for Oliver and (through him) for the readers. The Dodger's greeting of "Plummy and slam!" is followed by the narrative explanation that "This seemed to be some watchword or signal that all was right" (103), for example, while "Jerk the tinkler" is similarly translated for us, as designating "in plain English . . . an injunction to ring the bell" (155); at one point, indeed, the interactional dynamic of such scenes is made explicit, when Charley responds to a stream of Dodger slang by asking "What's the good of talking in that way? . . . he don't know what you mean," after which the Dodger is said to have modified "his conversation to the level of Oliver's capacity" (183–84). Dickens may even have intended to provide a direct key to such slang expressions, since the original serialization in *Bentley's* contained a footnote in the first volume, translating "swag" as "Booty," though the practice was discontinued in subsequent installments. What is most striking here, though, is that the use and effects of slang shift according to the different contexts in which these texts are performed or read. Scenes of translation in which Oliver acts as the butt of the joke would presumably have been received very differently in the popular theaters where the plays were performed, while the middle-class readers of *Bentley's* were aligned more closely with the novel's hero (as we have seen), and would probably have welcomed more footnotes.

Another way of putting this is to say that imitators like Almar simply capitalized on an opening provided for them by the original text, and realized the subversive potential of slang which Dickens had only gestured toward, but which had already begun to trouble his reviewers: in the words of the *North British Review,* writing with hindsight in 1845,

> In estimating the probable effect of these writings of Mr. Dickens, we must remember that, in the shape of plays, they have been represented at most of the theatres in the country. In the process of transmutation the better and more sober parts necessarily disappear, and the striking figures, amusing low life, smart vulgar conversation, and broad farce, are naturally preserved with care. . . . The higher rank thus laughs publicly at the scenes of most hurtful tendency; and it is these principally which are made widely known to the lower classes.

Dickens could not of course be held entirely responsible for his imitators and plagiarists, although the rest of this review essay—which mainly reiterates Thackeray's attacks on the representation of vice alongside ad hominem assaults on Dickens's use of slang and low humor—makes clear that he was considered partly to blame for having started a trend with *Oliver Twist,* which "has done much towards creating in the public a morbid interest in such heroes and their modes of life"; as a result, the review concludes that a taste for crime fiction "speedily becomes a craving, and the public learn to demand an insight into the haunts of crime, and to desire a familiarity with the habits and adventures of the profligate and brutal."[28] What is left uninterrogated, however, is the basis of this appeal, which is presented here as almost a natural (yet dangerously sub-versive) impulse on the part of the public, but was in fact explained and interpreted in a variety of ways for which we can find parallels in con-temporary critical practice.

### Subversion/Containment:
### The Function of Criminal Subcultures

As Deborah Epstein Nord has argued, the London underworld posed a particular problem for Dickens, in his representative position as spokes-person for the ascendant middle class. Where Pierce Egan's *Life in London* could still address itself to—indeed, represent—the aristocratic faction known as "the swells," who openly acknowledged a fascination for lower-class London, Dickens's comparable figure is "the shabby-genteel": aspiring to a higher social status, yet terrified of slipping back down the ladder of distinction; living more typically in those central re-gions of London (like Holborn, Clerkenwell, and Islington) where they might expect to come in contact with the poor, instead of in the com-fortable enclaves of the West End; and concerned (above all else) with the presentation of cultivated tastes, appearance, and manners. If, as Nord suggests, this class had "felt itself coming into at least partial possession of the city and, as a consequence, into a position of responsibility for its fate," then it makes sense to see Dickens's early works in particular as providing them with maps of the capital designed to foster relations of sympathy and understanding; indeed, we have seen in the previous chap-ter how the new periodicals of the period aspired to fulfill this same func-tion, dovetailing neatly with the fashion for panoramic sketches which Dickens himself had helped to popularize with *Sketches by Boz*.[29] But this sympathetic introjection of urban types reaches a limit, Nord argues, with the "dangerous classes" themselves, and with areas like Seven Dials from which Dickens appears to pull back: thus, he sets out to represent the true horrors of such regions, while simultaneously "retreat[ing] into a language of theatricality and artifice as a way of avoiding the harshness of his subject" (65–66). On this basis, Nord reads *Oliver Twist*—like the earlier *Sketches*—as concerned more with distance and containment than with exposure, and she designates the murder of Nancy as the moment which "purges the novel of danger and criminality" through a recourse to the exaggerated modalities of melodrama (81).

As part of a larger argument about the symbolic function of prostitution in urban fiction, this reading is compelling, since it helps to fix Nancy as one of the agents through which rich and poor characters are first able to associate, and then to dissociate themselves once more. Just as prostitution acts as a potent metaphor of contagion and social leveling in this period, so Nancy's East-West journey from her Spitalfields home to Mr. Brownlow's residence in Hyde Park initially suggests the permeability of class boundaries. But it also helps to restabilize and reestablish them, by focusing on the exceptional and transgressive nature of her actions. As Franco Moretti has shown, her progress seems magically truncated, skipping over the middle section of London which we normally think of as Dickens's home territory.[30] The more extensive journey that Sikes, Oliver, and Toby Crackit undertake to rob the Maylies' country house at Chertsey takes two chapters to complete and occasions a significant dislocation of the main narrative, whereas Nancy's much shorter excursion takes up an hour and two paragraphs, during which she is transformed from the familiar into the exceptional. On appearing in the West End, Dickens writes, she excites "a still greater curiosity in the stragglers" out in the streets and disparaging comments among the female servants in the house, feels an immediate sense of shame, and looks to return as soon as possible (358). Here, proximity and distance merge, in a process whereby the inhabitants of a nearby part of the city can come to seem so utterly alien.

And yet, we should not too quickly interpret this scene as arguing the success of a containment strategy, or as proposing a model of "separate spheres" for rich and poor. D. A. Miller's Foucauldian analysis of the novel uses this scene, for example, to suggest the ways in which various disciplinary procedures and tactics combine to establish a *cordon sanitaire* around crime. For him, Nancy's desire to return reinscribes an absolute opposition between the delinquent subcultures of Fagin's gang and the bourgeois lifestyle represented by Brownlow and the Maylies; only Oliver is allowed to bridge these separate spheres, and only because he had originally been misplaced and displays a conscious dedication to passing the course of ethical instruction which Brownlow lays out for him. In this sense, for Miller, the novel is well positioned to champion these bourgeois family values, and to join Oliver in decisively rejecting a deviant lifestyle which requires no further investigation: "Righteously 'exposed' in the novel," he concludes, "the world of delinquency is also actively occulted: made cryptic by virtue of its cryptlike isolation from the West End and suburban middle-classes."[31] On this basis, he reads *Oliver Twist* as demonstrating a classic containment-of-subversion technique, in which a potentially transgressive image of the criminal subculture is first produced and then effectively neutralized within the bounds of a traditional *Bildungsroman,* in which virtue is finally rewarded and crime doesn't pay: besides Oliver, only Charley Bates escapes—having renounced crime for the hard life of a Northamptonshire farmer—while the rest end up either dead or transported.

I find Miller's conclusion to be short-sighted, and symptomatic of a New Historicist fondness for premature totalization and theoretical conspiracy in which power and discipline always triumph in the end. Besides exaggerating the sense of security which such a *cordon sanitaire* might bring, his reading too readily assents to a moment of textual closure, while neglecting the ways in which the novel has in the process publicized counter- or subcultural values, codes, and slang which held an intense fascination for many of its original readers. Put another way, it misses the extent to which the middle class themselves—as personified by Brownlow and the Maylies—seek to breach the class divide, in search of useful local knowledge about how the other half lives and thinks, and to secure a precarious hegemony in the city. In this sense—for Dickens as much as Mr. Brownlow—Nancy's return can be read as a failure of urban incorporation, and a fatalistic triumph of local self-determination. Even those who now approach the novel from the perspective of Bart's musical would likely agree that the Artful Dodger is a far more appealing character than Oliver, and that the image of Fagin's underworld community presents a favorable—if ultimately self-defeating—contrast to the bourgeois households of Brownlow and the Maylies. If, as I have tried to suggest, this appeal was ambiguous and internally conflicted, then it was so in a very particular way which recalls the instabilities within the projects of urban planning and cognitive mapping which I have examined in the preceding chapter. It was certainly more complicated than the appeal of a kind of tabloid sensationalism which continues to inflect public discussions of crime today, and against which some of the reviewers of *Oliver Twist* would seem to be cautioning.

For conservative commentators, at least, both the excitement and the dangers of the Newgate novel were bound up with a larger ambivalence about the lower-class communities where crime was known to flourish, which manifested itself in the simultaneous impulses to imitate and annihilate criminals, and which craved an intimate knowledge of their habits while rejecting all responsibility or explanations suggestive of an environmental determinism.[32] Approaching *Oliver Twist* from this perspective allows us to see more clearly why it caused so much trouble for middle-class commentators, who were faced with the difficult choice between the desire for realist description on the one hand, and a counteracting moralism on the other. To reduce this novel's appeal to a single successful ruse of power (as Miller does) is, then, to subscribe to an instrumental vision of systemic control, in which there is no space for resistant modes of cultural reception and appropriation. It requires writing the narrative of Victorian crime fiction from the perspective of a Panoptic power, in place of the dialectical spirals of domination and resistance which Foucault described in his later work on *The History of Sexuality*. And finally, it makes a basic functionalist assumption that systems of power always work in the ways that they are designed, and with strictly rational and intended consequences.

To return briefly to the issue of language, a functionalist explanation might link Dickens's use of slang to a larger project of making criminal subcultures known to the Victorian public, including the fashion for journalistic exposé, as exemplified by Dickens's own articles on the London police, as well as sociological works like Mayhew's massive study of *London Labour and the London Poor*. Working through processes of infiltration, illumination, and categorization, such a strategy could present itself as providing a valuable service for the urban bourgeoisie, who might consider themselves forewarned by the knowledge they gain about London criminal life. Such a service was claimed, for example, by the publishers of earlier canting dictionaries and verse collections like Captain Grose's popular *Dictionary of the Vulgar Tongue,* following a traditional line of justification established by *The Newgate Calendar* and writers of crime fiction dating back to the eighteenth century.[33] Such claims to social utility are undermined in part, though, by the enormity of the task that such texts would be expected to perform. As Allon White suggests in a study of dictionaries, such a task would be a monumental and ultimately futile undertaking: "The language or 'antilanguage' of criminal subcultures," he argues, "could never be clearly identified or defined from outside. Part of its function was precisely its resistance to any comprehension by the high language." [34] Besides its complex heterogeneity, this kind of sociolect is also mobile and context-specific, and so easily able to stay at least one step ahead of the clumsy efforts of lexicographers.

Slang is, in this sense, precisely the product of a *subculture,* as the term has been used by Dick Hebdige, Phil Cohen, Paul Willis, and others working at Birmingham's Centre for Contemporary Cultural Studies. [35] Like them, I do not intend this term to designate a pure space of radical cultural alterity and opposition. Instead, I want to focus on how subcultural styles and codes develop in a dialectical relationship to the dominant culture, from which they cannot entirely disassociate themselves, much as middle-class commentators seem to have been drawn to the depiction in *Oliver Twist* of a criminal organization from which they might otherwise demand some distance. Indeed, it is this dual sense of inside/outside, in which the subculture remains parasitic on a larger "parent" culture from which it simultaneously makes claims of autonomy, which makes this a useful term for analyzing the complex imbrications of crime, class, and politics which arose in London culture during this period. The exact form of negotiation between the dominant and subcultures, and the efficacy of the latter in imagining alternative systems of value, were determined by a range of internal and external factors, but clearly depended on a larger political framework such as that provided in this period by the struggles of Chartism. To the extent that these struggles were fought over concepts like justice, rights, custom, and entitlement, they put into question any simple opposition between criminality and the law, while also charging the former with a political valence when practiced against unjust laws and oppressive state agencies.

Life in Fagin's gang is thoroughly suffused by crime, which provides the reference points both for their collective and personal identity. Newgate prison represents the most important of such points, giving rise to expressions like the following, used by "flash" Toby Crackit: "Damme, I'm as flat as a juryman; and should have gone to sleep as fast as Newgate, if I hadn't has the good natur' to amuse this youngster" (352). Even more significantly, the prison dominates leisure activities in the gang, as the Artful Dodger at one point proceeds "to amuse himself by sketching a ground-plan of Newgate on the table with the piece of chalk which had

served him in lieu of counters" (230). In this context, it is hardly surprising that Charley Bates should be so preoccupied by the Dodger's
forthcoming appearance in *The Newgate Calendar,* or that it might form
the basis for personal pride and the respect of others: "Oh, why didn't he
rob some rich old gentleman of all his walables," Charley laments, "and
go out *as* a gentleman, and not a common prig, without no honour nor
glory!"[36] In holding such values dear, of course, the criminal subculture
begins to resemble the dominant one, a point which Dickens was among
the first to realize. Here, for example, is his description of Fagin's neighborhood of Field Lane:

> Near to the spot on which Snow Hill and Holborn Hill meet,
> there opens, upon the right hand as you come out of the City, a
> narrow and dismal alley leading to Saffron Hill. In its filthy shops
> are exposed for sale huge bunches of second-hand silk handker-
> chiefs, of all sizes and patterns; for here reside the traders who
> purchase them from pickpockets. . . . Confined as the limits of
> Field Lane are, it has its barber, its coffee-shop, its beer-shop,
> and its fried fish warehouse. It is a commercial colony of itself:
> the emporium of petty larceny: visited at early morning, and set-
> ting-in of dusk, by silent merchants, who traffic in dark back-
> parlours, and who go as strangely as they come. (235)

This is actually Fagin's perception of Field Lane, as a kind of free-enter-
prise zone of commercial capitalism where he can profit from the labor
of others as ruthlessly as any of the expropriating owners and landlords
denounced by the rhetoric of Chartism.

But the criminal lifestyle also exemplifies some more positive values,
which in a sense form a precondition for Fagin's iron rule of exploitation. Nancy's impatience to return to Sikes from the security of Brownlow's residence, for example, demonstrates a naive sense of solidarity
which is taken to further extremes of self-sacrifice by Tommy Chitling,
who is prepared to go to prison for Bet in order to secure the trust of the
gang. This code of loyalty is best exemplified by Nancy's declaration
to Rose Maylie that "I have led a bad life too; there are many of us who
have kept the same courses together, and I'll not turn upon them, who
might—any of them—have turned upon me, but didn't, bad as they
are" (412). Regardless of the final outcome, this registers as a sincere and

ethical basis for a communal identity; indeed, even Fagin, who has been responsible for the downfall of many, recognizes a form of mutual self-interest with Sikes, who holds a similar power over him. Describing both the strengths and limits of this sense of identity, Richard Maxwell notes that "it embodies the possibility of group behavior in a world generally asocial," even if what holds the community together is the threat of the gallows under which each of its inhabitants operate. In this sense, its precariousness can be measured by the ease with which the entire social network can be unraveled, either through the force of honesty (as personified by Oliver, and in part by Nancy, who is, however, concerned only to inform on the outsider Monks) or through the self-interested actions of someone like Noah Claypole, who has clearly learned too well Fagin's lesson about looking out for number one.[37]

I certainly do not want to exaggerate the positive values of the underworld here, then, or even to suggest that Dickens himself necessarily subscribed to them. But it equally seems difficult to account for the appeal of this novel—especially to middle-class readers—without some reference to its distinctive representation of a criminal subculture, and to the values which it locates there. The closest contemporary comparison is probably to the gypsies, whom the early nineteenth century also treated with a combination of repressive legal measures and fetishized representations; like the gypsy camp, which often appeared as the site for an alternative model of community, the independence and solidarity of the criminal gang could easily be seen in opposition to the destructive social effects of *laissez-faire* capitalism.[38] Lower-class responses to *Oliver Twist* clearly picked up on these positive values, and seem as a result much easier to reconstruct, at least in their broadest outline. In terms of the inter-textual analysis I have been offering here, then, it might be possible to read play versions like that produced by George Almar or the anonymous plagiarism *Oliver Twiss* as accented readings of Dickens's novel, which put the story to use in radically different contextual formations and according to the tastes and interests of popular audiences.[39] Some of the alterations they made—like the increased role of a character like the Artful Dodger or a heightened use of slang—are easily accounted for by reference to an audience who no longer required an intermediary narrative presence to translate for them, and who did not necessarily experience the same investment in the figure of Oliver. Beyond these, the stage versions in particular enhance the violence and sexual content of the story, and emphasize some of its more obviously melodramatic aspects through a sustained use of the *tableaux vivants,* exaggerated gestures, and a starker opposition between the heroes and villains.[40]

Within this simplified binary structure, it is noticeable that none of the characters from the original novel change sides, even if some of the criminals are shaded more sympathetically. What changes most dramatically, though, are the attitudes expressed toward the law. Dickens's novel, for example, saves its harshest satire for the heartless magistrate Mr. Fang, and says little about the police themselves; indeed, their absence from the hunt for Sikes has often been noted, since it implies an uncomfortable sense of vigilante justice. Almar's play, on the other hand, uses the unlikely vehicle of Mr. Brownlow to adopt a more adversarial position in respect to the justice system as a whole, by placing the actions of Fang on a continuum with those of the lowest policeman on the beat, who (according to Brownlow) is always the last to arrive in situations where they are needed.[41] More surprisingly, the same Brownlow is given two highly critical speeches in the play, which are unimaginable given his representative status as the novel's kindly bourgeois. In the first, he upbraids Fang during the courtroom scene for his inconsistent application of the legal code, admonishing "D'ye think that laws are made like cobwebs, to catch alone the little flies, and let the greater ones break through?" while he cautions the officer arresting Oliver in the second not to hurt him: "Damn it sir, I say, don't hurt the boy, or by the Lord! I'll thrash the dust out of your blue jacket."

A similar shift can be detected in the popular plagiarism *Oliver Twiss,* which was published concurrently with the novel by Edward Lloyd in 1838–39. Louis James notes that the plagiarisms sparked by the phenomenal success of *The Pickwick Papers* and continued with a series of versions of Dickens's works by the anonymous "Bos," "Poz," "Buz," and "Quiz," as well as by named authors like G. M. W. Reynolds, tended to downplay the social criticism of the original novels, in favor of slapstick humor and melodramatic effects drawn from popular theater.[42] *Oliver Twiss,* however, goes to some pains to extend Dickens's attacks on the workhouse system, to correct some of his legal anachronisms, and to show how the story might be viewed from the perspective of Fagin's gang. Thus, while additional scenes are written around Jack White (Charley Bates) and the Knowing Cove (Artful Dodger) in the stocks, at a play on "the noble art of thieving," and at the famous Whitechapel gin-shop All-Max, "Bos" also corrects a significant legal oversight noticed by the reviewer at the *Quarterly Review,* that Fagin is never charged with a capital crime: in *Twiss,* as if to justify the powerful *dénouement,* Solomons (Fagin) confesses to having murdered a gypsy woman. Balancing out this additional crime, we might also note that he gives a full written confession to Oliver and Mr. Beaumont (Mr. Maylie) at the end, where he is merely shown lapsing into lunatic ravings in the novel. This pattern of humanizing the thieves, and even of explaining how and why they came to a life of crime, is repeated over the course of the text, in which both Solomons and Jem Blount (Sikes) are shown proclaiming sincere repentance for their actions; Solomons, for example, immediately regrets telling Blount of his betrayal by Poll (Nancy), and fights to prevent him from harming her.[43]

Beyond such elements of characterization, the most noticeable revision concerns the wider political context into which the story is inserted. In particular, what activities count as criminal are shown to depend upon community standards rather than the law itself. Two examples suggest the extent to which this occurs, as well as the reading formations within which these plagiarisms would have been read. The first instance appears when Blount and Poll recapture Oliver from his protectors. In the novel, Sikes and Nancy cast him in the role of an ungrateful brother, thereby exciting the sympathies of the crowd around them. In *Twiss,* a similar scene is staged in the presence of Mr. Beaumont, with Blount playing the role of Oliver's father. On hearing the former refuse to relinquish the boy, he appeals to the crowd, declaring that "I s'pose I must insist on my rights, that's all," at which point mud, stones, and brickbats are aimed at Beaumont. When Oliver identifies Blount as his persecutor, a policeman is summoned to arrest him, at which point "The mob . . . who had all along taken part with the ruffian, now exhibited still further manifestations in his favour, and a general attack being commenced upon the policeman, the prisoner soon found an opportunity to escape from his hold" (231–32).

Such a scene would be unthinkable in *Oliver Twist,* in which the sympathies of the crowd are more often enlisted—at times almost magically—in opposition to crime, whether at Sikes's last stand in Jacob's Island or during Fagin's arrest, when (as Tommy Chitling reports) "the officers fought like devils" to keep the crowds from attacking him. Aside from the gentle satire of the incompetent officers Blathers and Duff, who are criticized more directly as Traps and Grabble in *Oliver Twiss,* Dickens generally refrains from mocking the police in this novel, in part because the crowd is so effectively able to substitute for them in bringing Sikes to a form of mob justice. The attitude represented in *Twiss,* on the other hand, seems more in line with the actual level of popular discontent at the time, which (as we shall see in chapter 3) was often directed at the new police. Even more noteworthy is a scene which "Bos" interpolated wholesale, in which Solomons escapes from jail with Jem Blount's help and encounters a man beneath the hanged body of his youngest son. Prevented by his father from following his elder brothers into the army, the boy had fallen in with poachers and had killed a gamekeeper in self-defense after having been surprised on a raid. The story sounds like something borrowed from *The Newgate Calendar,* but what is most striking is Solomons's response to it, especially considering that he is experiencing feelings of remorse for his own crimes: "Well," he interrupts before the father has described the death of the keeper,

> so far as you have gone, the poor fellow has not been guilty of any great crime. If the wealthy of our land choose to lay claim to those things that are intended as much for the use of the poor man as for the rich one, we cannot be much surprised that men are to be found who will resist the laws that have been made for the purpose of depriving them of their share in the gifts of heaven. The poor man feels his wrongs, and boldly asserts his own claims. (558)

This remarkable speech could never have been spoken by Fagin, who is reduced to insensibility as the novel closes. It seems instead to emanate from outside the Dickensian text, from the radical tradition which was then being revitalized by Chartism and which justified "social crimes" in terms of an appeal to a higher order of rights and entitlement. Indeed, as E. P. Thompson and others have noted, the opposition of poachers to the so-called Black Acts represented one of the central sites of a radical struggle which was designed precisely to contest the legal definition of property and land rights, and to supplant it with moral justifications based on social need and customary usage.[44] It hardly matters that Fagin/Solomons seems very distant from these struggles, which took place largely in country settings, since my point here has been to emphasize some of the ways in which popular versions of the story became a vehicle for political protest and social analyses which arose from a very different place on the cultural map. Chartism in this sense represents an umbrella term here, under which a wide variety of linked statements and senti-ments were articulated, ranging from a democratic-populist perspective on property rights and usage to more direct expressions of class-conscious *ressentiment,* which were often aimed at the new police as representatives of a repressive social order.

Reviewing a popular stage adaptation of *The Pickwick Papers* by W. T. Moncrieff, Philip Cox has similarly found that it

> allows explicitly political ideas to circulate within the performed text and, moreover, that they circulate in a fashion which is less easy to contain than it would be with a written text. . . . Whilst the characters (and often their dialogue) are essentially the same, they have moved more obviously into the world of the audi-ence's lived experience, and their actions and decisions have be-come more explicitly involved with the uncertainties of con-temporary society.[45]

It is often difficult to predict exactly what form this will take, or what contemporary concerns will come to form the context for such adapta-tions. One more example might help to underscore the incredible range of contemporary issues on which the text of *Oliver Twist* was made to comment. In this case, the interpretive recontextualization arises not from working-class rereadings of Dickens, but from one of those middle-class readers of *Bentley's* who we can assume formed its intended audi-ence. Like "Buller, Senior," who was moved to describe his experience of reading the serial in poetry, "Father Prout" sent his response in verse to the editors, who published it in the first issue of 1838 just as Oliver and Sikes set out for the burglary at Chertsey. The final stanza, follow-ing a fairly standard encomium praising Dickens's ability to make his au-dience "weep with pathos deep, or shake with laughs spasmodical," reads as follows:

> Folks all enjoy your Parish Boy,—so truly you depict him;
> But I, alack! while thus you track your stinted poor-law's
> victim,

Must think of some poor nearer home,—poor who, unheeded
   perish,
By squires despoiled, by 'patriots' gulled,—I mean the starving
   Irish.[46]

Like its companion poem, this also sets out to describe the required emotional response of the *Bentley's* readers. Again, it refers to the truth of its
depiction of Oliver's life, yet ends by unexpectedly wrenching us back
to historical context: to "the starving Irish," just seven years before the
great potato famine, who were "gulled" and "despoiled" by squires and
patriots who might (we suspect) also be readers of the journal. The connection seems entirely unmotivated, at least according to any logic of
textual determination or authorial intent. Unless "Father Prout" had in
mind a more general sense in which the Irish were considered synonymous with the lowest of the London poor, then we must assume that he
mainly thought and grieved for "the starving Irish" in other contexts and
overlaid these concerns onto Dickens's text. This is the sense is which
I initially characterized *Oliver Twist* as displaying a remarkable adaptability, which enabled it to be recontextualized in so many different ways.
Steven Marcus has noted that its essential form is that of the parable, following the pattern of highly successful texts like *Pilgrim's Progress* in being easily adapted to illustrate a number of lessons.[47] From the Poor Law
and workhouses, through crime policy, Chartist agitation, the conditions
of the poor and those of the Irish—this is the political, symbolic, and
psychic terrain through which a text like *Oliver Twist* was forced to travel,
with a range of readerly appropriations, interventions, and revisions at
each turn. Indeed, the culturally sanctioned readings and responses of
critics and reviewers, manipulating the text to serve a range of political
interests and to participate in contemporary political and cultural controversies, seem to have no more respected an "essential" Dickensian text
than did the popular dramatists and plagiarizers with whom he publicly
fought about copyright. The diversity of these responses is testimony
both to the complexities of Dickens's novel and to its functional utility,
for if (in Barbara Hernnstein Smith's terms) it has survived because it
has maintained a continued relevance to these arguments, it has done
so by being not only "re-produced," but more importantly refashioned
in the images of its readers. The multiple texts and contexts of this re-
fashioning remind us that the novel acted (as Marcus puts it) "as an

indispensable agent in the understanding of society" in the time before modern sociology (77); to which we might add only that it sometimes also opened up a space where differing visions and readings of society could compete for legitimacy. Each of the versions and responses I have touched on here has clearly reconfigured and added to the continuing political life of *Oliver Twist,* a text which I have been reading here as belonging—like few others of its time—in the public domain of contemporary debate.

### You Are What You Read?

There is a certain irony in studying Victorian reading practices in relation to these Newgate crime novels, since they themselves actively foreground and participate in a larger controversy about cultural literacy and its political effects. Patrick Brantlinger has shown, for example, how the conventional connection made by Victorian reformers between illiteracy and crime is undermined by a simultaneous tradition of seeing popular literature itself as an agency in the corruption of youth.[48] A good example of this is *Oliver Twist,* in which, as he notes, almost all the underworld characters (Fagin, Sikes, and Nancy, as well as Oliver himself) unexpectedly demonstrate some ability at reading, and contemporary political conflicts about the social and educative uses of texts lie beneath the surface of the novel. In one scene, Mr. Brownlow shows his young charge the substantial collection of books in his library, promising that "You shall read them, if you behave well" (145). Such a model of cultural education, which D. A. Miller argues demonstrates Victorian fiction's function as one of the central mechanisms for propagating "the norms, protocols, and regulations of the middle-class family,"[49] might be opposed to an alternative that Foucault terms the "song of crime," in which the reader engages in a direct identification with the subject of a first-person criminal biography. This second tradition, as elaborated in connection with the memoirs of French parricide Pierre Rivière, encompasses a range of popular forms for the expression and consolidation of subcultural resistance, which are intended through a form of sympathetic introjection to "travel from singer to singer"; their subversive potential is thus encapsulated for Foucault in the presumption that "everyone is presumed able to sing it as his own crime, by a lyrical fiction" of subjective identification.[50]

This potential, which both Foucault and Miller believe was effectively suppressed by the 1830s, comes close to capturing the sense of danger which bourgeois commentators felt that the Newgate novel represented. The power of texts to kidnap and corrupt their readers is exemplified quite clearly by the figure of Fagin, who aims to directly "instill" into Oliver's soul "the poison which he hoped would blacken it, and change its hue forever" (185). His plan is to entrap Oliver into a criminal lifestyle which will ultimately make him ineligible to collect on his inheritance, advising him at first to make "models" of Charley Bates and the Artful Dodger. Evidently, Fagin also considers himself a suitable object of study: one night, for example, is spent in telling stories of the criminal exploits of his own childhood, which are "mixed up with so much that was droll and curious, that Oliver could not help laughing heartily, and showing that he was amused in spite of all his better feelings" (185). As the next stage of his campaign, Fagin gives Oliver a book to read at bedtime, which sounds like a cheap version of *The Newgate Calendar:*

> It was a history of the lives and trials of great criminals; and the pages were soiled and thumbed with use. Here, he read of dreadful crimes that made the blood run cold; of secret murders that had been committed by the lonely wayside: of bodies hidden from the eye of man in deep pits and wells; which would not keep them down, deep as they were, but had yielded them up at last, after many years, and so maddened the murderers with the sight, that in their horror they had confessed their guilt and yelled for the gibbet to end their agony. . . . The terrible descriptions were so real and vivid, that the sallow pages seemed to turn red with gore; and the words upon them, to be sounded in his ears, as if they were whispered, in hollow murmurs, by the spirits of the dead. (196–97)

There is certainly an echo of Foucault's "song of crime" here, as Oliver imagines a form of direct address. Brantlinger also suggests, however, that the book he is given—"soiled and thumbed with use"—represents a sort of criminal "antibible," which Fagin had earlier recommended his other converts to read. Fagin fails in this particular case, as Oliver reacts with horror and prayers to the criminal biographies he is forced to read, and retains a preference for the life represented by Mr. Brownlow and his library. What is notable, however, is that both Fagin and Brownlow rely on an idea of literature's unmediated impact on the reader, and of a use function of books which is able to exist independent of original authorial intentions. In such a context, Brantlinger notes how *Oliver Twist* enacts a figurative battle of the books, which in turn mirrored the more general War of the Unstamped Press initiated by the Seditious Publications Act of 1820, aimed quite literally at criminalizing reading of the radical and popular press. It was, he concludes, unregulated (and expressly countercultural) literacy which posed the problem, rather than illiteracy itself.

Ainsworth's *Jack Sheppard* also neatly foregrounds these battles in its dichotomy between Sheppard and Thames Darrell. Sheppard was a celebrated thief and jailbreaker in the 1720s, whose story rivaled Dick Turpin's for pride of place in the countercultural imaginary of the London poor. Darrell, however, is Ainsworth's invention, necessary in order to bring the story in line with one important source on which he based his narrative, Hogarth's famous series of drawings illustrating the fortunes of the idle and industrious apprentices. Early on in the novel, Jack is caught by his master carving his name into an overhead beam, while singing the song of "The Newgate Stone" and contemplating breaking his indentures for the life of a highwayman. A narrative sweep of the walls of the workshop at this point reveals "a goodly ballad, adorned with a rough woodcut, purporting to be 'The History of Chaste Susannah'; . . . an abstract of the various Acts of Parliament against drinking, swearing, and all manner of profaneness; and a view of the interior of Dr. Daniel Burgess's Presbyterian meeting-house in Russell Court, with portraits of the reverend gentleman and the principal members of his flock." But if all this propaganda is intended to inculcate a Christian and law-abiding spirit in Jack, it must compete against other influences, represented in this scene by a piece of paper displaying the words "the history of the four kings; or, child's best guide to the gallows," which had previously contained a piece of cheese Jack is now eating.[51] Later, we learn that Sheppard's bookshelves feature the *Accounts* of the Ordinary at Newgate, *Moll Flanders,* and flash songs called "The Thief-Catcher's Prophecy" and "Life and Death of the Darkman's Budge"; by way of contrast, the industrious Thames Darrell, who is ultimately revealed as the heir to the title and estates of an aristocratic Jacobin family, owns Plutarch's *Lives,* the *Histories of Great Commanders,* and the ballad of "Saint George for England" (1:130). Thus, the novel effectively preaches that you are what you read: Newgate stories, calendars, and novels lead Sheppard directly to the prison for which they are named, while patriotic military literature helps mold the heroic Darrell into a figure worthy of his inheritance.

Like the Artful Dodger, Jack's imagination is suffused with representations of crime, which have much the same effect as critics accused this novel of having over other impressionable London youths a century later. It is not surprising that he feels most at home in the criminal subculture of the Wapping Mint, into which he was born and to which he turns for support during his criminal career. The Mint was a kind of quasi-legal enclave of London established as a safe haven for debtors from the demands of bailiffs, which modeled itself after the right of sanctuary known as the benefit of clergy. Such claims had only a dubious legality, however, and the Mint was largely outlawed by capital statutes of 1722 and 1724 making the obstruction of an officer's duties a felony punishable by seven years' transportation.[52] In *Jack Sheppard,* its location changes between Southwark and Wapping, on either side of the Thames, so that it forms a mobile pocket of criminal association, much like Fagin's lair. It also represents a kind of counter-hegemonic seat of government, operating through a language of constitutionality, asylum, privileges, and fees. The Minters have developed their own definitions of customs and entitlements, the most important of which codify a debtor's right to claim the privileges of sanctuary and the penalties for its abuse, and Baptist Kettleby, the Master of the Mint, goes so far as to envision the following future:

> I hope to see the day, when not Southwark alone but London itself, shall become one Mint—when all men shall be debtors, and none creditors—when imprisonment for debt shall be utterly abolished—when highway robbery shall be accounted a pleasant pastime, and forgery an accomplishment—when Tyburn and its gibbets shall be overthrown—capital punishment discontinued—Newgate, Ludgate, the Gatehouse, and the Compters razed to the ground—Bridewell and Clerkenwell

destroyed—the Fleet, the King's Bench, and the Marshalsea remembered only by name. (1:210)

Kettleby's vision is utopian, and indeed logically impossible within a
system which requires that there is a creditor for every debtor, but it is
no less powerful as a result.[53] While the Mint itself had been broken up
by the time that Ainsworth was writing, some sense of its function as a
refuge survived in underworld rookeries like St. Giles, which similarly
established themselves as informal safe havens into which the police
would rarely venture. It is hardly surprising, then, that it was in places
like this that the Sheppard story found its largest audience, through the
same processes of popular imitation and dramatization which I analyzed
earlier in relation to Dickens. This again tends to undercut the basis for
a possible containment thesis, which might stress the ways that Ainsworth's novel, like other Newgate novels of its time, took for its subject
a famous eighteenth-century criminal. The historicizing impulse at work
here has led some critics to argue that these novels only evoke earlier
models of criminal resistance in order to effectively contain them as examples of the "bad old days" of the eighteenth century, prior to the establishment of a kinder and gentler disciplinary regime. This is the conclusion reached by Keith Hollingsworth, for example, who notes in his
analysis of *Sheppard* that while "a sense of injustice already present might
flow into sympathetic identification" with the hero, and "despite some
Chartist feeling in the populace,"

> [f]rowning Newgate, the grim hangman, and the gallows repre-
> sented old oppressions, maintained by the law of the rulers; and
> humanitarian feeling had made the middle class quite as uneasy
> about them as the class without property had been. . . . The
> owners of Newgate had been forced to yield some of their power
> in 1832; the death-dealing laws had been swept away in the half-
> dozen years just preceding this novel and these plays; hangings
> had become few, the gallows less obtrusive; policemen walked
> the streets of a safer London. Prison reform was respectable. The
> crudest terrors of Newgate, well enough remembered, could be
> thought of as safely in the past. Freedom and opportunity were
> in the air.[54]

This is really a remarkable apologetics, echoing the tone of the famous opening of Bentham's "Panopticon" essay, with its optimistic predictions of "Morals reformed—health preserved—industry invigorated—instructions diffused—public burthens lightened— . . . and all by the simple idea in Architecture!"[55] In fact, the political context in which this novel appeared was marked not only by the Chartist uprisings which coincided with its serialization, but also by a continuing campaign of resistance against the Metropolitan Police, who had only recently been introduced and were far from having secured public consent for their actions, as we shall see. London's Pentonville penitentiary, the nearest thing to a real-life Panopticon, was still three years away, while an earlier prototype, Millbank, had been vigorously opposed by prisoners throughout the 1820s and was widely considered a failure for which the harsher discipline of Pentonville was required to atone.

Hollingsworth's containment thesis would appear to stand on shaky grounds. In fact, contemporary reviews of *Jack Sheppard* consistently made reference to Chartism, and drew a conscious correlation between the cultural crisis which this text incited and the larger political crisis in which it appeared. The *Athenaeum,* for example, saw the novel as symptomatic of its historical moment, when "the classes most at their ease are occupied with the lowest and most trivial thoughts, [and] the classes below them, ignorant or careless of all book learning, and educated by the force of circumstances, far more stimulating than that of words, are brooding over the elementary principles of social existence." The period, in other words, reveals these classes as coming into a form of self-consciousness, at the same time that an unprecedented explosion of mass culture was appearing to satisfy the demands of an emergent reading public. Crowded into the major cities, this new readership required a literature which represented its unceasing struggle for "the means of existence," according to the reviewer, so that Ainsworth is shown to be merely responding to the dictates of the market.[56] The *Athenaeum* seems reluctant to spell out the consequences of this incendiary alliance between a newly literate class consciousness and a sensationalist popular culture, although the political stakes can be seen from a review article on "The Age of Jack Sheppardism" which appeared in the *Monthly Magazine* six months later. Starting from a generalized sense that "[t]he current state of literature is of a nature to produce the utmost amount of alarm in the well-constituted mind," the journal then drew a concise link between crime, politics, and cultural literacy by commenting that "[t]he times are out of joint, and Chartism rages while Jack Sheppard *reads.*" As Kathryn Chittick notes, the review ends on a note of desperation which would have been unthinkable a decade earlier, calling on Prince Albert and the aristocracy to "save the country's literature."[57]

These reviews suggest that Hollingsworth is both prematurely dismissive and short-sighted in his assessment of the political context of the Newgate genre, and that we need to take more account of the specific cultural forms by which these stories were disseminated and consumed. Here again, there is overwhelming evidence which bears out Patrick Brantlinger's argument that crime literature exemplified a kind of countercultural literacy in the 1840s, and that commentators feared this was active in the circulation of a subversive ideology. In *The Condition of the Working Class in England,* for example, Engels quotes from an 1843 Report of the Children's Employment Commission about working-class children in Wolverhampton that "[s]ome have never heard the name of Her Majesty, nor such names as Wellington, Nelson, Buonaparte, etc. But it is to be especially remarked, that among all those who had never even heard such names as St. Paul, Moses, Solomon, etc., there was a general knowledge of the character and course of life of Dick Turpin, the highwayman, and more particularly, of Jack Sheppard, the robber and prison-breaker." Mayhew also recorded a form of criminal literacy in *London Labour and the London Poor,* noting that stories of Turpin and Sheppard were popular in poor lodging-houses, and he editorialized about penny and halfpenny romances like "Charley Wag, or the New Jack Sheppard, a history of the most successful thief in London," stating that "to say that these are not incentives to lust, theft, and crime of every description is to cherish a fallacy."[58]

Once again, the popular theatrical versions of *Jack Sheppard* which circulated soon after its publication went further than the original novel in heroizing its protagonist. One version staged by J. B. Buckstone in 1839 even risks a rare and ironic moment of glorified violence by inventing an entirely new scene, in which a disguised Jack responds to the cult of personality which surrounds him by assaulting a street hawker who hands him a chapbook version of "the last dying speech and confession, birth, parentage and education, character and behaviour of the notorious housebreaker Jack Sheppard." Buckstone also omits Sheppard's execution entirely, and shows him present during a revised climax in which a criminal mob tries to burn down thief-taker Jonathan Wild's house. Another play from the same year has him cheat the gallows by dying during this assault from an earlier gunshot wound, while in a later version from 1855, Jack is hung offstage, before a final triumphal march to Wild's house to "settle accounts with that devil." Wild initially tries to bribe them, first with £10,000 and later with "all I'm worth," to which Sheppard's accomplice Blueskin replies in the play's closing lines: "We are giving you all you are worth. You are worth no better fate than what you shall now have. Justice is justice, and you deserve to die. Your coward soul shrinks within you, you tremble like a cur now you know you must die. Ah the powder—send the bar—set down the trap that will finish the business at once." The stage directions tell the rest: they "put the powder down . . . the house is blown up," and Wild and his men "are seen hanging from the burning rafters. Mob shout. Picture. Curtains."[59]

In this way, lower-class audiences were offered—and seem to have responded enthusiastically to—a melodramatic opposition between the heroic Sheppard and his villainous tormentor Wild. Such a rendering, though, quite clearly deviates from Ainsworth's own original plan, which drew inspiration from Hogarth's engravings of "Industry and Idleness." On this model, Sheppard is at least officially the villain of the piece: the final two plates of the Hogarth series, after all, show Tom Idle's procession to Tyburn to be hung, opposite his industrious counterpart's very different and triumphal procession as the new Lord Mayor of London. The excision of Darrell from the play versions and the reordering of the final scenes to end with the death of Wild thus produce a typological transformation of the source novel, through which Sheppard is able to emerge victorious, having (at least momentarily) cheated the gallows. In thus transforming the novel, these plays also soften the moral message of cultural determinism which Ainsworth wanted to draw from Hogarth, and which he symbolically represented through the different reading materials of Sheppard and Darrell. The novel contained another twist, however, which anticipated the processes of imitation and appropriation that later circulated around this text. While awaiting execution, Sheppard—now a celebrity on account of his spectacular prison escapes—is visited by a delegation consisting of the prizefighter Figg, portrait painter Sir James Thornhill, John Gay, and William Hogarth. While being painted by Thornhill, Jack briefly tells his life story, which inspires Gay to plan a drama set in Newgate, later presumably to become *The Beggar's Opera*. Hogarth also sketches Sheppard and offers to illustrate Gay's play, but later declares that "I've an idea as well as you, grounded in some measure upon Sheppard's story. I'll take two apprentices, and depict their career. One, by perseverance and industry, shall obtain fortune, credit, and the highest honours; while the other, by an opposite course, and dissolute habits, shall eventually arrive at Tyburn" (2:84). In a momentary confusion here, then, art begins imitating life imitating art, and it becomes increasingly hard to tell exactly what is original and what is a copy.

Such confusions, moreover, were not confined to the internal world of Ainsworth's text, but recur in the history of its reception. Thackeray, for example, noted in a letter to his mother at the height of the "Sheppard-craze" of 1839 that "one or two young gentlemen have already confessed how much they were indebted to Jack Sheppard who gave them ideas of pocket-picking and thieving [which] they never would have had but for the play." [60] In such a climate, it should not be surprising to learn how the craze, and the Newgate genre as a whole, came to an end. In May 1840, Lord William Russell, the uncle of a high-ranking cabinet minister, was murdered by his Swiss valet, B. F. Courvoisier. It was widely reported that the killer had seen a dramatization of Ainsworth's novel, and imitated one of its more gruesome murder scenes by slitting his master's throat. Courvoisier later denied this, but in the ensuing moral panic the Lord Chamberlain refused to license any more stage adaptations, and a press campaign denounced Ainsworth and the other Newgate novelists for authorial irresponsibility. The *Examiner* reported that Courvoisier himself had "ascribe[d] his crimes to the perusal of that detestable book, *Jack Sheppard*" in a confession, and went on to condemn the novel as an accessory after the fact: "certainly, it is a publication calculated to familiarise the mind with cruelties, and to serve as the cutthroat's manual," the newspaper editorialized, and proceeded to suggest that the text itself "deserved to be burnt by the hands of the common hangman." [61]

These events again need to be situated against a backdrop of political unrest, in which the murder of a lord by his own valet would have had quite alarming political overtones. Courvoisier was hung, but the process of mutual contamination between literature and life took one further turn. The execution, one of the best-attended of the period, was witnessed by both Dickens and Thackeray. The former recorded his impressions six years later in the first of a series of letters on capital punishment to the *Daily News*, in which he noted that the audience failed to receive any moral instruction from the spectacle, and acted as if at the theater. Thackeray published his own response more quickly, in an influential attack on capital punishment called "Going to See a Man Hanged" which appeared the following month in *Fraser's*. In it, he continued the campaign against the Newgate novelists which he had begun earlier in the year with his first novel *Catherine,* a satire which was timed to appear in simultaneous serialization with the monthly installments of *Jack Sheppard.* Yet he is strangely silent about that novel's possible influence on the murderer, and chooses instead to direct his attacks at his fellow spectator. Referring back to *Oliver Twist,* which he had identified in *Catherine* as the originator of the genre, Thackeray singles out the character of Nancy as "the most unreal fantastical personage possible"; Dickens has misleadingly emphasized only the character's virtues, he argued, whereas "not being able to paint the whole portrait, he has no right to present one or two favourable points as characterizing the whole."[62]

In this way, the outcry over the Newgate novel consistently turned back on itself, threatening to devour Dickens along with popular novelists like Ainsworth, Bulwer Lytton, and Reynolds, or at the least to blur the distinction between them. In the final chapter of *Catherine,* for example, Thackeray provides a brief history of the genre and its effects on audiences in the metropolis: Fagin, Nancy, Sikes, and the Dodger all "stepped from the novel on to the stage," he complains, with the predictable result that "the whole London public, from peers to chimney-sweeps, were interested about a set of ruffians whose occupations are thievery, murder, and prostitution." By degrees, according to what we might term a domino effect of criminalization,[63] public tastes are systematically degraded, and crave ever more sensational representations. "And what came of 'Oliver Twist'?" Thackeray asks. "The public wanted something more extravagant still, more sympathy for thieves, and so 'Jack Sheppard' makes his appearance. . . . We are not criticizing the novels, but simply speak of the Newgate part of them, which gives birth to something a great deal worse than bad taste, and familiarises the public with notions of crime."[64] According to such an organic and irreversible logic, it is difficult to exempt Dickens from criticism, especially since Thackeray is working with a theory of effects, not intentions. In doing so, he also naturalizes the public's taste for crime in terms of an irresistible and uncontrollable curiosity, which is presumably only checked by an equally public event like the murder of Russell. At such a moment, the line separating reality from fiction can be restored, while the ensuing moral panic helps to ensure that the reasons why it was blurred remain uninterrogated.

A more dramatic rendering of this genealogy of readerly incitement appeared where the Newgate genre had made its first public appearance, when "Father Prout" submitted another of his occasional poems to the editors of *Bentley's* in 1842. Like his earlier poem comparing Oliver's story with that of the starving Irish, this one also provides a useful meta-commentary on Victorian reading practices. Here, the reader's surrogate is Prout himself, who has become deeply disturbed by the culture's increasing sensationalism. The magazine is recast in the poem as a barber shop (presumably with echoes of Sweeney Todd), where Bentley has taken on a young Manchester apprentice. This latter figure—as foot-notes make clear—is a thinly disguised portrait of Ainsworth, who had recently resigned editorship of *Bentley's* to begin his own magazine. The apprentice soon begins to tell Newgate stories, with predictable results:

> But, as the tongues of giddy youth too much indulgence
>     loosens,
> His "*stories*" which came thick and thick, at last became a
>     nuisance.
> The shop frequenters often wish'd he'd hold his peace, or alter
> The staple of his tedious yarns, all ending in a halter.
> Soon, one by one they dropped away—for life cannot af-
>     ford us
> Sufficient time with maudling tales of cut-throats to be bored
>     thus;
> A listener by the button still he sometimes on the sly attacked,
> 'Till, finding that each new "*Romaunce*," like the reading of
>     the Riot Act,

Cleared out all decent customers, his master told him plainly
That "'twere better for the nonce eschew a practice so
   ungainly,"
That "men of sense and learning loathed an over-dose of
   folly."
Brief answer to his master made the varmint, "*Nix my dolly!*"

The complaint seems less directed at the magazine's sales than to the class of readers Ainsworth brings to it, as he drives away its "decent customers" with his incessant sensationalizing. In time, the apprentice in the poem is "disbentleyfied" (which helps to gloss over whether he is fired or quits, as Ainsworth himself did), and establishes his own barber shop at a cheaper cost, presumably to appeal to this more popular demographic. On hearing this, Father Prout pays a call but is apprehensive about letting the apprentice shave him, thereby enabling the author to reference Russell's murder two years earlier:

But PROUT, who had misgivings of the "gentle Sheppard's"
   razor,
Calmly deferred doffing his beard till BENTLEY came, or
FRASER,
For he had read his several tales of severing bone and muscle,
(So had the late COURVOISIER, who killed Lord William
RUSSELL.) . . . [65]

The barber's apprentice—representing Ainsworth—finally murders Father Prout, who figuratively personified the spirit of *Bentley's* itself, as well as the interests of its original readers, on whom (the poem somewhat disingenuously suggests) sensational crime novels had been forced. This version of events certainly runs counter to the more common narrative of the growing popularity of such texts, emphasizing in the process their potential effects on less sophisticated readers.

The poem's closing tableau seems an appropriate place to leave the Newgate novel, which—like a coiled serpent—was engaged in devouring itself and its practitioners. In the space of a few years, the genre had begun life in this newest of Victorian periodicals, then moved out into a wider public space of controversy following the sensational successes of *Oliver Twist* and *Jack Sheppard,* only to murderously return to its original base. Its trajectory is first centrifugal, as these novels are considered in connection to the key political issues of the period; but then finally centripetal, as a range of influential participants are drawn into a tightening (and almost incestuous) space of argument about the political functions and responsibilities of fiction. In this way, the Courvoisier case and its aftermath appear as something like a black hole into which various literary careers and ambitions swiftly vanish. Keith Hollingsworth's study of the genre suggests that it was largely played out by 1847, the year when Bulwer Lytton was finally so exasperated with the campaign against him which had been orchestrated in *Fraser's* that he actually contemplated challenging Thackeray to a duel![66]

This is not to suggest that writers like Ainsworth and Bulwer Lytton were consigned to the dustbin of history—both, indeed, had continued success in other genres, such as the historical novel. Instead, it is more accurate to conclude that the reputations of each of these authors suffered from the fallout of the controversy, along with that of their major opponent Thackeray, who felt as early as 1840 that the parody he had conceived in *Catherine* had missed its mark: he wrote to his mother that by imitating Ainsworth too closely, he might have signaled to readers "a sneaking kindness for his heroine," which defeated the entire object of the novel.[67] Dickens survives in the best shape of all, of course, but only after cutting his own ties to the genre and to *Bentley's*. After *Barnaby Rudge,* he stayed away from crime themes for some time, so that there is a striking sense of distance when we look ahead to a novel like *Bleak House* (serialized in 1852–53). As I shall suggest in the next chapter, the decisive defeat of Chartism enabled a new tone to emerge in much of the fiction and journalism of the 1850s, which confidently supported a restabilized rule of law. In such a changed context, Mayhew's massive *London Labour and the London Poor* (1851–52) already seemed like an anachronistic throwback to an earlier moment of intense anxiety and class conflict, and to be drawing upon outdated social maps. The shift can also be measured by looking at Dickens, who dramatically changes his position on capital punishment and writes in increasingly glowing terms about the new police. The history of the police force has been largely written from the particular perspective which he adopted, accepting the guiding principles of progressive acceptance and the inevitable attainment of a favorable public consensus. In the process, however, such accounts have tended to downplay or rewrite the early years of the British police, who were first introduced within a more hostile climate dominated by Chartism and faced intense popular opposition. In turning now to the issue of policing, both as a historical debate and as a topic in Victorian fiction, I want to keep in mind the effect of writing history from a retroactive and justificatory standpoint, and to set the standard triumphalist readings of the new police against an alternative model which is developed out of more recent research in British social history and cultural studies.

# 3 RESISTING ARREST/ ARRESTING RESISTANCE

Policing the Victorian City

ONE MORE RESPONSE to *Oliver Twist* helps to illustrate the ways that cultural texts were put to work in addressing the political controversies of the period. In 1849, at a meeting of the Marylebone Vestry, an alderman (and former Lord Mayor of London) named Sir Peter Laurie opposed using property taxes to finance training schools for poor children: such a scheme, he proclaimed, was as useless as a recent call by the bishop of London for improved sanitary conditions in Jacob's Island, a place which "only existed in a work of fiction, written by Mr. Charles Dickens ten years ago."[1] Laurie apparently believed that the novelist had sought to profit from the gullibility of his readers, and so had invented the dockland region of Bermondsey where Bill Sikes is eventually hunted down. The alderman may also have been on the counterattack, however, following Dickens's earlier caricature of him as Alderman Cute in *The Chimes* (1844). Widely known for his campaigns against the "separate system" of solitary confinement in prisons and against attempted suicides (which he saw as a means for getting media attention and charitable aid), Laurie had been repeatedly lampooned by Dickens—as well as by Douglas Jerrold in *Punch*—as epitomizing a heartless magistracy which aimed to "put down" the poor.[2]

It was relatively easy for Dickens to prove that Jacob's Island existed, and thereby continue his highly successful war of words with Laurie. Assuring his readers in a preface of 1850, Dickens humorously cast his opponent as believing that the material world ceased to exist when rendered in a work of fiction; in which case (referring back to *The Chimes*), he could only conclude that "Sir Peter Laurie having been himself described in a book . . . it is but too clear that there *can* be no such man!"[3] But the battle over Jacob's Island is of greater interest, I think, as an indication of how Victorian crime novels found themselves being taken up in contemporary debates about the *social* crimes of poverty and neglect. For Laurie to believe that Dickens had invented the region seems absurd; what it speaks to once again, though, is the novelist's peculiar status, as someone whose fictions were repeatedly taken on trust as representing the genuine realities of London slum life. Given the reformist ambitions that run through a text like *Oliver Twist,* the suspicion that he may have invented some of the details does not seem quite so ridiculous. Instead, it testifies to the enormous power which was accorded to fiction of the period, as both a conduit of public opinion and a serious contributor to contemporary debate.

In this light, Gareth Stedman Jones has noted the repeated targeting of areas made famous in popular crime novels during the first schemes of urban demolition in London, alongside notorious slum areas like St. Giles. "It is noticeable," he writes, "that the street clearance of the 1840s and 1850s included nearly all the quarters established with surreal horror by literary imagination" in the works of Dickens, Ainsworth, Bulwer Lytton, and G. M. W. Reynolds. The priority given to the destruction of Saffron Hill, Jacob's Island, and other sites of literary-criminal notoriety was presumably designed to counter the curiosity they excited among the novel-reading public: Stedman Jones cites a telling report from the *Quarterly Review* of 1855 about the crowds that gathered to witness the destruction of a street in Fleet Ditch, during which "its mysteries (far surpassing those of Udolpho) were exposed to the public gaze, with all its sliding panels, trap doors and endless devices for concealment or escape."[4] It was clearly important for the Victorian authorities to attempt to short-circuit the public curiosity that developed around sites like this, which recalled the fashionable slumming expeditions to St. Giles or Ratcliff Highway in the heyday of Pierce Egan. Even more disturbing, however, was the political valence with which areas like

Jacob's Island began to be imbued, presumably as symbols of a developing urban counterculture. In *The Mysteries of Paris and London,* for example, Richard Maxwell argues that the area became refigured as "a site of radical activity," noting a wall poster from 1846 in which the inhabitants of Dockhead in Bermondsey were invited to celebrate the repeal of the Corn Laws "on that highly interesting Spot, described by Charles Dickens."[5] This is only an isolated example, of course, but I think it bears out the larger argument of chapter 2, that early Victorian crime fiction performed an active function in the preservation and shaping of popular memory, especially as it accreted around specific geographical locations.

One further contribution to the Jacob's Island controversies should also be noted. The same year that Sir Peter Laurie made his attack on *Oliver Twist,* Henry Mayhew published an article in the *Morning Chronicle* which supposedly led to his being hired as London correspondent for its forthcoming series on "Labour and the Poor."[6] In it, Mayhew sought to capitalize on the Jacob's Island controversy by confirming the region's existence, especially as it had recently gained some notoriety as one of the worst hit by the cholera epidemic of 1849. In its close attention to detail and self-presentation as an authoritative eye-witness account, his article certainly confirmed and vindicated Dickens's own literary treatment of the area. Mayhew also characteristically incorporated a number of evocative phrases and images to strengthen the impact of the scene: the ditch which supplies inhabitants with their only source of drinking water is described, for example,

> as covered with a scum almost like a cobweb, and prismatic with grease. In it float large masses of green rotting weed, and against the posts of the bridges are swollen carcasses of dead animals, almost bursting with the gases of putrefaction. Along the banks are heaps of indescribable filth, the phosphoretted smell from which tells of the rotting fish, while the oyster-shells are like pieces of slate from their coating of mud and dirt.

In addition to punctuating his naturalist description with these powerful images, Mayhew also went further than either Dickens or Charles Kingsley—who set a scene from *Alton Locke* (1850) there, using descriptive language which may well have been borrowed from Mayhew—in assigning responsibility to negligent and profiteering landlords: "This, indeed," he concluded, "seems to be the great evil. Out of these wretches' health, comfort, and even lives, small capitalists reap a petty independence; and until the poor are rescued from the fangs of such mercenaries, there is but little hope either for their physical or moral welfare."[7]

This kind of bold authorial statement is rare in Mayhew's work, especially as it developed over the course of the *London Labour* project. His methods, which have occasioned a great deal of criticism, were more typically characterized by a positivist belief in the narrative power of statistics. When he came to define his approach in 1851, his self-image was that of a "mere collector of facts" who ultimately hoped to discover the basic economic laws governing the production of poverty, wage differentials, the division of labor, and so on. As Anne Humpherys has noted, moreover, these larger ambitions were usually postponed into an indefinite future, as Mayhew seems to have increasingly worked with an inductive methodology in which the facts are trusted to tell their own stories.[8] This is not to suggest that his work was value-free, either in the selection or the presentation of its evidence. But at the same time, I think it is worth giving some consideration to Mayhew's methods and intentions, instead of simply dismissing him out of hand for weaknesses which might equally apply to Victorian political discourse as a whole, or indeed to entire fields of the modern social sciences. In using his work as a brief introduction to this chapter, my aim is to spell out some of the prevailing assumptions of the period about poverty and politics, and to then trace how they recurred in contemporary debates about how best to combat urban crime.

It is undeniable (surely even predictable) that moralizing or racist assumptions find their way into Mayhew's complicated classificatory schema. Indeed, it is difficult to read the opposition he makes at the outset of *London Labour and the London Poor* between "wandering" and "civilized" tribes, complete with speculations about their respective physiologies, or his organizing distinction between those who *will, can't,* and *won't* work, and not sense the shadows of Darwin and Malthus.[9] But to argue, as Gertrude Himmelfarb has done, that Mayhew succeeds only in making his subjects into "a race apart," more closely resembling a Darwinian species than a class in Marx's sense, is to grotesquely misrepresent both the project and its historical context; indeed, it quite neatly sidesteps the profoundly anti-Marxist basis of her own argument, which aims to blame Victorian social reformers for producing a "culture of poverty" as the forerunner of what conservatives today like to term "welfare dependency."[10] Himmelfarb's criticism implies that a class analysis was readily available in any kind of systematic form at this time, when in reality socialists and communists were just as confused and divided over the issue of crime as reformers. In *The Condition of the Working Class in England,* for example, Engels still viewed criminal activity as a primitive but justifiable rebellion against conditions of capitalist oppression and immiseration. Just three years later, however, the *Communist Manifesto* dismissed such actions as the work of a potentially counterrevolutionary substratum, who were "dangerous" only to the extent that they might ultimately side with the bourgeoisie: "The 'dangerous classes,' the social scum (*Lumpenproletariat*), that passively rotting mass thrown off by the lowest layers of old society, may, here and there, be swept into the movement by a proletarian revolution," Marx and Engels declared; "its conditions of life, however, prepare it far more for the part of a bribed tool of reactionary intrigue."[11]

In such a context, it is unfair to condemn a more uneven and unsystematic thinker like Mayhew for dodging questions of precisely how his twin subjects, Labour and the Poor, were interrelated. Himmelfarb's own larger study of *The Idea of Poverty,* which holds Mayhew largely responsible for a confusion of these categories, gives ample evidence of a larger semantic and conceptual overlap that was only partially hidden by more generic terms like "the dangerous classes," "the people," "the ragged" or "the lower classes." Given her insistence that the Victorian public would instinctively know the differences and experience the "lines of demarcation" by which the respectable laboring poor were shielded from the crime around them, it is telling that Himmelfarb has no real answer for the evident misperception of Mayhew's text: "It is curious," she notes, "that so many reviewers of *London Labour* responded to these volumes with the same expressions of wonder and guilt that had earlier been elicited by the *Chronicle* letters," given that "many of those portrayed by Mayhew were, by his account, so exceedingly strange, deliberately cultivating their isolation and peculiarity, that the reader need have felt neither surprise nor shame at his ignorance. What is surprising," the passage concludes, "is how many reviewers did nevertheless react so guiltily, and more important, how many unwittingly identified the most distinctive street-folk with the generality of 'London Labour and the London Poor.'" Looking for answers, Himmelfarb is forced here (as at other points in her argument) to fall back on an imaginary "critical reader" who "might have wondered" at Mayhew's terminology and his use of facts; this abstraction, however, remains unconvincing when stacked against the considerable testimony she cites of actual readers who were apparently persuaded that the categories in the text's title were closely linked.[12]

One possible solution, of course, would be to see Mayhew in much the same light as I have tried to present Dickens here, as someone who was invested with a public trust to represent the truth about life in London's streets. But it is just as likely that his reader—like Mayhew himself, or Dickens, or just about any other social commentator of the period—felt that there had to be a connection between industrialization, declining wages, and the crime rate. Since Himmelfarb's agenda is to disconnect crime from the experience of poverty, she needs to operate within the more familiar Victorian binary distinguishing a respectable labor force from a demoralized residuum. The tendentious argument she goes on to rehearse, "that poverty was not a cause of crime," leads to a common conclusion of the period, which saw criminals as entirely self-motivated and outside of the bonds of society. Ironically, then, after she has criticized Mayhew for caricaturing London's "street-folk" in tribal terms, Himmelfarb ends by affirming a vision of the same citizens as "*in* the community, but neither *of* it, nor *from* it."[13] Against this line of argument, however, both Mayhew and Marx were careful to indict the wider society and the forces of capitalist accumulation for the existence of crime: "If the London costers belong especially to the 'dangerous classes,'" the former states, "the danger of such a body is assuredly an evil of our own creation"; and Marx and Engels were similarly insistent about the political causes of crime, even when they rejected attempts to romanticize the dispossessed as revolutionary outlaws.[14] In many ways, this is the key issue in midcentury debates about the etiology of crime, since there was a general agreement that its existence closely correlated with the quality of life in the slums: the question which followed was whether slum inhabitants themselves were to blame, or the social and economic conditions into which they were born and lived. As we shall see, different answers to this question helped to determine what combative schemes were developed and practiced, ranging from conservative calls for more police and slum clearance, through liberal reform measures aimed at improving environmental and social conditions, to Chartist or socialist platforms which saw those conditions as the by-product of political disenfranchisement and capitalist economics.[15]

Mayhew, for his part, was concerned much less with the prospects for amelioration than with the need to represent the actual conditions of poverty. He frequently refused charitable contributions from his readers, especially when earmarked for particular characters in his larger narrative. He also made only fitful attempts to organize workers in the various trades he studied, although it is worth noting that he often used meetings to elicit information about London trades for his *Morning Chronicle* reports, and once organized a mass gathering of tailors in order to underline the arguments against free trade which led to his break with the paper.[16] In many ways, though, he seems more interested in the London underclass as a distinctive social or cultural formation, rather than seeing it as a strictly determined economic class, and this helps to explain why the features he concentrates on—like the defining styles, customs, and slang of the people he includes in his survey—are those which would now characterize the study of urban subcultures. Lacking the methodological and analytical frameworks of modern ethnology, he often seems to be grasping for a new way of organizing information, while relying in the process on interviews with individuals whom he took to be representative of larger social forces and formations. In this respect, Deborah Epstein Nord and Anne Humpherys have credited Mayhew with developing a distinctive new style of presentation which borrowed from forms of anthropology as well as the techniques of realist fiction.[17] His reluctance to draw conclusions from the data he collected seems formally related to Mayhew's particular style of presenting interviews, in which the questioner recedes into the background: beginning from the second letter to the *Morning Chronicle,* as Humpherys notes, he effectively "evolved a new form of reporting, a fusion of himself, through his questions, and the respondent, whose answers were reported in the first person, in a long uninterrupted monologue, with the questions absorbed into the replies." This technique, she argues, is distinct from that developed by Dickens, who preferred (as we shall later in this chapter, from examples of his articles on the London police) to project his own thoughts directly into the mind of his addressee, thereby foregrounding his own authorial intervention.[18]

Mayhew's techniques are best represented by examining the most famous of his subjects, the London costermongers. These street-sellers most obviously embody Mayhew's contention that the capital was home to a distinct and wandering tribe, although he routinely reminds his readers that their social alienation was partly the fault of external forces. The costers claimed origins dating back to the sixteenth century, and had developed a semi-autonomous culture of dress, language, and customs that nicely illustrate the ambivalent relationship of subcultures to the larger society. Distinctive cries, for example, helped to convey the precise objects for sale, while a secret code was used for internal communications, in order to conceal the speaker's designs; the costers similarly participated in a larger economy of public entertainments, beer-shops, games, and fights, at the same time that they were felt to constitute a distinct body with its own standards of morality and culture. This second aspect, exemplified by a hatred of the police, their atheism, and "the most imperfect idea of the sanctity of marriage," is shown in Mayhew's biographies of a coster-lad and girl, whose "[lives] may be taken as a type of the many." The latter confirms that "I dare say there ain't ten out of a hundred gals what's livin' with men, what's been married Church of England fashion," while her male counterpart explains the coster code of conduct and allegiance: "I never heard about Christianity," he states,

> but if a cove was to fetch me a lick of the head, I'd give it him again, whether he was a big 'un or a little 'un. I'd precious soon see a henemy of mine shot afore I'd forgive him,—where's the use? Do I understand what behaving to your neighbour is?—In coorse I do. If a feller as lives next me wanted a basket of mine as I wasn't using, why, he might have it; if I was working it though, I'd see him further! I can understand that all as lives in a court is neighbours; but as for policemen, they're nothing to me, and I should like to pay 'em off well. No; I never heerd about this here creation you speaks about. In coorse God Almighty made the world, and the poor bricklayers' labourers built the houses arterwards—that's *my* opinion.[19]

This passage nicely demonstrates Mayhew's approach, as the opinions of the individual are supposed to represent the beliefs of the group. The questions posed concerning creation and the Christian treatment of others are incorporated into the narrative flow, and elicit responses which reveal a form of class consciousness in their insistence on the work of laborers or the distinction between neighbors with shared interests and the outside force of the police.

In Mayhew's account, the latter constitute the sworn enemies of the costers, because the Police Act of 1839 had granted them the authority to regulate the "stands" or "patches" from which street sales were conducted. To "serve out" or assault a policeman is therefore said to be "the bravest act by which a costermonger can distinguish himself," and was rewarded by communal funds to offset any time spent in prison, while the war against "the crushers" might be conducted through complex strategems and acts of retaliation (1:16). Indeed, Mayhew sees this animosity as central to their lives, noting at one point that it "is so intimately blended with what may be called the politics of the costermongers that I give them together." He mentions that they are "nearly all Chartists," but have only a simplified knowledge of the issues and are easily swayed by their leaders. Nevertheless, they frequently attend political meetings, and have a basic understanding of the balance of forces in society, which leads them to oppose the aristocracy and "the governing power" as in league with the detested police. While the Chartists typically viewed the new police as a secondary political force, charged with defending the rights of property and enforcing unfair trade practices, the London costermongers seem to have abstracted their political diagnosis out of a more direct experience of oppression at the hands of the police, and Mayhew accordingly concludes that "I am assured that in case of a political riot every 'coster' would seize his policeman" (1:20).

The threat of violence which these passages articulate goes a long way toward explaining why the campaign for the People's Charter was so incendiary, since it worked by generalizing a range of local grievances into a formidable mass movement. The enlistment of the costers, who otherwise seem to have little common interest with the organized working class, indicates why Chartism was able to successfully constitute itself as a struggle of "the people," since its strength lay in its ability to mobilize such disparate forces in a common cause. In this sense, we might point to a more widespread rhetorical linkage between a destitute and often criminalized underclass and the labor movement, as is evident not only from Mayhew's own organizational framework but also the statements of his subjects. In reality, however, the threat of a united front of Labour and the Poor rapidly dissipated after the fiasco of 1848, when the Chartist assembly promised violent confrontation would follow a third parliamentary refusal to grant the Charter, and we can only assume that the costers were numbered among those who failed to appear.

Their local struggles continued, however, as part of an ongoing opposition to the police which continued up to and beyond the eventual implementation of a national force in 1856, but which has been consistently minimized or written out of most accounts of the period. In retrieving these stories of a belligerent and often violent collective resistance in the next section, I want to critically examine the assumptions which ground those historical accounts of the new police, and to suggest that they have acted as an enabling fiction, aimed at legitimating a form of consensual agreement between ruler and ruled which was never fully attained. By outlining an alternative account which pays close attention to the shifting relationship between law enforcement agencies and the local communities they police, I offer a different explanation of why and on what terms the police were introduced in Britain, and how a range of antagonistic social forces successfully opposed, restrained, and delimited their authority. Finally, in turning back to Dickens at the end of this chapter, I hope to suggest some of the ways in which Victorian fiction after 1848 acted as a propagandist agent for the new police, a function which was quite clearly at odds with its earlier role as the vehicle for social protest and reform as described in chapter 2.

## Whig Historians and the New Police

The debates which attended the gradual introduction of a system of policing during the first half of the nineteenth century reveal a powerful alliance between civil libertarians and provincial magistrates, which in turn found a common interest with sections of the organized working class. As I reconstruct them here, the negotiations concerning the foundation of a nationwide force focused primarily on the comparative strengths and costs of maintaining a centralized authority at the expense of local and regional autonomy. Ranged alongside the arguments of radicals, Chartists, and reformers that an organized force would invariably function as a political arm of the State, provincial objections to a national police successfully delayed and modified government plans throughout the first half of the century. The reason these discussions are not more widely known, however, should be ascribed to the predominance of a Whig version of police history, articulated most clearly by scholars like Leon Radzinowicz and Charles Reith, who have employed the eventual existence of a more modest and delimited force by the end of the century as a powerful organizing *telos*. From such a position, a history of political struggle and contestation retroactively emerges in the form of an overarching masternarrative, in which rising rates of crime and urban unrest inevitably occasion a national consensus on policing.

For these police historians, evidence of working-class opposition is particularly inadmissible. Reith, for example, regards it as a purely residual reminder of eighteenth-century anarchy. His *British Police and the Democratic Ideal* opens by contrasting the late eighteenth and early nineteenth centuries as "an era of uncontrolled crime and mob disorder" with the period immediately following the passage of Robert Peel's Metropolitan Police Act of 1829, which is accordingly characterized by "the appearance of public orderliness in Britain, and of individual willingness to cooperate in securing and maintaining it." On such a basis, Reith is able to conclude that "It was the efforts of gangsterdom alone, and the success of its propaganda, which frustrated for nearly a century every attempt to end the menace of crime and disorder by creating police."[20] Similarly, the *locus classicus* of liberal police history, Leon Radzinowicz's four-volume *A History of English Criminal Law,* contains a chapter on this period entitled "Towards a National Standard of Police" and subheadings on "The Way to Efficiency" and "Eroding the Capital Laws": in each case what is being emphasized is a steady organic process of development that minimizes the very real conflicts and arguments which were evident at every stage.

In Radzinowicz's account, with its primary focus on parliamentary law, the main emphasis falls on the relationship between central and local levels of government. First, he notes how the model force introduced in London in 1829 was replicated for industrial cities like Birmingham, Manchester, and Bolton as the basis for a centralized infrastructure. Even here, though, he describes a series of compromises which successively diluted Peel's original formula for a standardized force, as local counties and boroughs continued to resist any proposal that they develop and fund their own police units. In response to these arguments about local government autonomy, legislators drew back from any central dictation of policy and left choices up to local parishes and magistrates: as late as 1842, Radzinowicz lists seven different forms of police in operation throughout the country, which collectively still fell short of the kind of omnipresent surveillance which Peel had envisioned. A new wave of agitation following the second presentation of the Charter in that year and the so-called Rebecca Riots of 1843 on the part of poor Welsh farmers occasioned a serious crisis in some areas, but they nonetheless continued to rely on support from the army of London's Metropolitan force rather than swear in their own paid constables. Although government legislation remained grounded in a permissive policy of voluntary compliance, Radzinowicz narrates his account with a tone of optimistic and retrospective complacency, which serves to undercut any sense that the successive crises of this period might have seriously threatened the stability of national order or the long-range policing project: "The condition of stalemate," he concludes, "was more apparent than real. The hope had always been that permissive rather than mandatory legislation, local rather than central control, would eventually make regular police forces generally acceptable. Taking the country as a whole, the results were disappointing, but there were some areas in which the permissive approach succeeded."[21] "Disappointing" but not disastrous: the calm narrative voice continues to assure us that the final outcome was never seriously in doubt, and that opposition merely served to delay the inevitable.

There is, however, a central paradox in these Whig accounts, since policing initiatives must be shown to arise from widespread public anxieties about rising crime and the need for protection, even as their progressivist narrative teleologies remain undisturbed by any note of doubt or contingency. In this sense, it is important to note that it is not the threat represented by Chartism, but rather the ending of transportation to Australia in 1853, that Radzinowicz offers as the reason for the final implementation of a centralized national force. The methodological assumptions of historians like Radzinowicz and Reith duplicate those of Victorian commentators, who also provided a retroactive justification for existing police powers by insistently demanding their incremental extension, without ever pausing to question the basis for the force's apparent ineffectiveness. In a useful analysis of conceptual approaches to the study of policing, Robert Reiner has noted a fundamental contradiction in how crime statistics have been deployed, which dates back to the mid-nineteenth century. Such statistics are of course notoriously bad indicators of actual levels of crime, since higher numbers might just as easily testify to a greater police efficiency or to a public trust in their abilities, which in turn leads to more reported incidents. Reiner argues that, as early as the 1840s, it became increasingly clear to opponents of the new police that "reformers were using rising crime statistics to justify the extension of a preventive police, the efficacy of which was called into question by those very figures."[22] Operating in tandem with journalistic exposés like those undertaken by Dickens, which routinely took the form of ethnographic journeys into enemy territory, this Victorian law-and-order discourse functioned to naturalize widely held assumptions about crime. Crucially, it aimed to justify the current methods and powers of the police to a public which might still harbor suspicions, and to minimize the dangers posed by criminal elements; at the same time, however, it highlighted the opposite case by calling for increased manpower, tougher sentencing, and greater surveillance, which were presumably required because the "war on crime" was being lost. The dilemma these writers faced was that any public celebration of the police's knowledge and efficiency inevitably led to questions about their apparent restraint: as *Fraser's Magazine* editorialized in 1857, "The public is aware that most, if not every one of the ticket-of-leave men who have spread the reign of terror in the well-lighted and crowded metropolis, are in the black list of the police and *wants to know* why they are not taken up."[23]

One reason why the police were reluctant to "take them up" was because the areas in which the majority of such criminals lived also sustained a counterculture grounded in an alternative interpretation of the legality of custom and rights, and in a rejection of the new police themselves. We have already seen examples of these attitudes among the London costermongers, the Chartists, and the criminals who were represented in the Newgate novels. At this remove, it is difficult to ascertain how many might have actively held to such beliefs, or to fully disentangle historical realities from the mediations of a culture which insistently produced criminals as the source of romantic idealizations and moral panics. It is nonetheless evident that a legitimate fear of mass opposition and resistance led Victorian authorities to modify plans for the new police, and to tightly circumscribe their remit and tactics. A concern for popular opinion, for example, predates discussion of an organized British force, as authorities registered widespread concerns about the French system of policing, which had routinely deployed paid inspectors as government spies under both pre- and post-revolutionary regimes. As early as 1763, Sir William Mildmay's *The Police of France* had warned of the potential intrusion of such a force into the lives of "free-born Englishmen," describing how the Parisian police "go under the name of military establishments, and consequently cannot be initiated by our administration, under a free and civil constitution of government"; in contrast to France, he argued, England was "a land of liberty, where the injured and oppressed are to seek for no other protection, but that which the law ought to afford, without plying for aid to a military power; a remedy dangerous, and perhaps worse than the disease."[24] These same concerns for civil liberties were addressed to successive parliamentary enquiries between 1789 and 1829. In 1822, for example, the report of the select committee Peel had established to investigate the policing of London argued that "It is difficult to reconcile an effective system of police with that perfect freedom of action and exemption from interference which are the great privileges and blessing of society in this country"; they concluded that the "forfeiture or curtailment of such advantages would be too great a sacrifice for improvement in police, or facilities in detection of crime, however desirable in themselves."

Seven years later, after widespread rioting and governmental upheaval, Peel finally got approval for his bill, but was forced to take these reservations into account. Most notably, he tried to alleviate fears of a political police by stressing the primacy of crime prevention over detection, since the latter was widely associated with the French system and held to infringe on civil liberties. On this principle, Peel introduced the famous beat system of foot patrols, and told police superintendents that

> potential criminals would be best deterred by "making it evident that they are known and strictly watched, and that detection will follow any attempts to commit a crime." To this end the seventeen divisions were subdivided into sections and again into beats,

each patrolled by a rota of constables at every hour of the day and night. At the centre of the division was a police station or watch house, at which an inspector was always on duty to keep order, to hold a reserve party ready to meet emergencies, to record charges, to detain persons or release them on recognisances, and to be responsible for any property brought in.[25]

It hardly needs to be said that such a system was extremely costly, and an inefficient employment of resources: as examples, Clive Emsley cites figures from forty years later, of 912 day beats and 3,126 night beats engaged in patrolling the streets of London.[26] It is not at all clear, though, how far Peel's careful compromises found popular acceptance. In 1833, for example, a London jury returned a verdict of "justifiable homicide" on a man charged with killing a police constable who had been engaged in forcefully breaking up a mass rally of the National Union of the Working Classes at Cold Bath Fields. Decisions like this one confirmed the suspicions of some conservative commentators that juries were dangerously democratic bodies, often acting on the basis of sectional interests instead of assuming the political neutrality of the law. Juries were very popular institutions, however, which were widely associated with earlier and more local forms of judicial administration. At the height of Chartist anxiety, for example, *Blackwood's Edinburgh Magazine* noted the government's reluctance to prosecute the London conventioneers for sedition, on the creditable grounds that a jury might refuse to convict. This observation gives rise to a series of oppositions, which combine to suggest a nation moving in the direction of a repressive and centralized authority: "Is the unpaid juryman in the end to be everywhere supplanted by the stipendiary judge; the church-warden by the poor-law commissioner; the parish constable by the paid policeman; the yeomanry by an armed gendarmerie; the militia by a powerful regular army? . . . These are vital and momentous questions."[27] At a moment of national crisis, the choices seemed clear: either a reaffirmation of the more communitarian tradition of judical administration represented by juries, constables, and a volunteer army; or the ruthless enforcement of legal authority, as embodied in the professional apparatus of a police force and a standing army.

In such an equation, it is the police and not the jury system which appears to be guided by political interests. By posing the options in this way, *Blackwood's* usefully codified the long-standing civil libertarian objections to the new police, while also implying that they would inevitably be required to act on dubious principles if the prime purpose was to suppress the Chartist threat. In this context, the jury's decision in the case of Cold Bath Fields closely coincided with a larger and more damaging scandal, in which police sergeant Popay was accused of infiltrating the National Political Union, amending their resolutions to reflect a more inflammatory rhetoric, suggesting that they practice with firearms and broadswords, and then reporting back to police authorities. The investigating parliamentary committee seems to have responded to a widespread sense that Popay had overstepped the bounds of his duties by acting as an *agent provocateur,* and it reproved him for "carrying concealment into the intercourse of private life."[28] In such a context, policy decisions were consistently influenced by a general mistrust of the police, and in particular by opposition to any system resembling the detested French model of governmental spies and informers. We have already seen how such sentiments were responsible for the initial decision to prioritize preventive techniques, and they also seem to have determined what form detective work would take when it was eventually introduced. At its inception in 1842, the Metropolitan Police's detection unit consisted of two inspectors and six sergeants, and more than twenty-five years later it had only grown to a total of sixteen men. The Popay scandal was replayed three years later when undercover police were again accused of acting as spies, and from then until 1862 such tactics were used only in cases of "urgent necessity" and required special orders from police superintendents. Indeed, even a champion of legal authority like Leon Radzinowicz summarizes this period by suggesting that "the need to absolve the police from any suspicion of spying took precedence over the general needs of detection and prevention."[29]

In *Policing the Crisis,* Stuart Hall and others at the Centre for Cultural and Community Studies at Birmingham University use the moral panic generated over mugging in Britain in the early 1970s as the occasion for a wide-ranging theoretical discussion of the social role of the police. Informing their analysis is Gramsci's analysis of hegemony, which suggests that a historical function of the police has been to mediate between the State and its citizens, by acting as both a repressive apparatus and as public servants. As such, they argue,

If the individual policeman [sic] is constrained by his organisation, he is also constrained by the society of which he is a part.
Formally, the police enforce and apply the law and uphold public order; in this they see themselves and are seen as acting "on
society's behalf." But in a more informal sense, they must also be
sensitive to shifts in public feeling, in society's anxieties and concerns. . . . Even where, formally, they apply the law, how, where,
and in what manner it is enforced—key areas of police discre-
tion—are influenced by the prevailing "social temperature."[30]

In the terms of a Gramscian analysis, then, the police need to combine
the twin functions of coercion and consent through which State power
is exercised within Western democracies. In this way, they are consistently forced to play different—and often conflicting—roles, as both the
agents of law eforcement and public servants. The best account of how
the ensuing tension impacts on crime policy is offered by Phil Cohen,
who has undertaken a series of studies of policing strategies and their application to urban subcultures. In "Policing the Working-Class City," for
instance, he offers a fascinating analysis of the history of policing in the
London borough of Islington, which was home to many of Mayhew's
costermongers. Echoing Raymond Williams's influential redefinition of
determination as the setting of limits and the exertion of pressures, Cohen identifies community opposition as a limit imposed on the police, in
the sense that districts like Islington "sustained popular cultures which
incorporated quite highly-developed countervailing norms of law and
order, which could only be eliminated by outright repression." Such
subcultural resistance thwarted attempts by the police to gain consent for
their actions until as late as World War I, Cohen argues, given that a condition for their success was that they be perceived as "the neutral administration of a rational system of justice" rather than an overtly repressive
extension of bourgeois state power into working-class communities.[31]

In order to understand the ensuing tension, Cohen offers a useful
theoretical account of the police's dual function. On the one hand, he
suggests, the policeman performs "a purely expressive function of community welfare and is expected to do so impartially, as a public servant, in
contexts occupied solely by what appear to be individual citizens in need
or distress"; at the same time, however, he performs a more repressive

role of protecting property by distinguishing between its "legitimate" and "illegitimate" possessors.[32] Again, this implies a combination of coercive and consensual operations, but what is most valuable is the way Cohen understands the points of contradiction between the police's different roles. These, he suggests, can signify areas of contestation and resistance, generated by and through the oppositional dynamics existing between the State and its citizens; the contradiction is located, in other words, within the exercise of law enforcement itself, rather than at the site of the individual policed subject or at the interstices of a range of conflicting discourses, as it might be theorized in a more Foucauldian framework of power relations.

In fact, consent was eventually—and only provisionally—obtained in the early years of the twentieth century by turning a blind eye to a range of cultural activities like gambling or street football which were officially classified as "criminal," since the application of a strict policy of law enforcement in communities like Islington would have inevitably resulted in mass arrests and open class warfare. As a result, the police were effectively faced with what Cohen terms "the impossible choice of enforcing law *or* order," and this is a double bind which continues to haunt modern-day policing in the form of discussions centered around the concept of community policing: any attention to strict law enforcement, he argues, inevitably means that "more manpower has to be poured into 'community relations' to restabilize the public image of the force. The more technologically sophisticated, and hence impersonal, the systems of surveillance, the more home-beat coppers are needed on the ground."[33] In this way, the subcultural opposition maintained by groups like Mayhew's costermongers needs to be seen—just as much as the arguments of civil libertarians against undercover detective work, or those of provincial magistrates against centralized authority—as embodying a kind of constitutive limit on the potential operations of the new police.

Where these limits had been negotiated and agreed at local levels, an uneasy consent might be granted for the police's actions, but violent opposition consistently erupted when they were seen to act out of overtly political motives, or when systems of legal enforcement were imposed by centralized authority. Mayhew recognized the contours of this ongoing struggle between the police and the community as well as anyone, and sought to explain the costers' belligerence by pointing to the provocation of the police: "Denied the right of getting a living by the street authorities," he notes, the costers viewed the law as "a mere farce, or at best, but the exercise of an arbitrary and despotic power, against which they consider themselves justified, whenever an opportunity presents itself, of using the same physical force as it brings to bear against them."[34] This sense of a rational calculus of interests—according to which the activities of the police are shown to overtly negate the costermongers' own understanding of the rights of labor—is what connects their opposition with the larger struggles of the Chartists, and helps to distinguish Mayhew's text from those of other contemporary commentators. Like the Whiggish police historians who constitute their direct descendants, these commentators tend instead either to ignore groups like the costers (by focusing in their place on the more respectable discourse of civil liberties) or to pathologize their actions as the logical consequence of ignorance or moral laxity. Such claims are certainly present in Mayhew, although not to the extent suggested by his critics; what is more distinctive and remarkable, though, are passages like that cited above, which suggest how Mayhew might have viewed the conceptual connections between London labor and the poor.

By the time that the national police network was consolidated in 1856, a powerful journalistic movement was in place, which had developed out of earlier attempts to document conditions of poverty in North or East London but now circulated a very different set of assumptions and prescriptions for action. As I suggested in chapter 1, early efforts to represent the London poor proceeded on the basis of an abstract sense of common interest, which was not always readily apparent but at least hoped for: if this underclass held only limited or faulty moral standards, then these were attributable to the conditions in which they lived, and thus in part the responsibility of those who lived elsewhere. We can still find echoes of this position in Mayhew's own writings, and more strongly in a text like Engels's *Condition of the Working-Class in England,* but it is increasingly supplanted by a new language which sought to moralize the "respectable" working class, and to blame the underclass below them for their poverty. This second position appeals to supposedly core values of decency, honesty, respect for the rule of law, and so on, and thus works to construct the very consensus to which it looks for moral authority. As we have seen from debates concerning the origins of the British police, this consensus had not been attained in the first half of the nineteenth century, and increasingly required a legitimating public discourse. In response to this challenge, a number of novelists, commentators, and journalists addressed issues of policing in the aftermath of the Chartist defeat of 1848, among whom Dickens occupied an important but ambiguous position. In turning back to Dickens now, and specifically to his articles on the detective police, I propose to read these ambiguities as symptomatic of the struggles of the 1850s to reformulate the discourse of public policy, and to rethink the bonds of social responsibility by which the classes were connected.

## Dickens on Duty

It might initially seem strange to find Dickens in this company, given what I have written in the previous chapter about *Oliver Twist* as a vehicle for articulating political criticism. In broad terms, though, we could say that British fiction turns away from the overtly interventionist tactics which it pursued during the 1840s. The shift is evident not only in an examination of crime literature, but also in the sequence of industrial novels which aimed to answer the famous "condition of England" question, which had been placed on the national agenda by Carlyle's 1839 essay on Chartism.[35] One of the earliest responses, Disraeli's 1845 novel *Sibyl; or, the Two Nations,* directly encodes its answer in the subtitle, even as it begins to outline the alternative strategy of one-nation Toryism. Elizabeth Gaskell's *Mary Barton* (1848) and Charles Kingsley's *Alton Locke* (1850) both attempt to articulate working-class grievances and the appeal of the Chartists, although each ends on a note of optimistic inter-class connection: in the former, between labor agitator John Barton and the mill owner whose son he has murdered, but from whom he eventually receives forgiveness; and in the latter case, between the eponymous "tailor-poet" and Chartist, and the wealthy benefactors who embody Kingsley's idealized Christian socialism. By the time of Gaskell's *North and South* (published serially in Dickens's own *Household Words,* in 1854 – 55), the secondary character of strike leader Nicholas Higgins is more accommodating and morally upright, serving mainly to facilitate the novel's central romance between its Southern heroine and an enterprising Northern mill owner. These are simplified plot summaries, of course, but they help to suggest the trajectory of the genre during the 1840s and

'50s away from the presentation of class conflict, and increasingly toward the production of symbols of reconciliation.

Dickens follows a somewhat different trajectory, but one which touches at various points upon that sketched here. It is by now customary to divide early from late Dickens around the publication of *Dombey and Son,* in the watershed year of 1848, as the humanism of the early novels gives way to a more systematic critique of social institutions like the factory system, business, or the Chancery courts.[36] But what is also striking is the way that the critical edge of these later satires is blunted by a newfound respect for law and order. In schematic terms, the earlier critique of the legal system—and its effect on those who are subjected to its authority—is increasingly particularized, and focuses with greater precision on specific institutions (like Chancery) and agencies (like the magistracy). In many ways, this shift parallels Dickens's changing attitudes toward capital punishment, to which he was absolutely opposed around the time of *Oliver Twist* and the Courvoisier hanging; by 1849, when he witnessed the execution of Maria and George Manning (found guilty of murdering their lodger), he proposed a modified position in letters to the *Times,* which chiefly call for the abolition of public executions as having no value as a deterrent; even this pragmatic compromise was ultimately abandoned when he called for the death sentence for the surgeon and poisoner Thomas Smethurst ten years later.[37]

It is tempting to ascribe the changing status of the police in Dickens's writing to the same rightward drift. In *Barnaby Rudge* (1841), for example, he wrote that the growth of the London mob at the time of the Gordon Riots had been "fostered by bad criminal laws, bad prison regulations, and the worst conceivable police,"[38] and characters like Blathers and Duff in *Oliver Twist* do little to correct the impression that the police were incompetent at best, if not actively counterproductive. But Dickens's main concern may have been to dignify the new police system at the expense of the older patchwork of constables, parish beadles, and the Bow Street Runners. His gentle satire of Blathers and Duff—which was intensified twenty years later in *Great Expectations* (1860–61)[39]— is designed, in other words, mainly to highlight the contrast between policing past and present, a comparison which is also at the center of his influential articles on the London detectives. These essays, which appeared in 1850–51 in *Household Words,* open in fact with a statement of this difference: "We are not by any means devout believers in the old Bow Street Police. To say the truth, we think there was a vast amount of humbug about those worthies. Apart from many of them being men of very indifferent character, and far too much in the habit of consorting with thieves and the like, they never lost a public occasion of jobbing and trading in mystery and making the most of themselves." The blame for this false reputation, interestingly, is said to lie with Dickens's old enemy the magistracy, along with journalistic "penny-a-liners" who exaggerated the ethics and efficiency of the early detectives; in reality, he insists, they had been ineffective for the purposes of crime prevention, and disorganized in their attempts at detection. As such, this prototypical force compares badly with the Metropolitan detective squad which had recently been instituted, but already performs "so systematically and quietly, does its business in such a workmanlike manner, and is always so calmly and steadily engaged in the service of the public, that the public really does not know enough of it, to know a tithe of its usefulness."[40]

In the exact manner of those hack writers he accuses of puffing the Bow Street Runners, Dickens then proceeds to extol all of the virtues of the detective squad, which at this time consisted of two inspectors and six sergeants for the whole of London. The most famous of these articles, "On Duty with Inspector Field," describes a night spent on patrol with one of the inspectors (who has often been taken as the model for Bucket of *Bleak House,* a novel to which I shall turn shortly), and is narrated in such an uncharacteristically obsequious tone that many critics have accused Dickens of a form of star-struck hero worship.[41] The essay exemplifies a recognizable fantasy of police power, in which they are attributed a remarkable degree of investigative efficiency; indeed, Dickens would have us believe that the contrast between old and new systems— as personified by the compelling authority of Field—was so great that this squad of eight was able to subjugate London's entire criminal underworld. As if to prove the point, they bring the author to a cellar in Rat's Castle, at the heart of St. Giles. Dickens duly notes that the population there "is strong enough to murder us all, and willing enough to do it; but let Inspector Field have a mind to pick out one thief here, and take him; let him produce that ghastly truncheon from his pocket, and say, with his business-like air, 'My lad, I want you!' and all Rat's Castle shall be stricken with paralysis, and not a finger raised against him, as he fits the handcuffs on!" (516).

On the night that the author accompanies him, however, no arrests are made. Indeed, Field himself resembles less the feared and omniscient detective of crime literature (for which he apparently posed as a real-life model) than the modern-day community policeman, whom Phil Cohen describes as serving the compensatory function of softening the more overtly repressive aspects of legal authority. At one point on the tour, for example, he leads Dickens into an outhouse in St. Giles which is home to "ten, twenty, thirty—who can count them" Irish, takes pains to find the landlord, and gives him money to buy them all coffee in the morning (517–18). He seems, moreover, well-known and respected by the criminals they encounter, as "pickpockets defer to him; the gentle sex (not very gentle here) smile upon him. Half-drunken hags check themselves in the midst of pots of beer, or pints of gin, to drink to Mr. Field. . . . One beldame in rusty black has such admiration for him, that she runs a whole street's length to shake his hand," and so on (518–19). There is one sense in which detection takes precedence over crime prevention here, although not that intended by the detectives' supporters, as two parallel scenes nicely illustrate. In the first, the party visits a crowded room in a poor lodging-house where, as a precaution against theft, the sheets have been inscribed with the warning "STOP THIEF!" (520). Later, in another lodging-house owned by a belligerent landlord, Bark, they again examine the bedding: here, however, the message reads "STOLEN FROM BARK'S!" (525). Where the first is presumably designed to *prevent* theft by rendering the sheets useless for resale, the second would seem to offer an alternative—and probably more likely—assessment of its inevitability: resigned to the fact of theft, Bark would prefer to maximize the chances of getting his property back in the event that the thief is ever arrested. Such an outcome would seem to be a remote possibility at best, however: a squad of eight Metropolitan detectives were, after all, facing what amounted to a critical mass of criminality, concentrated in labyrinthine rookeries like Rat's Castle, and engaged in a wide array of illegal activities.

Given the odds, Dickens's faith in Field seems misplaced, or maybe a willful exaggeration aimed at inculcating much-needed public confidence in the new detective force. Immediately following the first scene described above, for example, he imagines himself in the position of a thief wrapped up in these same imprinted sheets, the inscription of which must function as "my first-foot on New Year's day, my Valentine, my

Birthday salute, my Christmas greeting, my parting with the old year.
STOP THIEF!" Dickens continues to imagine the thief's life:

> And to know that I *must* be stopped, come what will. To know
> that I am no match for this individual energy and keenness, or
> this organized and steady system! Come across the street here,
> and . . . examine these intricate passages and doors, contrived
> for escape, flapping and counter-flapping, like the lids of con-
> juror's boxes. But what avail they? Who gets in by a nod, and
> shows their secret working to us? Inspector Field. (520; empha-
> sis in original)

The italicized "must" here is presumably intended to denote the inevitability of capture. Given the context of this passage, however, a second
possibility presents itself—that it signifies instead an urgent *necessity,* and
thus a tone closer to ideological prescription than to realist description.

Working from contemporary sources, Kellow Chesney has recently
given a very different account of life in these rookeries, where intersecting underground passageways posed a formidable obstacle to police surveillance, and necessitated a shift in their tactics: "In places," he notes,

> cellar had been connected with cellar so that a fugitive could pass
> under a series of houses and emerge in another part of the rook-
> ery. In others, long established escape routes ran up from the
> maze of inner courts and over the huddled roofs: high on a back
> wall was a double row of iron spikes, "one row to hold by, and
> another for the feet to rest on," connecting the windows of ad-
> jacent buildings. To venture into the passage mouths that led into
> the back settlements was risky: to chase a wanted man through
> the escape ways could be really dangerous, even for a party of
> armed police.[42]

In this way, and much like the local opposition of the costermongers earlier, the architecture of the rookery forms a geographical barrier, beyond
which the police would be wise not to venture. This may also help to
explain why when they *do* go there in "On Duty with Inspector Field,"
the visit seems almost stage-managed for the novelist's benefit, and why
Field's apparently omniscient powers are hidden beneath the kindly ve-
neer of communitarian charity.

The difference between the mundane nature of the police's work and the fantasies of omniscience which they encouraged is significant for understanding the ways in which the new force was ultimately legitimated. As I have already suggested, the public discourse about policing in the 1850s made two very different points at the same time: principally, it aimed to justify existing police powers, in a political climate in which they still faced a great deal of antagonism, by offering glowing reports of their effectiveness in fighting crime; but it also implied that greater results would accrue from an extension of those powers, even at the risk of representing the police as presently outmanned. In this context, articles like "On Duty with Inspector Field" played an important role in shaping public opinion about crime and policing. These articles, which appeared in periodicals throughout the decade, routinely took the form of a journey into the geographical heart of London's underworld, usually undertaken in the company of the police.[43] Already, we can detect a concern here to disrupt potential lines of sympathy with the inhabitants of the rookeries, which had been encouraged by Mayhew and the earlier "slumming" literature which grew up around Egan's *Life in London*. As Randall McGowen argues in an analysis of these later articles, the concept of a "criminal class" which recurs throughout this decade was designed to short-circuit public sympathies: on the one hand, he notes, this "class" was shown to be large, shadowy, and threatening, with a division of labor and forms of specialization paralleling those which existed within civil society; on the other hand, however, its inhabitants were presented as entirely extrinsic to that society, existing outside of the prevailing norms of moral and social behavior, and thus fairly easy to recognize.[44]

Here, we can see many of the contradictory ideas about crime which this journalistic discourse aimed to explicate. If criminals represented a distinct "class," this was because they must be seen to have no organic connection with the local populations within which they lived. There had to be a lot of them in order to justify public expenditure on a growing judicial-policial apparatus; but if they were too many, they threatened to blend back in with a more generalized sense of the poor, and thus potentially excite popular sympathy. Furthermore, the danger they represented had to be known to the public, who needed to feel themselves surrounded; at the same time, though, the criminal underworld operated through secret codes of language and gesture, which the general population might miss, thereby placing themselves in a position of greater vulnerability. Finally, the *police* must be able to decipher these secret codes, and know who the criminals are, even if they cannot always act on that knowledge because of limited resources or unnecessary restraints on their ability to act. When faced with this series of double binds, each of which might be traced out in an essay like "Inspector Field," the Victorian press made an important distinction which operated in tandem with ideas of a "criminal class"—it singled out the new category of the "hardened" or "habitual" criminal for attention, in opposition to the merely "casual" or juvenile offenders who might still be prevented from joining the ranks of the hardened.[45] Following a number of highly publicized incidents of garotting in 1862, Police Commissioner Mayne responded to widespread anxieties over the safety of London's streets in precisely these terms, by proposing a close watch on released felons. As James Winter reconstructs his thinking, Mayne felt that "habitual criminals were unredeemable" and required a more constant supervision even when at liberty: "Did it make sense, he asked, that his men should do everything they could to expose suspected villains but then assist in concealing those who had already been imprisoned for actually carrying out their villainous intentions?"[46]

The invention of the category of "habitual" offender at this time had a number of consequences. Most importantly, it helped to weaken arguments about the social causes of crime, by suggesting that only some of the urban poor reacted to economic deprivation through illegal means. The majority, it implied, were honest and hard-working, so the criminality of a hardened minority could then be ascribed to laziness, character defects, or an inherent (and often inherited) immorality. As a result, an elaborate theory of genetic causality emerged to supplant previous ideas of social or economic determination, in which the responsibility for crime was seen to lie with the offending individual and not the larger society that had been indicted by Marx, Mayhew, and others. Indeed, one logical inference was that these habitual offenders—who might be genetically disposed to a life of crime—should no longer be given the presumption of innocence: as M. D. Hill proposed in *Suggestions for the Repression of Crime* (1857), "when, by the evidence of two or more reliable witnesses, a jury has been satisfied that there is good ground for

believing . . . that the accused party is addicted to robbery or theft, so as
to deserve the appellation of robber or thief, he shall be called upon in
defense to prove himself in possession of means of subsistence, lawfully
maintained."[47] The terms of debate had clearly shifted away from the police's potential to infringe on the civil liberties of the individual, and toward a prior assumption of guilt which might presumably have been directed at just about any of the residents of the London rookery visited by
Dickens and Field. The novelist would not have concurred with the dra-
conian measures proposed by Hill, although an essay from 1868, asking
rhetorically why any "notorious Thief and Ruffian" should ever be "left
at large" when he invariably leaves prison "as notorious a Thief as he was
when he went in," shows just how conservative he later became on issues of crime and punishment.[48] Such proposals found a logical basis in
new forms of thinking about the etiology of crime which were popular-
ized by the Victorian press, and ironically arose out of a widespread frus-
tration that the police failed to live up to heightened expectations of their
abilities, which had been generated in the first place by those same journalistic sources. The tensions in an essay like "On Duty with Inspector
Field," in which the London detectives are simultaneously presented as
cogs in a ruthlessly efficient disciplinary machine and as the impartial dis-
pensers of a humane and rational justice, are symptomatic of these exaggerated expectations, at the same time that they indicate why and on
what basis they were raised in the first place.

Even though it shares many of the ideological features of this mid-
century law-and-order discourse, "On Duty with Inspector Field" also
points to one of its key limitations—its inability to propose any long-
term remedies for conditions in the worst of London's slums, beyond
calling for a steady increase in police powers of surveillance. As I have
shown, the overriding tendency was to separate crime from the social
conditions in which it developed, but another passage from the Inspector Field essay suggests that Dickens was also thinking in broader terms
about the problems posed by the rookeries. "How many people may
there be in London," he asks,

> who, if we had brought them deviously and blindfolded, to this
> street, fifty paces from the Station House, and within call of Saint
> Giles's church, would know it for a not remote part of the city

in which their lives are passed? How many, who amidst this compound of sickening smells, these heaps of filth, these tumbling houses, with all their vile contents, animate and inanimate, slimily overflowing into the black road, would believe that they breathe *this* air?

This comes closer to the Dickens of *Oliver Twist,* with its challenge to "respectable" Londoners to remedy their ignorance of neighboring parts of the capital. Indeed, the reference to St. Giles's church recalls Jerrold's novel and an earlier convention of urban reporting that I discussed in chapter 1. Here, at least, the fault lies with bureaucracy and ruling-class negligence, not the poor themselves: "How much Red Tape may there be," Dickens asks, "that could look round on the faces which now hem us in . . . and say, 'I have thought of this. I have not dismissed the thing. I have neither blustered it away, nor frozen it away, nor tied it up and put it away, nor smoothly said pooh, pooh! to it when it has been shown to me'?" (514–15).

If we had to reconcile this powerful critique of callous indifference with the obsequious praise for London's detectives elsewhere in the same essay, we might conclude that the latter is earned at the direct expense of heartless politicians and magistrats like Peter Laurie, who aimed to "put down" poverty through simplistic schemes of slum clearance. After the successful launch of Urania House for Fallen Women in Shepherd's Bush, Dickens was involved in helping Angela Coutts to find a site in the East End for model workmen's homes in 1853, and at one point considered asking for Field's help.[49] As a result, he was actively engaged with issues of housing and sanitation during this period. What is striking, however, is that his progressive critique of legislation—that it effectively created homelessness by destroying substandard housing without considering what should replace it—did not extend to the similar tactics deployed by the London police, who dealt with an impoverished (and often itinerant) underclass by simply moving them from one spot to another. *Bleak House,* a novel he wrote immediately after the essays on the London detectives and while actively engaged with issues of sanitary reform, clearly illustrates the internal contradictions within Dickens's work at this time, as he struggled to reconcile his support for the police with a larger dissatisfaction at political inaction to remedy the conditions of life in the London slums.

## Inspector Bucket and the London Poor

Inspector Field has often been taken as a model for *Bleak House*'s Inspector Bucket. Besides their physical similarities, some of the scenes from the earlier essay reappear in fictionalized form in the later novel, and we might almost suspect Dickens of accompanying the detective as a way of conducting research for his novel. In *Bleak House,* for example, he provides a surrogate for the disbelieving reader (and the kind of person who might actively dismiss London's slums from consideration) in the figure of Mr. Snagsby, who accompanies Bucket through the rookery of Tom-all-Alone's just as Dickens had visited Rat's Castle under the guidance of Field. Underscoring the parallel, the anonymous narrator describes Snagsby as passing "along the middle of a villainous street, undrained, unventilated, deep in black mud and corrupt water—though the roads are dry elsewhere—and reeking with such smells and sights that he, who has lived in London all his life, can scarce believe his senses."[50] The reason for their visit is to find the crossing-sweeper Jo, about whom I will be saying much more in a moment. Their failure to find him causes a telling problem for D. A. Miller, a New Historicist critic who wants to offer this passage as testimony to the ways in which the detective police have "saturated" the criminal underworld. The problem that he faces—as we have already seen in the case of Dickens's visit with Field—is that the considerable knowledge of crime amassed in this way does not readily translate into any arrests: offenders may well be "known" to the police, but that does not appear to deter them from committing crimes, as Peel's conception of preventive policing suggested it should. This dilemma can only be averted by reinterpreting the scene according to a perverse logic, according to which the underworld is only an effect of the operation of an all-pervasive power, which produces, maintains, and contains such sites specifically in order to police them more efficiently: thus, for Miller,

> If the saturation does not appear to have much curtailed delinquency, or even, strangely, to have prevented Tom-all-Alone's from continuing to serve as a refuge for those wanted by the police, these perhaps were never the ends of police penetration. What such penetration apparently does secure is a containment of crime and power together, which both become visible mainly

in a peripheral place "avoided by all decent people." The raison d'etre of Tom-all-Alone's is that it *be* all alone.[51]

This reading may be ingenious, but it is ultimately disingenuous, I think. As many critiques of Foucault have argued by now, if such failures can in fact be adduced as evidence of surreptitious success, and criminals contained by simply being left alone, then there really is no imaginable outside or reverse of power: such a theoretical model, as Fredric Jameson noted, "would seem slowly and inexorably to eliminate any possibility of the *negative* as such, and to reintegrate the place of an oppositional or merely 'critical' practice and resistance back into the system as the latter's mere inversion."[52] What also interests me about Miller's reading, though, is how much it depends upon an over-valuation of police efficiency, and thus on the same strategies by which Victorian journalists sought to defend the new police. Underwriting this interpretive strategy is a prior methodological assumption, according to which Miller has opted to read *Bleak House* as a key text within the development of the detective fiction genre, as if a direct line of descent might be traced, which would link Bucket to (Sam) Spade.

The problem with reading Dickens's text as a detective novel is that this assumption inevitably leads to an overemphasis on the linear unfolding of its mystery plots, and on the role of Bucket in their resolution. In this sense, Miller's approach dictates that anything which might point to a critique of the institutions and apparatuses of power will be automatically dismissed, as irrelevant to a reading which presumes the novel's adherence to the developing conventions of classical detective fiction—among which, of course, the omniscience and omnipotence of the protagonist are crucial. Even within its own terms, this argument is problematic, since the novel transgresses a number of these conventions. One contemporary reviewer, for example, highlighted the difficulty of reading the character of Inspector Bucket:

> Here comes a man whom it is even exciting to watch; it is the celebrated detective officer, Buckett [sic]. Mark him well. He can find out anything. See him in the streets, in the day time. Follow him at night. Notice how he behaves to various characters. Now, he is in operation—he will infallibly reach what he is seeking. What is it? Again, it is nothing—or nothing which greatly influences what has thereafter to be unfolded.[53]

*Bleak House,* this reviewer suggests, violates one of the central rules by which detective fiction will be governed: that the truth the detective seeks, and invariably finds (usually the "Whodunit?") is in itself significant, pointing us toward textual closure. It is a weakness that Hortense highlights in the scene where Bucket arrests her for the lawyer Tulkinghorn's murder, asking whether the detective's powers might "restore him back to life" or make "an honourable lady" and "haughty gentleman" of the aristocratic Dedlocks; if not, she concludes, then "you can do as you please with me. . . . I pity you, and I des-pise you!" (799). When we consider the range of social, moral, and metaphysical problems raised by the novel, crime detection begins (as she suggests) to look like a minor skill indeed.

As I have indicated, a critical preoccupation like Miller's with closure inevitably produces a highly tendentious interpretation of this novel, in which that same skill becomes overinvested with significance. In a sense, though, the sheer *size* of the novel dictates that any reading will be inadequate to its full complexity. Its earliest reviewers consistently referred to its proliferation of minor characters like Skimpole, Boythorn, the Turveydrops, Jellybys, and Smallweeds, with many complaining that such "exaggerated" caricatures played no central part in either the Dedlock family or Chancery plots. One critic for the *Eclectic Review* went on to link the confusions of the novel's plot to the formal requirements of serial publication, noting that "the public has had to content itself with receiving it in monthly portions—a somewhat tantalizing process to the reader, whose interest is absorbed in the windings of the narrative, and who rises from every number with perplexing surmises as to what will be the end of such a character, or what is the meaning of indistinct allusions to something that has yet to be disclosed." The main problem with serialization is that it renders it "almost impossible to produce that which when completed shall be deemed a good book," and the review concludes with a common criticism of Dickens, as "not very capable, we should think, of looking right through his story, and marshaling his characters and incidents in the proper order. He sees so much of every part, and takes such delight in dwelling on it, that he is apt to forget the relations it bears to others."[54]

Reviewers seem to have been authorized to berate Dickens for his apparent neglect of the text's "proper order" by their perception that he had failed to fulfill a promise—suggested by the preface and opening installments—to deliver a critique of the Chancery system, and became sidetracked instead by the mystery plot concerning the death of "Nemo" (Captain Hawdon). In another sense, however, I would argue that the opening offers a set of tropes through which to connect its heterogeneous cast of characters. In an important chapter on Tom-all-Alone's, for example, Dickens attempts to link the major plot lines by asking what connections might exist between Sir Leicester Dedlock's Lincolnshire home and "the whereabouts of Jo the outlaw with the broom, who had that distant ray of light upon him when he swept the churchyard-step? What connexion can there have been between many people in the innumerable histories of this world, who from opposite sides of great gulfs, have, nevertheless, been very curiously brought together!" (272). The novel provides literal answers to this question (especially that Jo acts as a conduit enabling Lady Dedlock to find the grave of her lover Hawdon), which are also partially metaphorical ones, since Jo also passes along a case of smallpox to the product of their union, Esther Summerson. These in turn relate to larger questions raised in the "condition-of-England" debates about the environmental and hygienic problems of the London slums, and their link to wider forms of social unrest (including crime): questions about who is ultimately responsible for such problems, and whether—in its most abstract application—it is even possible to talk about a common humanity, as had been proposed by romantic writers in the 1820s and '30s.

In this more general sense, Dickens set out in this novel to answer Carlyle's "condition-of-England" question by investigating the networks and connections underlying British class relations. An early indication of the novel's interest in the totality of the social body appears in the opening chapter, which maps the geo-social space of London:

> Fog everywhere. Fog up the river, where it flows among green airs and meadows; fog down the river, where it rolls defiled among the tiers of shipping, and the waterside pollutions of a great (and dirty) city. . . . Fog creeping in the cabooses of collier-brigs; fog lying out on the yards, and hovering in the rigging of great ships; fog drooping on the gunwales of barges and small boats. Fog in the eyes and throats of ancient Greenwich pensioners, wheezing by the firesides of their wards; fog in the stem and bowl of the afternoon pipe of the wrathful skipper,

down in his close cabin; fog cruelly pinching the toes and fingers of his shivering little 'prentice boy on deck. (49)

The fog is only the first in a series of organic metaphors suggesting the interconnectedness of the diverse elements of English society represented in the novel. Just as the fog makes no social distinction between the ship's captain and a lowly apprentice, so news of Lady Dedlock's illegitimate child proceeds via the conduit of rumor at the end of the novel through jewelers, stables, Parliament, and lending libraries, while smallpox travels just as inexorably from Jo through a servant, Charley, to her mistress, Esther.[55] This idea of contagion is central to *Bleak House,* moreover, given its apparent purpose of addressing the need for slum clearance and sanitary reform, advanced in part through the familiar argument that the "evils" of rookeries like St. Giles ultimately threatened the palaces of St. James.

In these passages, Dickens deliberately employed an earlier rhetoric of urban life, in which the stress fell on the interdependence of rich and poor. Where the law-and-order discourse of the 1850s sought to distinguish a "hardened" and immoral underclass who were essentially to blame for their own poverty, earlier commentaries (as we have seen) had deployed the alliterative association between St. Giles and St. James to suggest the latter's responsibility for conditions in East London. In seeking to recover the topical context of *Bleak House,* John Butt and Kathleen Tillotson point to a speech that Dickens delivered in May 1851 (six months before he began work on this novel) at a dinner of the Metropolitan Sanitary Association. In the speech, which I cited in chapter 1, he conveys the common interests of rich and poor in terms of a palpable threat, that "the furious pestilence raging in St. Giles's no mortal list of lady patronesses can keep out of Almack's."[56] What is perhaps more striking, though, is Dickens's insistence that the filth of St. Giles would be carried to Mayfair via "an easterly wind." The geographical arrangement of London, as well as its architectural and social history, depends upon a prevailing wind blowing west to east, which would carry the ill effects of industry out toward the Essex marshes; consequently, the east wind which John Jarndyce consistently predicts in *Bleak House* would bring that filth back to the center from which it emanated, again in either literal environmental terms or through the metonymies of crime and social unrest which also festered in the East End.[57] If we recall that a cholera epidemic had recently swept through East London, we can read in this a timely reminder that contagious diseases respected neither the social distinctions of class nor the artificial boundaries by which the East End is imaginatively cordoned off from the commercial center and the West End.

Indeed, both senses are combined in the contagious fever that passes from Jo to Esther, and thus to the aristocratic Dedlock family. This point is underscored by the anonymous narrator, who personifies the urban poor (in the figure of Tom-all-Alone's) as exacting a form of vengeance on an uncaring ruling class: "There is not a drop of Tom's corrupted blood but propagates infection and contagion somewhere. It shall pollute, this very night, the choice stream (in which chemists on analysis would find the genuine nobility) of a Norman house, and his Grace shall not be able to say Nay to the infamous alliance. There is not an atom of Tom's slime . . . but shall work its retribution, through every order of society, up to the proudest of the proud, the highest of the high"(683). Like the rumors which spread news of Lady Dedlock's final humiliation, infection appears here as an agent of anarchic or apocalyptic social leveling. This is the sense in which Terry Eagleton has written of the novel as shaped by a pattern of formal unity which directly belies its exposure of social tensions. In a manner which is typical of his later novels, Eagleton argues, Dickens is forced "to use as aesthetically unifying images the very social institutions (the Chancery Court of Bleak House, the Circumlocution Office of Little Dorrit) which are the object of his criticism. It is, ironically, these very systems of conflict, division and contradiction which provide Dickens with a principle of symbolic coherence."[58] Eagleton's point, I think, is not that these formal images—to which we might add fog, rumor, infection, and the east wind—serve to moderate or smooth over social tension, but that they enable its expression.

What is most interesting about Bleak House, however, is the way that these apocalyptic implications are articulated alongside an ambivalent defense of policing and the function of law. Much of this ambivalence is centered on Chancery, and its ability to exert a centrifugal force which ensnares not only those characters associated with the Jarndyce family and Bleak House itself, but also Lady Dedlock (who is tangentially implicated in it) and Tom-all-Alone's (which is inevitably, if quite inexplicably, "in Chancery"). On the one hand, then, the very fact of being named in *Jarndyce v. Jarndyce* affords some form of equality under the law; on the other, however, the expenses of a continuous legal involvement are clearly regressive, and successively destroy Tom Jarndyce, Richard Carstone, as well as unrelated litigants like Miss Flite and Mr. Gridley. In this context, Inspector Bucket's cheering promise to the latter on his deathbed, that "You'll lose your temper with the whole round of 'em, again and again; and I shall take you on a score of warrants yet" (407), contains a sinister echo of his repeated injunction that Jo should "Move on." What both Jo and Mr. Gridley experience is a ceaseless harassment, which is repeated until the point of death with decreasing odds of victory or escape.

Some of the same ambiguities of the novel's discourse on the legal system are localized in the figure of Bucket, the dispenser of this "equality under the law." As we have seen, Dickens wanted to contrast the detective's efficiency and incorruptibility with previous systems for policing London prior to 1829, in similar terms to those found in the *Household Words* essays. The beadle who presides over the inquest into the death of Hawdon is, for example, clearly a throwback to an earlier time: "The policeman considers him an imbecile civilian, a remnant of the barbarous watchmen times; but gives him admission, as something that must be borne with until Government shall abolish him" (195). Bucket's superiority rests upon an apparent blindness to social distinctions, and an impartial performance of his professional duties: thus, he boasts of an intimate acquaintance with the crimes committed in the homes of "gen-teel families" like the Dedlocks, which would presumably rival his intimate knowledge of Tom-all-Alone's (776). Moreover, he increasing appropriates the disembodied and disinterested position of the narrator in classical realism: "Time and space cannot bind Mr. Bucket," we are told (769), since he is apparently possessed of "an unlimited number of eyes" (368) which enable him to maintain a Panoptic surveillance over the entire social space of the novel. Indeed, as Miller argues, it is this ability to transcend or generalize the shortsighted micro-investigations of amateur detectives like Mrs. Snagsby and Mr. Guppy that offers the possibility of finally unraveling and closing the novel's major hermeneutic mysteries: the murder of Tulkinghorn and the parentage of Esther Summerson, if not the outcome of *Jarndyce v. Jarndyce.*

Both the elevation and disembodiment involved in Bucket's assumption of a privileged position of supervision are literally signaled at the moment when he is about to set off in search of Lady Dedlock: Bucket, we are told, "mounts a high tower in his mind, and looks out far and wide. Many solitary figures he perceives, creeping through the streets; many solitary figures out on the heaths, and roads, and lying under haystacks. But the figure he seeks is not among them" (824). By the time Bucket manages to find Lady Dedlock she is already dead, on the steps of the cemetery containing the body of Captain Hawdon, her former lover. It is surely significant that this heroic act of willful self-abstraction fails to produce the desired results, while at the same time offering a key image of his Panoptic power.

If his celebrated abilities seem to have been oversold, the same also might be said for the professed impartiality which grounds his performance. Reflecting a contemporary ambiguity in the functioning and payment of the police from the days of the Bow Street Runners, Bucket seems at least part of the time to be working in the service of Sir Leicester Dedlock, who instructs him before the start of his search that "If I have not . . . in the most emphatic manner, adjured you, officer, to exercise your utmost skill in this atrocious case, I particularly desire to take the present opportunity of rectifying any omission I may have made. Let no expense be a consideration. I am prepared to defray all charges. You can incur none, in pursuit of the object you have undertaken, that I shall hesitate for a moment to bear" (773). Even the detective's motives seem suspect when he declares, on (wrongly) arresting George for the murder of Tulkinghorn, that "I tell you plainly there's a reward out, of a hundred guineas, offered by Sir Leicester Dedlock, Baronet. You and me have always been pleasant together; but I have got a duty to discharge; and if that hundred guineas is to be made, it may as well be made by me as any other man" (735). Bucket's knowledge of the aristocracy, it seems, arises less from any direct professional investigation of them than from time spent in their pay.

At this point, it is worth recalling the intense debates concerning the political role and function of the new police. In reality, as the real-life Inspector Field's nocturnal excursions into London's rookeries confirm, a detective like Bucket would probably have spent considerably more time in surveillance of Tom-all-Alone's, or the radical political societies and reform organizations that seem strangely absent from the world of *Bleak House*. In this sense, Bucket's failure to find Lady Dedlock in time or to initially identify Tulkinghorn's killer are finally less significant than his more striking inability to develop strategies for reforming or transforming Jo, outside of his repeated instructions that he "hook it" or "move on." The young crossing-sweeper—who is almost physically constituted by the London mud from which he makes his meager living[59]—comes in this way to represent the entirety of "outcast London," a class which the anonymous narrator compares to wild dogs that might degenerate far enough as to "lose even their bark—but not their bite" (275). This is not to suggest that Jo actively embodies the resistance to disciplinary power and authority that I focused on earlier in this chapter; what he stands for is more precisely the *problem* of the underclass, which remained stubbornly unassimilable to structures of social organization and control. Bucket's failure to contain Jo, so graphically illustrated by the enforced migration of the "Move on" injunction, seems in this sense symptomatic of a larger failure to contain the threat of urban poverty.

In such a context, *Bleak House* offers a powerful critique of the failures of social reform to have any ameliorating effects on slums like Tom-all-Alone's, comparing the "telescopic philanthropy" of Chadband, Mrs. Pardiggle, and Mrs. Jellyby with a corresponding abnegation of local responsibilities which Esther Summerson feels it her duty to overcome. Shortly before his death, Jo is described in terms which make this contrast clear: "He is not," the anonymous narrator declares, "one of Mrs. Pardiggle's Tockahoopo Indians; he is not one of Mrs. Jellyby's lambs, being wholly unconnected with Borrioboola-Gha; he is not softened by distance and unfamiliarity; he is not a genuine foreign-grown savage; he is the ordinary home-made article" (696). Esther makes a similar point when she accompanies Mrs. Pardiggle on a visit to a brickmaker's family: her companion, she notes, acted "as if she were an inexorable moral Policeman carrying them all off to a station-house," and Esther conceptualizes her own good works in the very different terms of local reformism, commenting that "I thought it best to be as useful as I could, and to render what services I could, to those immediately about me; and to try to let that circle of duty gradually and naturally expand itself" (154–58). Even these more immediate interventions are problematized, however, as her charitable advances toward the brickmakers' families are resisted by the husbands, one of whom later declares that "I'm not partial to gentlefolks coming into my place, as you've heerd me say afore now, I think, miss. I let their place be, and it's curous they can't let my place be. There'd be a pretty shine made if I was to go a-wisitin *them*, I think" (834; emphasis in original). This last sentence raises the specter of Tom's vengeance, but the brickmaker's insistence that each class remain apart also carries with it echoes of Disraeli's "two nations." Esther feels the same sense of distance when she first visits them along with Charley, remarking that "[w]e both felt painfully sensible that between us and these people there was an iron barrier, which could not be removed by our new friend [Mrs. Pardiggle]. By whom, or how, it could be removed, we did not know" (159); moments later, as one of the wives comforts another on the death of her baby, Esther concludes that "I think the best side of such people is almost hidden from us" (161).

While clearly preferable to telescopic philanthropy, Esther's sense of local responsibility also leads directly to her own disfigurement after she contracts smallpox from Jo. Bruce Robbins has compared this sequence of events with the "irresponsibility" of Harold Skimpole: "At some risk to herself," he notes, "Esther takes the sick Jo into her house; fearful for himself, Skimpole accepts a bribe from Bucket and helps turn Jo out of the house. But Skimpole is in effect placing the burden on the public, where Dickens would agree it ultimately belongs; and Esther, taking the burden upon herself, falls ill, nearly dies, and is scarred for life."[60] In a sense, Robbins's point is unarguable: that the exertions of any one person, whether Esther Summerson or Inspector Bucket, can be no match for long-standing and wide-ranging social problems. Unfortunately, the phrase by which he summarizes Skimpole's position, with its promotion of the panacea of "placing the burden on the public," is one that *Bleak House* seeks to expose as also inadequate for what Jo represents. Far from endorsing such a prescription for "public" action, it seems more likely that Dickens would recognize its depersonalization of political responsibility as another kind of telescopic philanthropy, seeking by its generality to keep the problem at arm's length or simply to move it on to someone else's attention. The novel ends in a kind of stalemate, then, as Jo remains radically incomprehensible and unreformable in spite of the best efforts of Esther, Bucket, Mrs. Pardiggle, and the British Parliament.

This conclusion would seem the logical result of Dickens's critique

of political and philanthropic failures to reform Tom-all-Alone's. In a colonial metaphor that we have already encountered in Engels, and which
will be amplified in later chapters, the novel makes clear that Evangelicals
like Mr. Chadband have less impact here than on the imperial outposts
of Africa and India. Jo confirms their ineffectiveness on his death-bed,
recalling that "[d]ifferent times, there was other genlmen come down
to Tom-all-Alone's a-prayin, but they all mostly sed as t'other wuns
prayed wrong, and all mostly sounded to be a-talking to theirselves, or
a-passing blame on the t'others, and not a-talkin to us. *We* never knowd
nothink. *I* never knowd what it was all about" (704, emphasis in original). Even more importantly, this philanthropic sectarianism is shown as
leading to parliamentary procrastination: "Much mighty speaking there
has been," the anonymous narrator notes,

> both in and out of Parliament, concerning Tom, and much
> wrathful disputation how Tom shall be got right. Whether he
> shall be put into the main road by constables, by beadles, or by
> bell-ringing, or by force of figures, or by correct principles of
> taste, or by high church, or by low church, or by no church. . . .
> In the midst of which dust and noise, there is but one thing per-
> fectly clear, to wit, that Tom only may and can, or shall and will,
> be reclaimed according to somebody's theory but nobody's
> practice. And in the meantime, Tom goes to perdition head
> foremost in his old determined spirit. (683)

In passages like this, Dickens extends his initial attacks on the procrastination of Chancery to cover a wider range of governmental institutions.
In doing so, however, his efforts run counter to his otherwise enthusias-
tic endorsement of Victorian methods of policing, which often operated
according to a similarly single-minded application of abstract principles.
After all, the blind eyes being turned by politicians and priests alike seem
consistent with Bucket's own "Move on" strategy, at least in terms of
their respective effects on people like Jo. By looking at the relationship
between Jo and the detective, we can begin to uncover some of the constitutive tensions in the novel, and to suggest some important limits
to the discursive and disciplinary mechanisms of Panoptic surveillance,
which a critic like D. A. Miller sees as functioning smoothly in this text.
     For if, as John Bender has argued, Panopticism centrally involves a

form of sympathetic introjection, one that (following the formal structures of fictional realism) works to reform individuals from within, then
what is striking about the novel's treatment of Jo is how it denies him the
interiority and consciousness necessary for such a reformation to take
place.[61] In a long meditation on Jo's distance from social norms that elsewhere guide the novel, the narrator comments, "It must be a strange
state to be like Jo! To shuffle through the streets, unfamiliar with the
shapes and in utter darkness as to the meaning, of those mysterious symbols, so abundant over the shops, and on the corner of streets, and on the
doors, and in the windows!" As the passage progresses, Jo's alienation
from such systems of linguistic representation is increasingly associated
with a parallel alienation from forms of political and legal representation:

> It must be very puzzling to see the good company going to the
> churches on Sundays, with their books in hand and to think (for
> perhaps Jo *does* think, at odd times) what does it all mean, and if
> it means anything to anybody, how comes it that it means noth-
> ing to me? To be hustled, and jostled, and moved on; and really
> to feel that it would appear to be perfectly true that I have no
> business here, or there, or anywhere; and yet to be perplexed by
> the consideration that I *am* here somehow, too, and everybody
> overlooked me until I became the creature that I am! It must be
> a strange state, not merely to be told that I am scarcely human
> (as in the case of offering myself for a witness), but to feel it of
> my own knowledge all my life! . . . Jo's ideas of a Criminal Trial,
> or a Judge, or a Bishop, or a Government, or that inestimable
> jewel to him (if he only knew it) the Constitution, should be
> strange! His whole material and immaterial life is wonderfully
> strange; his death, the strangest of all. (274; emphasis in original)

Dickens refers here to a very real alienation from a constitutional
framework of English law which continued to deny electoral rights to
the poor, but also to the limitations of the abstract idea of equality under the law: Jo's ignorance, combined with his lack of the financial resources at the disposal of Sir Leicester Dedlock, reveals this to be at best
an ideological fiction enabling the continuation of business as usual. Far
from being (in Louis Althusser's famous phrase) "interpellated as a subject" by the narrative form and structures of *Bleak House,* Jo remains
unassimilable even to strategies of realistic representation, as mysterious

as the symbols which he himself is unable to read.[62] In contrast to the ethnographic expeditions into working-class neighborhoods undertaken by Mayhew, Dickens, and others, the purpose of which was, as Randall McGowen suggests, to "get to know the criminal class," Jo is here imaginable only through his outward appearances and the narrator's guesswork. Like the rookery for which he stands, Jo seems finally and radically irreducible to any totalizing schemes of novelistic and social organization that Dickens might be thought to be extolling elsewhere.

Thus, where most recent critics have concentrated on the figures of Bucket or Esther Summerson, and thereby offered up the novel as either a prototypical detective story or an early experiment with dialogical narration, my own emphasis on the character of Jo places *Bleak House* more firmly in the tradition of the "condition-of-England" novels. There is some measure of corroboration to be had for this in looking at contemporary reviews of this text, which were often bemused by Inspector Bucket (as I have already mentioned) but continually reverted to the figure of Jo. The *Westminster Review* rather prematurely declared that Jo "will be remembered always as one of the choice things that do honor to our literature," while "[t]he gem of *Bleak House*" (for the *Eclectic Review*) was "'poor Jo,' the crossing-sweeper, hapless representative of a class whose very existence from generation to generation cries shame on the land in which they dwell." Similarly, *Putnam's Magazine* noted with some irony that

> Poor Joe [*sic*], down in Tom-all-alone's, has already become a proverb. We read the deaths of a good many eminent men without emotion . . . but we cannot withhold a tear when we read the death of poor Joe, and when he is 'moved on' for the last time we too are moved. Yet we know all the time that poor Joe is an unreal phantom—a mere shadowy outline, raised by a few strokes of a pen; yet we weep over him and give him the sympathies which we would withhold from the real Joes we encounter in our daily walks.[63]

That response described here, which combines an excessive sympathy for a fictional character with a cold-hearted response toward his real-life counterparts, is also a form of "telescopic philanthropy," of course, and may well indicate the strength of a desire for fantasies of reconciliation in the aftermath of Chartism: "sympathy" is, for example, the keynote of Gaskell's *Mary Barton,* which argues both for its difficulty given the prevailing social structures of the period and also its absolute necessity in order to close the gaps and divisions which had been highlighted throughout the 1840s.

A dissonant note was struck by the reviewer at *Blackwood's,* who contrasted Jo's apparent centrality in the emotional responses of Victorian readers with his relative irrelevance to the novel's formal plot and structure, concluding that "[t]he poor boy Joe is a very effective picture, though we fail to discover a sufficient reason for his introduction."[64] The tension alluded to here is one which I have attempted to address throughout the course of my reading of *Bleak House,* a novel which poses a problem but withholds its solution in the manner of a postmodern detective story seeking to thwart our desire for textual closure. One final inter-textual source would seem to confirm a need among some of the novel's earliest readers to move Jo from the text's periphery to its center. In chapter 2, I discussed several theatrical versions of Ainsworth's *Jack Sheppard,* and suggested that they represented a form of rereading, which tended to revise or highlight a range of textual elements to accord more closely with the interests of the play's intended audience. Along similar lines, H. Philip Bolton has analyzed nearly fifty theatrical adaptations of *Bleak House,* and notes the remarkable popularity of Jo. It may be understandable that the earliest versions, two of which were licensed for performance while the novel was still being serialized, should focus on his death, which is perhaps the most dramatic scene up to that point. Two of the earliest versions—from May through June of 1853—each end on this note, and appear to have excited a controversy for the Lord Chamberlain's office about the recitation of the Lord's Prayer which accompanies Jo's final move. The history of the novel's adaptation resumes in the 1870s with American versions entitled *Chesney Wold,* which ran for eighteen years, and *Jo; or Bleak House,* which crossed over to the London stage and was widely performed from 1875 to 1896, including tours in Australia, South Africa, India, and China; then we have titles like *Jo, the Waif of the Streets, The Life and Death of Jo, Dickens' Jo; or the Dedlock Disgrace, Jo v Jo,* and *Poor Little Jo,* by which point in the late seventies the sentimental note had to compete with theatrical burlesques which simultaneously satirized "Jo-mania." One 1882 program copy reproduced by Bolton inadvertently picks up on the character's inability to read the signs around him by advertising his name in 2½-inch lettering, so large that even he might have a chance of deciphering it.[65]

The theatrical popularity of the character clearly survived the publication of the rest of the novel, which in May 1853 still had about a quarter left to appear, including the arrest of Madame Hortense, the death of Lady Dedlock and many others, the resolution of Esther's parentage, and her marriage to Allan Woodcourt. Of course, the success of those earliest versions may have dictated the format of later ones, which still build up to Jo's death and elevate him even more centrally in their titles. One version by George Lander, performed in London between 1876 and 1890, includes a telling revision of the death scene, which Lander stages to coincide with Lady Dedlock's own death, discovered by Esther and Bucket at the gates of the cemetery where Hawdon is buried. In Dickens's original, Jo dies much earlier, in George's shooting gallery, possessed (according to Allan Woodcourt) by "an extraordinary terror" of Bucket, who "in his ignorance, he believes . . . to be everywhere, and cognizant of everything" (694). The scene's considerable pathos stems from Jo's "confession" to Mr. Snagsby, in which he asks that "when I was moved on as fur as ever I could go and cou'dn't be moved no furder, whether you might be so good p'raps, as to write out, wery large so that any one could see it anywheres, as that I was wery truly hearty sorry that I done it and that I never went fur to do it" (702); the irony is that Jo never really knows why he was "moved on" by the police in the first place, even as he now agrees to "move on" one last time. In Lander's play, shortly before he recites "The Lord's Prayer" with Mr. Snagsby, Jo offers an uncharacteristically cogent and articulate denunciation of the political system which has hounded him, declaring

> Oh! they have moved me on. "You ain't a goin' to stop here and breed fevers," says one. "You're poisonin' our place," says another. "You're a hidle rogue, and a wagabone," says another. When I goes to the workhouse, they say—they says, "we're full; go somewhere else." Yes, the workhouse chucks me out and the bobbies won't run me in—they only moves me on. And so I wanders about like a dog—like a dog.[66]

This last line serves as a reminder of one of Dickens's own metaphors, comparing the character of Jo to a wild dog that might temporarily lose its bark but not its bite. This potential for violent retribution clearly lurks beneath the surface of Jo, even if he is incapable of exacting it, and Lander's play indicates its prime targets: symbols of authority like the magistracy and Poor Law commissioners, social health reformers, and the police. This version even allows Inspector Bucket to hear the speech and witness the results of his "Move on" strategy. As Snagsby and Jo begin their recital of the Lord's Prayer, the detective mutters "I can't bear this" and turns away, in what appears to be an admission of responsibility which Dickens's novel can never quite make clear. It is an alternative conclusion which we should bear in mind, I think, as a corrective to modern desires to lionize Bucket as an emblem of a Panoptic power which is beyond challenge or resistance.

Where *Oliver Twist* moved its eponymous hero toward an inevitable (if unlikely) happy ending, his juvenile equivalent in *Bleak House* suffers a pathetic death after persistent harassment from the police, far out of reach of any reform measures that might be thought up by a remote and uncaring Parliament. If the challenge that Dickens and other novelists of the period picked up from sociological and governmental investigations was to describe the problem of poverty, then *Bleak House* was a success. Solutions, however, were beyond the limits of fiction, especially considering the sheer scale of the problem. As we move into the latter half of the nineteenth century, urban literature turns away from realistic representation, in favor of a revived Gothic style, and away too from the underclass as the site of crime. Increasingly, fictional criminals originate from within the privileged classes themselves, and detectives also become individuated superheroes like Sherlock Holmes. With the social displacement of crime, though, the question of causality shifts as well: where the 1840s and '50s saw debates about whether the poor or the wealthy were responsible for the social and moral conditions that bred criminality, late-Victorian discussions shifted to a psychological terrain, in which deviance could be recoded as a pathology. In the process, the topography of crime also shifted: in fiction, at least, offenders were more commonly residents of London's West End, like Dorian Gray or Doctor Jekyll, even if their crimes were usually committed farther to the east, in Whitechapel and the neighborhoods surrounding the London docks.

# 4 "Lords of the Street, and Terrors of the Way"

The Privileged Offender in Late-Victorian Fiction

If Dickens is the most celebrated writer of London in the first half of the nineteenth century, his successor is clearly Sir Arthur Conan Doyle. Even now, our perceptions and images of the capital seem to have been filtered through a reading of the Sherlock Holmes stories, while Baker Street has assumed a place on the tourist itinerary that is vastly disproportionate to its actual importance. As Franco Moretti shows, however, in his *Atlas of the European Novel,* something interesting happens when we plot the locations of these stories on a map. Using as a point of comparison Charles Booth's color-coded maps of poverty and crime, both of which tended in the 1880s to cluster in South and East London (as Henry Mayhew also might have predicted), Moretti notes a strikingly inverse pattern of criminal activity in Conan Doyle: "A small cluster of crimes in the city, a few more here and there; but the epicenter is clearly in the West End. The working class areas lying south of the Thames, so prominent in Conan Doyle's first two novels . . . have practically disappeared; as for the East End, Holmes goes there precisely once in fifty-five stories." [1]

I will come back to that exception shortly, but first I want to endorse Moretti's conclusion that such an asymmetry is remarkable, especially when we consider that Holmes makes his debut the year before the

Whitechapel murders of Jack the Ripper, yet also understandable: unlike actual crime, which was readily explicable according to a theory of economic and environmental determinism, the literary crimes encountered in detective fiction needed (in Moretti's words) to be "an *enigma:* an unheard-of event, a 'case,' an 'adventure'" (137; emphasis in original). A fictional super-detective like Sherlock Holmes might well have compensated readers for the failures of the real London police, as spectacularly demonstrated in the case of the Ripper; that compensation requires, however, a prior act of displacement, by which crime itself and the motives behind it can be reconceptualized. As a product of a particular pathology, crime can be solved, isolated, and eradicated, thus producing the welcome feeling of a world returning to normal with the capture and arrest of a fictional offender—a satisfactory conclusion which, as we have seen in the case of *Bleak House,* is impossible to produce if its author takes seriously the interconnections between social class, environment, and crime.

To return to Moretti's map, then, we can understand why Conan Doyle's criminals so often reside in the fashionable West End, and even beyond London itself, in the residential suburbs of Surrey, Kent, and Sussex. Taking only the twelve stories that constituted the first volume of Holmes adventures, we typically find ingenious offenders who are often related to their wealthy victims or engaged in complex acts of revenge for previous acts committed overseas. Only two might plausibly belong to the "dangerous classes," as the term would have been understood earlier in the century by Mayhew or Dickens: a repentant hotel employee who collaborates in a jewel theft in "The Adventure of the Blue Carbuncle," and the bank robber John Clay in "The Red-Headed League," who is a professional London criminal but also has an Oxford education and claims to be descended from royalty. The exceptional case where Holmes actually ventures into the East End is even more instructive. "The Man with the Twisted Lip" opens in an opium den in the docklands. Doctor Watson has been charged with finding and rescuing an old friend Isa Whitney, who has become addicted to the drug: "Hitherto," according to his wife, "his orgies had always been confined to one day, and he had come back, twitching and shattered, in the evening. But now the spell had been upon him eight-and-forty hours, and he lay there, doubtless among the dregs of the docks, breathing in the poison or sleeping off the effects. There he was to be found, she was sure of it, at the Bar of Gold, in Upper Swandam Lane." This unsavory place, we learn, is "a vile alley lurking behind the high wharves which line the north side of the river to the east of London Bridge," where Watson finds the opium den nestled between "a slop-shop and a gin-shop."[2]

The site is an East End cliché, which would have been familiar to readers from a half-century of descriptions of "darkest London" by Engels, Dickens, Mayhew, and countless others. On arriving, Doctor Watson easily finds Isa Whitney and persuades him to take a cab home to his wife, at which point the story starts to follow another missing-persons case. As he leaves the opium den, Watson passes a tall and thin old man, who whispers to him, "Walk past me, and then look back at me." To his surprise (but not that of the attentive reader), this stranger turns out to be Sherlock Holmes, who reveals himself with a characteristically dramatic flourish. The detective, whose own drug use had already been documented two years earlier in *The Sign of Four,* jokes about his reason for being there, saying "I suppose, Watson . . . that you imagine that I have added opium-smoking to cocaine injections, and all the other weaknesses on which you have favoured me with your medical views." As if to compound the impression, he then goes on to state somewhat cryptically that he had previously used the den "for my own purposes," and needed the disguise in order to avoid the vengeance of its proprietor (232). Finally, though, he confesses that he is on business rather than pleasure, having been engaged by another anxious wife to find another missing husband.

The case revolves around a reworking of *Doctor Jekyll and Mr. Hyde,* a contemporary story which I will examine later in this chapter. A respectable gentleman from Lee in Kent named Neville St. Clair has gone missing, and was last seen by his wife at an upper window of the opium den. When the police are summoned, they find only a beggar named Hugh Boone and evidence that St. Clair might have been thrown into the Thames. In the end, the beggar turns out to be the bourgeois in disguise, and so no crime has actually been committed. Holmes, however, feels annoyed at himself for failing to arrive at this obvious conclusion for some time, even to the extent of dismissing evidence that St. Clair is still alive and trying to convince his wife of his death. Rereading the story, one finds the first clue in Holmes's own description of the purported victim: "Some years ago," he tells Watson, ". . . there came to Lee a gentleman, Neville St. Clair by name, who appeared to have plenty of money. . . . He had no occupation, but was interested in several companies and went into town as a rule in the morning, returning by the 5:14 from Cannon Street every night" (233). For someone who is normally attuned to the close relationship between money and labor,[3] the inference should have been clear at once: that St. Clair was merely performing the role of an archetypal suburban commuter. Since Holmes himself was fond of disguise, and indeed opens this very story with a convincing imitation of an opium addict, he is probably correct in concluding that he deserved "to be kicked from here to Charing Cross" for failing to see through the masquerade.

The simple reason for his failure is that St. Clair and Boone seem so dissimilar, in social as well as physical terms. The distance between them is quite literally conveyed during the seven-mile drive which Holmes and Watson make from Upper Swandam Lane (a "dull wilderness of bricks and mortar," alongside the "murky river" of the Thames) to "the fringe of the belt of suburban villas" in Kent: indeed, if the opium den represents a classic location of East End poverty, Lee is surely as stereotypical a representation of the suburban green belt surrounding the inner city, the site of many other fictional crimes depicted on Moretti's map. Inhabitants of these different social spaces would not have been expected to meet, much less cohabit in a single body: in this sense, Mrs. St. Clair expresses the proper degree of discomfort and anxiety as she accidentally wanders into Upper Swandam Lane and sees her husband where he clearly should not have been. His story, as he finally conveys it to Holmes and the police who have been holding Boone under arrest, contains its own share of clichés. After a respectable education, including some time spent on the stage, he had worked as a reporter and gone undercover for an exposé on begging in the city. Due in part to his education and wit, he was able to make more in seven hours of begging than he got in a week's work at the newspaper, and so takes it up full-time after being pressured to pay back a £25 debt: "Well, very soon," he continues,

> I found that I was saving considerable sums of money. I do not mean that any beggar in the streets of London could earn £700

a year—which is less than my average takings—but I had exceptional advantages in my power of making up, and also a facility of repartee, which improved by practice and made me quite a recognized character in the City. All day a stream of pennies, varied by silver, poured in upon me, and it was a very bad day in which I failed to take £2 [his weekly wage at the newspaper].

As I grew richer, I grew more ambitious, took a house in the country, and eventually married, without anyone having a suspicion as to my real occupation. My dear wife knew that I had business in the City. She little knew what. (243)

On this basis, it would seem to make sound economic sense to collapse the distance between begging and the bourgeoisie, although Holmes ultimately insists that he reopen it by giving up the character of Boone. The issue of how St. Clair is to make up the shortfall in wages is never raised, since his main compensation is that he can henceforth be honest with his wife and children.

The ideological subtext is clear: that some beggars might really be able to drive Rolls Royces, in which case the "culture of poverty" (to use Gertrude Himmelfarb's phrase) is founded on a deception. Given that his success requires charitable donations from the general public, the exposure of St. Clair's masquerade might help to return poverty to its rightful place, by restoring a sense of the difference between the deserving and undeserving poor. Indeed, this may well have been what he had intended to convey in his original magazine articles, given the historical role that journalism has played in recycling messages like this. As a fable of late-Victorian life, the story works to restabilize the family and a social order which was grounded in the separation of spheres: city center / suburban periphery; self-supporting middle-class / mendicant underclass; and so on. As Audrey Jaffe has noted in her reading of this story, the cultural proximity of Boone and St. Clair was closer at the time than might first have been thought: popular ideology, for example, maintained that "a beggar might very well be a gentleman," while the latter term was sometimes used with skepticism, to designate a privileged social position which required no productive labor to sustain itself; finally, "the increase in both financial speculation and unexpected, devastating crashes made it appear likely, at least from the gentleman's perspective, that a gentleman might someday have to beg."[4]

But if this suggests that the bourgeois family and social order were in need of some ideological support, it still seems odd that Holmes should be called upon to provide it, given that he apparently has little investment in either. His bohemian traits are well documented, and significantly combine with an exemplary ability to move across boundaries of class which are geographical as well as social. His major tactic for accomplishing this, moreover, is disguise: in "A Scandal in Bohemia," for example, he masquerades as a groom, later commenting to Watson, "There's a wonderful sympathy and freemasonry among horsey men. Be one of them, and you will know all there is to know" (167–68). In the same vein, he admonishes his companion in "The Adventure of the Solitary Cyclist" for not going undercover in a rural pub, since "[t]hat is the centre of country gossip. They would have told you every name, from the master to the scullery-maid" (532). In this sense, Jaffe notes that Holmes is involved in the multiplication of identities just as much as Neville St. Clair, and employs subjective transformation in order to gain access to marginal areas of the city like the opium dens, which would otherwise be off-limits. As a "gentlemanly amateur" in the field of detection, he also holds the privileged position of avoiding productive labor in the periods when he is not engaged on a case, and of setting his own terms for employment and recompense; indeed, the work (as he often remarks) represents its own reward, which means that he can often defray expenses, let the culprit go free, or even work on cases in which no actual crime has been committed.

Like Neville St. Clair's, Holmes's "business" takes place primarily in the city. In one of those moments of *ennui* that descend on them between cases, Watson opens "The Resident Patient" by proposing a vacation in the New Forest or on the beaches at Southsea; "as to my companion," however, "neither the country nor the sea presented the slightest attraction to him. He loved to lie in the very centre of five millions of people, with his filaments stretching out and running through them, responsive to every little rumour or suspicion of unsolved crime." Surely enough, a page or so later, Holmes counter-proposes "a ramble through London" (423–24). This passage suggests that he has fulfilled the dream on which the Metropolitan Police were founded, of rendering the capital perfectly visible. As I noted in chapter 1, the image of a spider's web, with its radii projecting centrifugally from a fixed center, was often used to describe London itself, and the influence which it exerted on the rest of the nation; here, the same figure applied to Holmes suggests that his knowledge is coextensive with the city itself, and that his "filaments" are able to reach into its darkest corners. In this context, we might note the supplementary force of the Baker Street Irregulars, a band of street urchins whose name mimics the early police force of the Bow Street Runners. In *The Sign of Four,* they help to track Jonathan Small along the Thames waterfront, thereby extending Holmes's access through the use of surrogate agents: "They can go anywhere, see everything, overhear everyone," he comments with approval and even envy (127).

From Holmes's perspective, then, all of London is potentially knowable, and importantly *totalizable:* he does not respect distinctions between the East and West Ends, or its suburbs and slums, since his disguises grant him equal access to all points on the map. These same fantasies of Panoptic surveillance are also interestingly attributed to Professor Moriarty, the "Napoleon of crime," who is described in "The Final Problem" as similarly sitting "motionless, like a spider in the centre of its web," from which "a thousand radiations" connect him with at least half of the crimes committed in London (471). It therefore seems entirely appropriate that he and Holmes—each with their respective networks of power and influence—should compete for control over and above the emptied-out and depoliticized space of the capital. These fantasies are of course just that, but aimed in a real sense to compensate for the public's low assessment of the London police: a master-criminal like Moriarty—who can be destroyed with one push over the Reichenbach Falls—is certainly preferable to a threatening underclass which was sometimes estimated as constituting more than 10 percent of the population.

As I suggested in chapter 3, it is part of the emerging project of detective fiction to make this substitution, by giving the reader the fantastic and entertaining skills of Inspector Field or Bucket in place of a plan for combating urban poverty. In this chapter, I identify three discursive maneuvers by which this was accomplished in late-Victorian culture, all of which are mapped out in "The Man with the Twisted Lip." First, criminal activity was refigured as the province of the middle and upper classes in urban crime texts like Robert Louis Stevenson's *Doctor Jekyll and*

*Mr. Hyde* (1886) and Oscar Wilde's *The Picture of Dorian Gray* (1891), as well as in the Sherlock Holmes mysteries. Martin J. Wiener has noted that the professionalization of policing brought with it a corresponding upgrade in the public image of the criminals who needed to be apprehended:

> As crime detection, in both fact and fiction, was being removed to an expert and esoteric realm, suspicions appeared that there existed much hitherto unsuspected expert and esoteric crime. The increasing sense of conquest of the external criminality of the streets combined with the blurring of the stark moral certainties of the early nineteenth century to turn middle class attention inward . . . from the unruly populace to persons and scenes of apparent respectability.[5]

By shifting criminal agency away from the beggar Boone to the bourgeois St. Clair, for example, "The Man with the Twisted Lip" offers up a new version of the privileged offender, a figure that was also coming into literary vogue with characters like Dr. Jekyll and Dorian Gray, both of whom also adopt disguises in order to commit a variety of crimes.

My second point concerns motive. The social and/or environmental background of the underclass rendered this issue largely moot, since they were generally thought to commit crimes in order to offset hunger and need, even if these conditions might ultimately be held to be the fault of the criminals themselves. By contrast, the villains against whom Sherlock Holmes struggles act for love, out of greed, or from sheer malice: besides revenge, the most popular motive is to safeguard an inheritance which might otherwise be lost, as paternal guardians routinely attempt to murder their charges ("The Speckled Band"), to imprison them to prevent a marriage from taking place ("The Copper Beeches"), or pose as a deserting suitor in order to bring about the same result ("A Case of Identity"). As this brief survey suggests, criminal motives often have to do with the arcane financial details of inheritance settlements, which may have been a topic of concern for readers of the *Strand Magazine,* in which these stories first appeared, but had little to do with "the criminal class" as it had been discursively constituted at midcentury. "The Man with the Twisted Lip" is instructive here, too, since the final relocation of criminal agency in St. Clair reverses the conventional logic by which the fictitious beggar Boone might seem more warranted in turning to crime. His bourgeois counterpart, by contrast, would seem to have little to justify his double life, beyond the initial pretext of repaying the £25 debt. That debt represents three or four months' salary at his old job, it is true, but as the deception continues it seems clear that St. Clair is primarily motivated by the desire to maintain his suburban lifestyle and status. A further clue reveals itself when we notice that he found the work of a journalist "arduous," and that of begging relatively easy. The comparison simultaneously indicts him as one of those shiftless gentleman who probably deserved to go broke, and suggests that begging is both pleasurable and profitable. By implication, then, beggars like Boone would *not* have good reasons for taking to crime, since they are relatively well-compensated for their work. In this sense, the story effects the same denial of criminal agency to the working class that we find in other Holmes stories. In looking for a substitute, Conan Doyle and others reworked the figure of the privileged (and usually amoral) offender, who had a long pedigree by this time dating back to the rakes and libertines of the epistolary and Gothic traditions.[6]

Finally, these texts offer a critique of charity, as one of the central forces through which the distinction between the deserving and undeserving poor began to unravel.[7] As Gareth Stedman Jones has argued, philanthropic relief surprisingly emerges within the dominant discourses of 1860s and '70s as a major obstacle to the management of East End poverty. I shall examine his argument in a moment, and show how the problem of charity arises out of the uncertainties I described in the previous chapter concerning slum clearance, crime, and the moral character of the London poor. First, though, I want to briefly mention some of the ways in which a critique of middle-class philanthropy is articulated in each of the texts under discussion here. In "The Man with the Twisted Lip," for example, it is clear that begging can only be profitable because Hugh Boone appeals to gullible city-dwellers, who are perhaps comforted by his educated patter and respond with a steady "stream of pennies, varied by silver." In terms of political economy, however, this weakness has more serious consequences, to which the story implicitly alludes. Since debates over the Poor Law and the Speenhamland system back in the 1830s, a motivating factor in Victorian social policy had been to ensure that welfare payments would not equal or exceed the typical wages of the honest laborer, since it would then provide a disincentive to work. The worst-case scenario imagined by both conservatives and reformers—of a massive defection from the workforce to the dole—is actualized on a smaller scale in this story, then, as St. Clair abandons the respectable work of journalism for the higher rewards of charity. His own moral weakness is partially shown to be at fault, of course, but the mildness of the story's final rebuke (and the suggestion that St. Clair be returned to his family) also recognize that his decision was made out of a rational calculation of economic interest. Conan Doyle even supplies the precise figures (£2 per week from journalism, against 26s. 4d. from a day's begging) so that the reader might recognize the scale of the problem: economic and social priorities have clearly been inverted when beggars can afford the homes in the suburbs which should be the reward for honest labor. What makes this story a unique product of its historical moment, however, is that the blame is shown to lie not with government policies but instead with the well-intentioned acts of charity from which Boone is able to make such a fine living.

A different aspect of the problem is presented in *Doctor Jekyll and Mr. Hyde,* in which Stevenson investigates some of the darker motives which might underlie these casual acts of kindness. Jekyll, the narrator tells us, "has always been known for charities," but there is something suspicious in the way he turns to philanthropic activity for his salvation, especially after having committed an act of murder in the character of Hyde.[8] The key is offered earlier in the text by Mr. Enfield, who witnesses Hyde's first violent act and remarks on the oddity of his connection to Jekyll, "one of your fellows who do what they call good" (33). The doubt expressed in this construction is immediately amplified, as Enfield hypothesizes that Hyde is blackmailing Jekyll for "some of the capers of his youth"; Jekyll's own friend and lawyer Mr. Utterson (to whom these comments are addressed) afterwards concurs, noting somewhat cryptically that the doctor had been "wild when he was young; a long time ago to be sure; but in the law of God, there is no statute of limitation" (41). From each of these statements, and others that I shall look at later, a picture of Jekyll emerges as the consummate Victorian hypocrite, who aims to conceal his desires through his standing in the community and the commission of philanthropic deeds, only to find them effectively desublimated in the person of Mr. Hyde. Indeed, Jekyll's autobiographical narrative, which closes the text, makes this point very clear: "the worst of my faults," he notes,

was a certain impatient gaiety of disposition, such as has made
the happiness of many, but such as I found it hard to reconcile
with my imperious desire to carry my head high, and wear a
more than commonly grave countenance before the public.
Hence it came about that I concealed my pleasures; and that
when I reached years of reflection, and began to look around me
and take stock of my progress and position in the world, I stood
already committed to a profound duplicity of life. Many a man
would have even blazoned such irregularities as I was guilty of;
but from the high view that I had set before me, I regarded and
hid them with an almost morbid sense of shame. (81)

The text never specifies the nature of these "irregularities," except to repeat that they are "undignified" and occasioned Jekyll a difficult life, one
which had been marked by an enormous degree of "effort, virtue, and
control" (84). Readers have however speculated on them ever since the
novel first appeared, and have seized on the smallest hints from the narrative, as well as from Hyde's recorded actions. In the interpretation I
shall offer, the key evidence is to be found, though, in *where* those actions occur (in a poor neighborhood of Soho, where Hyde takes separate lodgings) rather than what they are. My argument, in other words,
is that there is a close connection between the forms of charitable philanthropy by which Jekyll attempts to disguise his desires, and the social
spaces in which they re-emerge through the agency of Hyde.

The connection is confirmed in the third text I examine in this chapter, Oscar Wilde's *The Picture of Dorian Gray,* which presents a very precise topography of London life in the 1880s and '90s. Here, it is the
aristocratic Lord Henry Wotton (of Curzon Street, in fashionable Mayfair) who offers a forceful critique of charity, by dissuading the impressionable Dorian Gray (of Grosvenor Square, also in Mayfair) from performing duets as part of his Aunt Agatha's campaign to improve life in
Whitechapel. On being asked to defend his cynicism, in the face of the
"very important problem" of the East End, Wotton replies—in a phrase
that Wilde himself would repeat in his essay on "The Soul of Man under Socialism"—"It is the problem of slavery, and we try to solve it by
amusing the slaves."[9] As I shall show, there was a strong political basis for
this argument which many were making at the time when Wilde's novel

first appeared. What is more troubling, however, is the way that this critique of misguided philanthropy appears in a text that simultaneously highlights the exploitation of the East End. Like Henry Jekyll, Dorian Gray adopts a disguise (as "Prince Charming," no less) when he traverses the city in search of pleasure, and he finds it precisely where Neville St. Clair found a living wage, in the opium dens which ran alongside the river in the East London docklands. This has led some critics to read *Dorian Gray* as embodying a casual stance toward the problems of the East End, which would seem to arise quite naturally out of Wilde's own position as an archetypal West End socialite. My own reading, however, takes a very different approach, which consists first of taking Lord Henry's critique of charity at face value. On this basis, I argue that the novel presents a forceful assault on all forms of fashionable slumming, as disguising a fundamental contempt for poverty and an egoistic search for personal gratification. Like Neville St. Clair and Dr. Jekyll, Gray adopts an expropriatory attitude toward the East End, in which he effectively takes from the poor instead of giving.

Each of these new "Lords of the Street" adopts a different position on the issue of charity: Henry Jekyll hides behind it, to shield his more sinister activities as Mr. Hyde; Neville St. Clair makes his living from the contributions of others; while Dorian Gray claims to follow Wotton in condemning philanthropy on political grounds. There is, however, a common attitude underpinning each of these positions, which seeks to exploit the resources of "darkest London" for pleasure, and to access poorer areas of the city through a careful masking of the class background of these privileged offenders.

### Charity, Housing, and the De-moralization of the Poor

If the relative prosperity of the 1850s created the favorable conditions in which an opposition could be drawn between the deserving and undeserving poor, the economic climate in the following decade quickly threatened to undermine such distinctions. During the unusually severe winter of 1860−61, there were bread riots in East London, as all riverside work had to be suspended for six weeks. A similar combination of bad weather and economic depression led to more serious rioting in 1866−67, when the agitation of the under- and unemployed moved beyond the confines of the East End: 100,000 of them invaded Hyde Park, causing a panic in Parliament which contributed to the passing of the Second Reform Bill. Amid talk of "crime waves" and "plagues of beggars," the concept of the respectable poor began to lose some of its ideological force, and had to compete for attention with newer rhetorical tropes which emerged to explain the social process by which the working class was sinking to the level of its lowest "residuum." It was, for example, the rioting of 1866 which helped to inspire Matthew Arnold's *Culture and Anarchy* (1869), with its repeated images of a critical mass of hooligans, each intent on asserting "his right to march where he likes, meet where he likes, enter what he likes, hoot as he likes, threaten as he likes, smash as he likes. All this," he concluded, ". . . tends to anarchy."[10] Interestingly, however, it was charitable benevolence which was widely seen as one of the worst culprits, and as contributing more to this process of "de-moralization" than to its alleviation. Partly as a result of the internal migration caused by earlier schemes of slum clearance, the poorer London boroughs bore a disproportionate burden during times of hardship, and the existing mechanisms of Poor Law relief were revealed to be inadequate for the needs of impoverished Londoners. In an attempt to fill the vacuum created by the temporary collapse of the welfare system, a group of well-intentioned West End club-men formed the Society for the Relief of Distress in 1860, and distributed £3,000 in alms; during the more serious crises of 1866–67, the Mansion House Relief Fund distributed over £15,000 in the East End.[11]

As with other aspects of Victorian social policy during this time, there was a paradoxical logic at work in the critique of charity. It had originally been offered in response to enormous hardship, when economic conditions were already helping to pauperize the London working class, and yet the availability of charitable relief was also held responsible for the conditions which it sought to redress. The key to understanding how such a logic might have originated can be found in the term "de-moralization," which was widely used to describe what was happening to the poor at this time. What it serves to underscore is that the process was understood in terms of morality rather than economics. Since the operation of market forces was sacred to most policymakers and commentators, the impoverishment of the working class could only be the fault of wealthy philanthropists. In this way, the entire focus of debate shifted away from the character of the poor (on which their deserving or respectable status depended) to that of the almsgiver, who may have had acted out of a guilty conscience or concentrated too narrowly on immediate needs, and so helped to exacerbate the problems that she or he hoped to alleviate. Ironically, the accusation was one of acting "indiscriminately" (much as the free market does) in giving out charity to anyone who wanted it: in this way, the undeserving benefited as much as the deserving poor, who would quickly learn to modify their behavior. This discursive substitution of morality for economics is best exemplified by a sermon preached at Oxford in 1869 by Brooke Lambert, a Whitechapel clergyman. "Some of us East End clergy," he claimed, "dread the coming winter like the return of some intermittent fever. The amount of charity which has flowed from West to East has demoralized the clergy and pauperised the yet honest poor"; as soon as the respectable worker experiences charitable relief, according to Lambert, "he becomes in nine cases out of ten, a whining supplicant, ready to cringe for all he can get."[12] The priorities are clearly spelled out here: the cure of philanthropy is to be dreaded as far worse than the disease of poverty, or even the more literal fevers of cholera, which had recently broken out again but appear in Lambert's text only as a metaphor for the more alarming epidemic of charity.

A similarly inverted set of priorities dictated the positions of the Charity Organisation Society (C.O.S.), which aimed to address the social and environmental consequences of earlier slum clearance programs by proposing more of the same. This organization was founded in 1869, a year in which the annual Poor Law report forcefully articulated the "de-moralization" thesis by noting that the honest poor tended to follow the example set by those who exploited the unsystematized provision of charitable relief. The C.O.S.'s first innovation, then, was to install officers in each district to coordinate such activities and treat claimants on a casework basis. Its major contribution to social policy was an 1873 report on London's housing crisis, which would form the basis for the Artisans' Dwelling (or Cross) Act passed two years later. Reflecting a symptomatic confusion of morality and economics, the report described "the *inability or unwillingness* of a large proportion of the poorer classes to pay the rent requisite to obtain sufficient accommodation," thereby suggesting the limitations of suburban development and the model housing schemes organized by the Metropolitan Association for Improving the

Dwellings of the Industrial Poor, which had priced themselves out of the range of potential tenants.[13] But it also underscored the problem of earlier clearance schemes like those undertaken by the railway companies or during the building of New Oxford Street: that they exacerbated the housing crisis by evicting tenants without giving any consideration to their resettlement. As Dickens noted in "On Duty with Inspector Field," the result was that the homeless simply moved into adjacent areas, thereby helping to create new slums in turn: "Thus," he noted, "we make our New Oxford Streets, and our other new streets, never heeding, never asking, where the wretches whom we clear out, crowd."[14] Given the cost of suburban transportation, most chose to stay closer to the commercial centers where work was available, and so the problem was effectively moved a short distance to the east, where areas like Whitechapel and Shoreditch began to supplant St. Giles and Seven Dials in the popular imagination as areas most representative of "darkest London."

At a proposed cost of £2,000,000 for the whole of London, the Metropolitan Board of Works was authorized to seize unsanitary and overcrowded properties by compulsory purchase, to demolish existing buildings, and then tender the land to contractors to develop substitute accommodations. In theory, the Cross Act would have removed some of the worst housing in London, without displacing the population or adding to the burden in other sections of the city. To counter the concept of de-moralization, the Board of Works developed a new theory of "leveling up," which aimed to move the urban poor in the opposite direction. The zero-sum game proposed by the Cross Act, for example, assumed that while the occupants of the condemned housing might be temporarily displaced, the new buildings would attract better tenants from the area, thereby creating a housing vacuum within which poorer residents might be resettled. In practice, however, the Cross Act was undermined by its reluctance to deal with London as a totality, or to imagine its wholesale reconstruction on the scale of the Parisian projects undertaken by Baron Haussman in 1853 and 1870. As J. A. Yelling has shown, the act was also limited by its conception of the slums themselves, which were considered to be the archaic remnants of a previous model of urban planning, and thus to represent "a finite stock of housing no longer suitable for present purposes"; in proposing their systematic demolition, then, Cross had no basis for imagining that new slums might be created in their place.[15]

If the initial purpose of these policies had been to reverse the process of de-moralization and restore a sense of the obligations of the privileged to help their less fortunate counterparts, the net result was that the gap separating rich and poor, and the West and East Ends of London, was as wide as ever: the "leveling up" which was supposed to follow from slum clearance schemes never materialized, in part because of a strict adherence to *laissez faire* economic principles. By the early 1880s, the problem of East End poverty needed to be revisited—or *rediscovered*—all over again, first in a new wave of journalistic exposés like George Sims's *How the Poor Live* and Andrew Mearn's *The Bitter Cry of Outcast London* (both 1883). These texts drew on the earlier models of Mayhew, Dickens, and others: we find, for instance, the same invocation of a journey into uncharted and foreign lands, into what Sims terms "a dark continent that is within easy walking distance of the Post Office";[16] the same indictment that a social gap "has been daily widening which separates the lowest classes from our churches and chapels, and from all decency and civilization," according to Mearns;[17] the same sense of shock that all of this could happen "not a mile from the full tide of all the pomp and vanities of fashion" (Sims, 72). Indeed, Sims seems aware of how repetitive the process has become, commenting at one point that he would like to be able to inject a note of the picturesque in order to break up the monotony; yet both authors provide almost identical eye-witness accounts of a landlord, who had executed entirely inadequate repairs with paper and a piece of wood broken off from a soapbox, and then raised his tenants' rent to offset his costs (Sims, 70; Mearns, 101). It is easy to conclude from all of this that there was really nothing new to this new "discovery," and indeed that Dickens or Mayhew might have told the same story thirty years earlier.

In other ways, however, these texts of the 1880s are distinctive. To begin with, they make a decisive break with the earlier model followed by Dickens, of touring the slums in the company of the police. Sims, for example, is immediately asked if he is a policeman, and explains that "[i]t is unpleasant to be mistaken, in underground cellars where the vilest outcasts hide from the light of day, for detectives in search of their prey" (69, 66)—judging from "On Duty with Inspector Field," we can only assume that Dickens would have taken this as the ultimate compliment. Despite the melodramatic undertones of this last passage, both Sims and Mearns are also generally careful to refrain from moralizing, even about the causes of crime. Mearns, for example, notes the unfortunate necessity for the honest to cohabit in cramped conditions with the criminal, and maintains that "[t]here can be no question that numbers of hardened criminals would never have become such, had they not by force of circumstances been packed together in these slums with those who were hardened in crime" (97). A couple of pages later, he calculates in the manner of "The Man with the Twisted Lip" that a seven-year-old boy would need to make 1,296 matches per day in order to recoup the 10s. 6d. he could make from thieving. This sense of rational self-interest undercuts the environmental causality Mearns had outlined earlier, of course, but what is more noticeable is that neither explanation relies on a theory of genetic or moral deficiency. More importantly, both authors are quick to assign blame in quite specific ways: Sims points the finger at "increased wealth and civilization," to whom "we owe the wide gulf which today separates well-to-do citizens from the masses," and even provides an illustrative sketch of a rich slumlord "with a big gold chain across his capacious form, and an air of wealth and good living all over him" (67, 73). Meanwhile, Andrew Mearns targets the English clergy for a large share of the blame. In both cases, the Cross Act is criticized for exacerbating the problems that it initially sought to alleviate.

The crisis, it seems, could no longer be managed by caring individuals, but needed to be addressed by large-scale administrative institutions and apparatuses. Sims, who had posed as a School Board inspector in order to avoid the suspicion of being a policeman, notes the success of the Education Act of 1870 which granted state aid for religious and public elementary schools, and sets out the critique of personal philanthropy in a section entitled "Legislation Wanted, Not Almsgiving": "I have been grievously misunderstood," he writes, "if anything I have said has led to the belief that all Englishmen have to do to help the denizens of the slums and alleys is to put their hands in and pull out a sovereign or a shilling," and he goes on to commend the C.O.S. for exposing cases of fraudulent charities in the capital (85–86). Finally, circling back to his starting point via comparative descriptions of the British government's attention to the problems of Zulus, Egyptians, and Bulgarians, Sims conveys both a main cause of the separation of the classes and the danger of its eventual explosion, by noting that nothing is ever done to address the social conditions of poverty "until its victims have begun to start a crusade of their own—to demonstrate in Trafalgar Square, and to hold meetings in Hyde Park" (88). As Matthew Arnold had noted with alarm, this was precisely what the unemployed had done seventeen years earlier, because bringing the problems of East London into the center was the one guaranteed way of pushing the organizing oppositions of the city to the point of collapse, and thus of transforming local grievances into a perception of national crisis.

By the late 1880s, as Judith Walkowitz notes, the East-West polarity which had traditionally structured popular mappings of London began to break down, under the weight of a whole host of "new social actors." This refiguring of the capital as a contested terrain, she argues, allowed a variety of political constituencies to emerge, some of which I shall examine in the next chapter: "new commercial spaces and journalistic practices, expanding networks of female philanthropy, and a range of public spectacles . . . enabled workingmen and women of many classes to challenge the traditional privileges of elite male spectators and to assert their presence in the public domain."[18] Alternatively, however, we might read many of these developments as a continuation of older practices, by which middle-class professionals had penetrated the East End and reported back, with the aim of generating new schemes of management and control: indeed, discrete sections of the city (and especially Whitechapel) must have seemed positively overrun by the bourgeoisie, in their various guises as rent collectors, clergymen and Salvation Army evangelicals, housing and education inspectors from the Board of Works or the School Board, and crusading journalists.

It is worth keeping these various forms of penetration in mind when approaching literary texts of the period like *Doctor Jekyll and Mr. Hyde* and *Dorian Gray*. But one subgenre of journalistic commentary should also be mentioned, as resonating in particular ways with the *Doppelgänger* theme which they both explore. Beginning with James Greenwood's 1866 serial on "A Night in the Workhouse," an entirely new form of exposé developed that sought to infiltrate the East End communities themselves, and then adopt the appearance and viewpoint of the poor as their own. "Slumming," which would reach the height of its vogue in the 1880s and '90s, assumed that these problems could best be experienced from the inside, even if only temporarily; at its worst, of course, it was exploitative, voyeuristic, and self-aggrandizing. Perhaps as befits an early forerunner, Greenwood seems oblivious to the ethical issues involved in the charade, and even opens by playfully drawing attention to the split subjectivity which it requires: on arriving at the workhouse in a carriage, he describes "a sly and ruffianly figure, marked with every sign of squalor" who descends, and prolongs the tension for a lengthy paragraph before confessing that "[t]his mysterious figure was the present writer."[19]

We shall see this play on first- and third-person narration repeated in *Doctor Jekyll and Mr. Hyde,* but first I want to underscore the obvious difficulty of passing off these first-hand accounts as authentic sociological evidence. Sir William Hardman of the *Morning Post,* for example, considered that Greenwood should get the Victoria Cross for braving one night in a workhouse (which others made a semi-permanent home), even though he has the luxury of giving away the bread he is given for dinner, and has his carriage waiting for him the next day; similarly, Olive Christian Malvery went undercover as a costermonger at the turn of the century, but had to hire someone to push her cart of vegetables (after first paying a Covent Garden porter to load it); and even the adventurous Jack London, before passing as "the seafaring-man-who-had-lost-his-clothes-and-money" among *The People of the Abyss* (1903), hired a private detective to keep track of him.[20] It is not only that such actions compromise the exercise of "slumming" itself (which always has a finite timespan, in any case), but also that they help to underline the necessary distance that still separates the author from her or his object. By doing so, they suggest a more serious danger that the kind of split subjectivity which this entails might go unremarked, in a process where speaking *for* the poor can easily become speaking *as* them. The ventriloquistic slippage involved is dramatically illustrated by another text of this subgenre, written by the Cambridge graduate (and later New Liberal politician) C. F. G. Masterman, who used his experiences in the evangelical settlement movement to authorize an account of life in South London with the symptomatic title of *From the Abyss: Of the Inhabitants by One of Them* (1902). By this point, the processes of sympathetic introjection had developed to a point of transferential overidentification on the part of the well-intentioned "slummer," thereby highlighting the political space and context that more cynical operators like Jeykll, Gray, and Neville St. Clair exploited. By using the kinds of disguises perfected by slummers like

Greenwood, these bourgeois interlopers could emerge as lords of all the streets in London, and use the cover of respectability to alibi a range of crimes, from St. Clair's fraudulent performances to the more sinister terrors embodied in the figure of Mr. Hyde.

### Stalking the City Streets:
### Jekyll, Hyde, and Jack the Ripper

Just as attention begins to focus on charity as a potentially "criminal" act (or, at least, one that might ultimately encourage crime), so the wealthy and privileged emerge in late-Victorian fiction as a new class of criminals. The two processes are clearly linked: after all, the individuated and masterful criminality of a Professor Moriarty cannot easily make sense within an explanatory framework that would insist that the widespread experience of poverty and unemployment contributed to rising crime rates among the urban poor. Popular literature, as I have suggested in the case of Sherlock Holmes, could perform a compensatory function, especially at a time when public confidence in the London police was low. But I do not think that this fully explains the appearance at this time of privileged offenders like Doctor Jekyll, Dorian Gray, or Neville St. Clair. In a sense, their appearance represents a return to the earlier tradition of the Gothic novel, with the difference that the aristocratic rakes and libertines who populate those texts have been taken out of the European castles and country houses and transplanted into the modern metropolis.

By reinventing the figure of the privileged offender, though, writers like Stevenson and Wilde also advance an internal process within the history of crime fiction, by which the rich and poor, the lawful and the criminal, continually switch places. In *Delightful Murder,* the economist Ernest Mandel describes an earlier stage in this process, during which the "bandit hero" of folklore and popular ballads is transformed into the nineteenth century's criminal. As part of the same "dialectical somersault," Mandel notes that "yesterday's villainous representative of authority" can also emerge as the new hero, as the bourgeoisie secures its hegemony:

> the rising place of crime stories in popular literature corresponds to an objective need for the bourgeois class to reconcile awareness of the "biological fate" of humanity, of the violence of passions, of the inevitability of crime, with the defence of and

apology for the existing social order. Revolt against private property becomes individualized. With motivation no longer social, the rebel becomes a thief and a murderer.[21]

The final twist in this dialectical spiral, I am suggesting, is to dispense with the antagonism of class entirely, as the bourgeoisie in effect produces its own enemies in a process that *Dr. Jekyll and Mr. Hyde* most concisely illustrates. Jekyll's science, as Marie-Christine Leps puts it, aims "not to understand 'criminal man' and discover means to eradicate his presence from society (to ensure the triumph of good over evil), but rather to discover ways of allowing himself, an upright citizen, to become a criminal and enjoy deviance with impunity."[22]

The respectable doctor, it should be remembered, had developed a taste for "undignified" pleasures even before he stumbled on the formula which might enable his physical transformation. From Jekyll to Hyde, then, is not a process whereby "evil" overcomes "good," in the way that the story is usually interpreted in popular culture. Neither is this simply a moral or even subjective transformation, but instead one that entails complicated sociocultural consequences. As Hyde, Jeykll can act on desires which he has had to suppress since his youth, although the precise nature of those desires is never specified in the text. An important hint, however, might be found in examining Hyde's own lodgings, in a "dismal quarter of Soho" which seemed to Mr. Utterson like "a district of some city in a nightmare":

> as the cab drew up before the address indicated, the fog lifted a little and showed him a dingy street, a gin palace, a low French eating-house, a shop for the retail of penny numbers and two-penny salads, many ragged children huddled in the doorways, and many women of many different nationalities passing out, key in hand, to have a morning glass. . . . This was the home of Henry Jekyll's favourite; of a man who was heir to a quarter of a million sterling. (48)

All of the details here—the gin, cheap serials, ragged children, and multi-ethnic population—suggest an archetypal London slum, even though Soho itself was never targeted for clearance during this period. Like nearby St. Giles, it is located at the heart of the city center, and so would have had a very different cultural resonance than Whitechapel

or the Wapping docks. Indeed, Soho sits in between fashionable Mayfair and the Strand, and might well have been a favored spot for slumming interlopers who did not want to venture too far East; today, it
is well known as the center of London's sex industry, and filmmakers
seem to have had that reputation in mind as they have consistently portrayed Hyde in a cultural milieu of lower-class music halls, brothels, and
opium dens.[23]

But if we do not know the nature of Jekyll's indiscretions, we can
certainly identify him as a slummer who has sought to infiltrate the area
for his own purposes: once inside the house, for example, Utterson notes
that it is "furnished with luxury and good taste," complete with a closet
of wine, silver plate, good carpeting, and even "a good picture" on the
wall.[24] Hyde's residence, then, is an interesting combination of an ele-
gant interior style, hidden behind a dingy and dismal external facade—
and in this, of course, it perfectly suits its owner, who also disguises a
genteel persona by adopting a degraded and disgusting outward appearance. All of these elements, and their complex interaction, can be found
even earlier in the story, in the first description of Hyde's actions by the
onlooking Mr. Enfield. The scene takes place on a small and quiet by-
street of a busy quarter of London:

> The inhabitants were all doing well, it seemed, and all emulously
> hoping to do better still, and laying out the surplus of their grain
> in coquetry; so that the shop fronts stood along that thorough-
> fare with an air of invitation, like rows of smiling saleswomen.
> Even on Sundays, when it veiled its more florid charms and lay
> comparatively empty of passage, the street shone out in contrast
> to its dingy neighbourhood like a fire in the forest; and with its
> freshly painted shutters, well-polished brasses, and general clean-
> liness and gaiety of note, instantly caught and pleased the eye of
> the passenger. (30)

Given what we know of Henry Jekyll, this seems a fitting place for his
surgery. Like the street, he hopes to better himself, with philanthropic
charity signaling the self-improvement he intends. As we have seen,
however, the performance seems a little forced, as if engineered mainly
for the recognition of others; and here again, Jekyll resembles the street,
which sounds exactly like a metaphorical prostitute in this passage, putting on airs (and fresh paint) to attract admirers.

In fact, Jekyll lives and works around the corner from this street, in "a square of ancient, handsome houses, now for the most part decayed from their high estate, and let in flats to all sorts and conditions of men: map-engravers, architects, shady lawyers, and the agents of obscure enterprises" (40). The area seems to be going down, not up, and to be filled with residents whose professional lives are taking them in the same direction; at any rate, what is most important is that it is a mixed and marginal neighborhood, combining signs of economic health and decay in a manner which seem entirely appropriate when we remember that Jekyll is already partly Hyde even before he effects his first transformation. In contrast to his more wholesome companions, like "Mr. Utterson of Gaunt Street" (39) or Doctor Lanyon of Cavendish Square, Jekyll's precise address in never given. In fact, the street as I first described it is actually home to Hyde:

> Two doors from one corner, on the left hand going east, the line was broken by the entry of a court; and just at that point, a certain sinister block of building thrust forward its gable on the street. It was two storeys high; . . . and bore in every feature the marks of prolonged and sordid negligence. The door, which was equipped with neither bell nor knocker, was blistered and distained. Tramps slouched in the recess and struck matches on the panels; children kept shop under the steps; the schoolboy had tried his knife on the mouldings; and for a close on a generation, no one had appeared to drive away these random visitors or to repair their ravages. (30)

Out of this darkened doorway—of an uncharacteristically dirty building, in an uncharacteristically bright street, in a mixed area of London— emerges Mr. Hyde, at a considerable pace, to collide at the corner with a poor child and set the story in motion. Even this seems fitting, since it is presumably an intersection that points in two different directions: either to Jekyll's or to Hyde's entrances, both of which are specified as two doors from the corner, but which ultimately open out into the same building.

The story's initial location closely correlates with the internally conflicted figure of Henry Jekyll, then, as we can reconstruct him from his own narrative: a successful man with a comfortable income, though perhaps not as great as we might expect, given his inheritance of "a large fortune" (81); hamstrung by the need to hide his "undignified" pleasures through a professional life of "self-denying toils" (91), yet also egoistically dependent upon the opinion of his peers, among whom he was "well known and highly considered" (85); and so committed from an early age to "a profound duplicity of life" (81). But if Jekyll seems to be relatively consistent in his self-description, and a recognizable character in terms of his social class, geographical location, and outlook, Mr. Hyde has proven much more difficult to pin down. Since we are purposely denied any details of the pleasures that he was created to enjoy, we are forced to work from external appearances. The problem is that witnesses routinely find him hard to describe, even though all of them take an instant dislike to him. Enfield first suggests this indescribable impression, noting that "[t]here is something wrong with his appearance; something displeasing, something downright detestable. I never saw a man I so disliked, and yet I scarcely know why. He must be deformed somewhere; he gives a strong feeling of deformity, although I couldn't specify the point" (34). Later, Utterson has the same impression, listing Hyde's dwarfish size, displeasing smile, murderous bearing, and husky voice, before concluding that "all these points were against him, but not all of these together could explain the hitherto unknown disgust, loathing and fear" which he excited (40). To Doctor Lanyon, "there was something abnormal and misbegotten in the very essence of the creature" (78).

In this way, of course, Jekyll has found the perfect disguise for committing his crimes. As Hyde, he should be able to pass quite convincingly among his fellow residents in Soho. Indeed, all of the physical details we are offered of his appearance—and the various attempts of the other characters to describe him as "savage," "trogolodytic," acting with "apelike fury," and so on—combine to suggest the atavistic archetype of "criminal man," as proposed by Cesare Lombroso, founder of the Italian school of criminal anthropology. As Stephen Arata has suggested, the physiognomy of this type would have been familiar to Stevenson's readers, in part through the work of Havelock Ellis (who translated Lombroso, and also published his own studies of criminal pathology), but also because of "the ease with which the new 'scientific' categories mapped onto older, more familiar accounts of the urban poor from Mayhew onward. . . . Equating the criminal with atavism, and both with the lower classes, was a familiar gesture by the 1880s, as was the claim that deviance expressed itself most markedly through physical deformity."[25] In this sense, Hyde can be taken as representative of the residuum, that enlarging criminal underclass among whom he presumably lives and plays when settled into his Soho hideout. But when we recall the tasteful manner in which that house was decorated, another possibility presents itself—that Hyde typifies the depraved and degenerate aristocrat who was emerging as the focus of studies by Max Nordau and others. As Alan Sinfield summarizes this influential theory of decadence at the other end of the social scale, it was normatively "associated with idleness, immorality, aristocracy and aestheticism"; for Nordau, for example, "[d]egenerates are not always criminals, prostitutes, anarchists, and pronounced lunatics; they are often authors and artists" like Wagner, Nietzsche, Zola, and Oscar Wilde.[26] Mr. Hyde's aesthetic sensibility and good taste (as classically revealed through his penchant for interior decoration) might also qualify him for the role of a degenerate product of the leisure class.

The two possibilities considered so far—that Hyde resembles either a Lumpenproletarian or a decadent aristocrat—also resonate with the few actions of that character which are recorded in the text. For appropriately enough, the apparently arbitrary victims of his crimes are the poor neighborhood girl with whom he collides on the street corner and the M.P. Sir Danvers Carew. As Arata notes, Stevenson created a composite figure in Hyde, "who embodies a bourgeois readership's worst fears about both a marauding and immoral underclass and a dissipated and immoral leisure class," but it is also these same classes that bear the brunt of Hyde's rages.[27] The observation helps to remind us that Hyde can have no real class status of his own, since the identity he assumes is one which is entirely forged out of Jeykll's lived experience. The disparity between them narrows as the text progresses, and pronominal distinctions becomes increasingly difficult to maintain. Describing the confrontation with Lanyon, for example, Jekyll writes that an attendant "led me to a private room, and brought me wherewithal to write. Hyde in danger of his life was a creature new to me; shaken with inordinate anger, strung to the pitch of murder, lusting to inflict pain. Yet the creature was astute; mastered his fury with a great effort of the will." Shortly, the confusion of first- and third-person is addressed in the text, but Jekyll's explanation of "He, I say—I cannot say, I" hardly clears up the matter of exactly who is acting—and for whom—in these scenes (93–94). It is moreover noteworthy that it is now Hyde who exercises self-control, the failing of which had caused Jekyll to invent him in the first place.[28]

Hyde's impersonation of Jekyll (or is it the other way around?) remains convincing right up until the end. Mr. Utterson, who acts as an unofficial detective in the text despite a quite singular lack of imagination, makes the same assumption that hindered Sherlock Holmes in "The Man with the Twisted Lip," refusing to acknowledge the close connection between Jekyll and Hyde. Just as Holmes seizes on anything that might confirm the death of Neville St. Clair, Utterson concocts a series of theories to explain away the evidence. Even at the end, when the servant Poole believes that Hyde has barricaded himself in Jekyll's laboratory, Utterson strains to recognize the latter's voice and footsteps, while insisting that he might be seized by "one of those maladies that both torture and deform the sufferer; hence, for aught I know, the alteration of his voice; hence the mask and his avoidance of his friends; hence his eagerness to find this drug."[29] It is hardly necessary to cast Utterson as a dupe of scientific positivism here, for what causes his blindspot is the entirely *social* error of failing to imagine a material connection through which men like Jekyll and Hyde might associate with each other. The latter apparently has nothing in common with the interacting network of bourgeois professionals (Jekyll, Utterson, Lanyon, and Enfield) constituted in the text, so Utterson's instinct is to consign Hyde to another class altogether. He experiences Hyde's proximity as a threat, and would prefer that his friend Jekyll maintained a more appropriate distance from his deformed Other; hence, his overwhelming need to relegate Hyde to the criminal underclass, as Jekyll's illegitimate offspring or his blackmailer.

In rethinking how the two figures are connected, I prefer to read Hyde's criminal actions—perpetrated, as we have seen, against representatives of political privilege and the London poor—in the broadest terms, as embodying the desublimated anger of the late-Victorian bourgeoisie. The text is centrally concerned, in other words, with processes of repression, as Jekyll labors to preserve his respectable appearance. Describing his first transformation into Hyde, he expresses a sense of relief that he no longer needs to keep up the front: "I felt younger, lighter, happier in my body; within I was conscious of a heady recklessness, a current of disordered sensual images running like a mill race in my fancy, a solution of the bonds of obligation, an unknown but not innocent freedom of the soul" (83). The language here is sexualized, but what it conveys is a release from the claims of society and an ensuing sense of personal liberty. Chief among those social obligations from which Jekyll can now claim exemption is the necessity of helping the poor. His own narrative clearly links the two topics, noting that the temporary renunciation of Hyde (following the murder of Carew) caused him to devote greater energies to the relief of others: "I resolved in my future conduct to redeem the past," he writes to Utterson, "and I can say with honesty that my resolve was fruitful of some good. You know yourself how earnestly, in the last months of the last year, I laboured to relieve suffering; you know that much was done for others, and that the days passed quietly, almost happily for myself" (92). The problem, though, is that these actions are undertaken for himself, in order to compensate for Hyde's crimes. A sense of duty and obligation may return to Jekyll here, but these will still be experienced as constraining; at best, they help to restore his public image, in which he seems so egotistically invested. Indeed, just as he turns to philanthropic work in reaction against the excesses of Hyde, the reverse occurs less than a page later, when the latter explicitly re-emerges as a consequence of Jekyll's feelings of self-aggrandizing satisfaction. Jekyll recalls that, in Regent's Park,

> I sat in the sun on a bench; the animal within me licking the chops of memory; the spiritual side a little drowsed, promising subsequent penitence, but not yet moved to begin. After all, I reflected, I was like my neighbours; and then I smiled, *comparing my active goodwill with the lazy cruelty of their neglect.* And at the very moment of that vainglorious thought, a qualm came over me, a horrid nausea and the most deadly shuddering. . . . I was once more Edward Hyde. A moment before I had been safe of all men's respect, wealthy, beloved—the cloth laying for me in the dining-room at home; and now I was the common quarry of mankind, hunted, houseless, a known murderer, thrall to the gallows. (92–93; my emphasis)

This passage encapsulates my reading of Stevenson's text. The differences separating Jekyll from Hyde are material—the doctor's wealth and table, versus the "common" and "houseless" Hyde—but they also require a constant re-affirmation by other people. Charity is one way of gaining "all men's respect," but it immediately threatens to tip over into an arrogant egomania, in which Jekyll feels himself to be the superior of those whose judgment he craves in order to maintain his sense of self. At that moment, he turns back into Hyde, who is licensed to kill and can set about undoing all of Jekyll's good deeds.

Despite his superficial resemblances to the proletarian "criminal man" and to the aristocratic aesthete, Mr. Hyde is finally revealed to be the pure product of the late-Victorian middle class, as a materially desublimated personification of its guilty conscience. Instead of being located elsewhere, in the decadent or the dangerous classes which were the simultaneous subjects of contemporary psychopathologies, crime and violence are shown to be the particular province of bourgeois professionals who claimed to represent the larger interests of society as a whole. Appearing in the middle of a decade which saw the distance between rich and poor quite significantly widen, Stevenson's text could only confirm the critique of charity that had already gained ground in recent years, while also highlighting the exploitative subtext of slumming enterprises, in which the caring middle classes sought to close the gap through their physical presence among the London poor.

These conclusions would not have seemed obvious to the first critics and reviewers of *Doctor Jekyll and Mr. Hyde,* who mainly praised its formal construction and prose style while advancing mild concerns about its impact on popular audiences. Two years later, though, the five murders ascribed to "Jack the Ripper" seemed to correlate closely with the recorded actions of Mr. Hyde, and thus incited a retroactive rereading of Stevenson's text. Where before it had seemed to properly caution against hypocrisy and excess, it was now considered a blueprint for a horrifying series of unsolved killings. At a general level, as Judith Walkowitz notes, the mysterious nature of the case and the unprecedented brutality of the crimes themselves meant that commentators frequently resorted to literary analogs from Poe and de Sade, in addition to more direct comparisons with Jekyll and Hyde.[30] Soon after the second victim, Annie Chapman, was discovered, the *East London Advertiser* speculated that "a murderous lunatic [is] concealed in the slums of Whitechapel, who issues forth at night like another Hyde, to prey upon the defenceless women of the 'unfortunate' class"; a month (and two murders) later, the same paper looked for parallels in Gothic fables and vampire legends, noting that "the most morbid imagination can conceive nothing worse than this terrible reality; for what can be more appalling than the thought that there is a being in human shape stealthily moving about a great city, burning with the thirst for human blood, and endowed with such diabolical astuteness, as to enable him to gratify his fiendish lust with absolute impunity?"[31] The language here mimics that of Stevenson's favorable critics, who praised him for creating a similarly impenetrable enigma in fiction; for the *Times*'s reviewer, for example, the novelist "evolves the ideas of his story from the world that is unseen, enveloping everything in weird mystery, till at last it pleases him to give us the password. . . . A crime committed under the eyes of a witness goes unavenged, though the notorious criminal has been identified, for he disappears as absolutely as if the earth had swallowed him."[32]

At its most literal level, the connection between Jekyll and Jack the Ripper was made in September 1888 after the second murder, when a sensationalistic dramatization of Stevenson's story was closed down. Indeed, some newspaper correspondents even suspected the actor Richard Mansfield for the murders, because he performed the role of Hyde so well![33] At the same time, *Punch* accused sensational theater advertising campaigns of sharing some blame for the murders, due to their potential effect "on the morbid imagination of unbalanced minds"; this view was endorsed by the novelist Walter Besant, writing in the in-house journal of the East End People's Palace, where he noted, "It is one thing—and a very desirable thing—to legitimately stimulate the imagination, to the lack of which we may attribute nearly all the cruelty and selfishness in the world; . . . but it is quite another thing, and an extremely dangerous one, to stimulate the depraved appetites to be found in most human beings by hideous and brutal representations of crime and violence." To underscore the link between popular audiences and the site of the murders themselves, Besant concluded in the paternalistic tones which had become second nature to privileged slummers and philanthropic settlers, that "there can be absolutely no justification for these hideous posters which are perpetually appealing to these instincts, especially strong in the uncultured and ignorant."[34]

This helps to suggest the discursive parameters within which the Ripper murders were initially situated and discussed. Like his victims, the killer was held to originate among the "uncultured and ignorant" residuum of East End life, and to use a first-hand experience of the labyrinthine streets and courtyards of Whitechapel to elude capture. Indeed, a measure of how useful such local knowledge was can be gathered from the inability of the police to effectively patrol and cordon off specific geographical areas; according to one of the detectives in charge of the case, for example, they once

> formed a circle around a spot where one of the murders took place, guarding they thought, every entrance and approach, and within a few minutes they found fifty people inside the lines. They had come in through two passageways which my men could not find. And then, you know these people never lock their doors, and the murderer has only to lift the latch of the nearest house and walk through it and out the back way.[35]

The inference was that any one of "these people" might be the Ripper's accomplice, if not the murderer himself.

The more basic assumption that he was an East Ender went unchallenged for some time. After the first two murders, Samuel Barnett of the Toynbee Hall settlement wrote to the *Times,* suggesting practical reforms (for adequate lighting, police supervision, the removal of local slaughterhouses, and closer control of tenement houses) and arguing that the East End as a whole should not be judged by what was occurring in its worst sector. The newspaper's lengthy response argued instead on the basis of a theory of economic and biological determination, which significantly refused to distinguish between the moral and de-moralized poor: "We seem to have listlessly acquiesced in the existence of these kitchen-middens of humanity," it editorialized,

> to have treated them as though society must keep a receptacle for the collection of its waste material. We have long ago learned that neglected organic refuse breeds pestilence. Can we doubt that neglected human refuse as inevitably breeds crime, and that crime reproduces itself like germs in an infected atmosphere, and becomes at each successive cultivation more deadly, more bestial, and more absolutely unrestrained? . . . We speak often enough of the political residuum; but we speak and think far less

often of the moral residuum ever present with us, though, as we may hope and believe, slowly decreasing in quantity, in which lust and vice are altogether unbridled and even crime is almost unrestrained.

This is consistent with the general shift we have seen in the framework within which crime was comprehended in the 1880s. No longer mainly a question of morals, its etiology is located here in biology, much as Dickens had sought to draw attention to pestilential London slums like Tom-all-Alone's.

The Ripper appears in the *Times*'s account, much like Mr. Hyde, as the archetype of "criminal man." He is produced by a degenerate environment in which he finds support, but which he also exploits and corrupts still further: "In these infamous dens," the editorial continued, "are bred and nurtured the miserable wretches to whom at last such crimes as those of Whitechapel become possible. Humanity there loses its native stamp and takes on the temper and impulses of a beast. . . . We cannot expect to get rid of the criminal classes altogether, but at least we should be able to prevent their collecting together and infecting an whole neighbourhood." Inevitably, the *Times* rejected Barnett's practical proposals—on the grounds of cost, and because "what is called charity is too often blind, and as often does more harm than good"—and called for more police surveillance and clearance schemes.[36] And indeed, the demolition of entire areas of Whitechapel, proposed early on by the *Daily Telegraph* under the slogan of "A Safe Four Per Cent" profit margin, might be taken as one of the lasting results of the Ripper murders, which one local historian has argued had a greater impact than "fifty years of road building, slum clearance and unabated pressure from the police, Poor Law guardians, Vestries and sanitary officers."[37]

In this context, it is hardly surprising that initial suspicions fell on the usual East End suspects: East European émigrés, anarchists, Russian Jews, and even the prostitutes themselves. The ethnic subtext of the case was quickly established by a series of possible eye-witness reports of "foreigners" having been seen with the victims, and by initial accusations against John Pizer ("Leather Apron"), a local Jewish shoemaker. Even before a third body was found at the end of September 1888 outside the headquarters of the Jewish socialist International Working Men's Educational

Club, the *East London Organiser* reported that "It was repeatedly asserted that no Englishman could have perpetrated such a horrible crime . . . , and that it must have been done by a JEW."[38] But what seems more surprising is that these scapegoating suspicions failed to hold. By the time of the fifth murder (of Mary Kelly), the *Star* was already reporting on local rumors that "the Government do not want the murderer to be convicted, that they are interested in concealing his identity, that, in fact, they know it, and will not divulge it."[39] The report was skeptical of such conspiracy theories, although they were based on widespread speculations that the Ripper was really a respectable gentleman, who used his social position to shield himself from police inquiries: the *East London Advertiser* encapsulated a change in public opinion in October, for example, when it editorialized that "we have to consider whether the murderer is a maniac in the narrow sense of the word, and is not rather a man with a maniacal tendency, but with quite sufficient control of himself and of his faculties to impose upon his neighbours, and possibly to mix in respectable society unquestioned by a single soul."[40]

These new suspicions can be dated from a series of article in the *Pall Mall Gazette* comparing the Ripper to Jekyll/Hyde, after which the image of the "Mad Doctor" began to coalesce, drawing on popular prejudices against the medical profession from over a decade of antivivesectionist campaigning. In this way, the public's imagination of the killer shifted away from the homicidal Mr. Hyde archetype, in favor of a more calculating deception like that practiced by Doctor Jekyll. The belief that the murderer had specialized medical knowledge originated at the second inquest, when the coroner testified that specific organs had been removed, possibly for sale; henceforth, potential eye-witnesses invariably mentioned the Ripper's fine clothing, as well as his trademark surgical bag. One medical suspect was children's campaigner Doctor Barnado, who had been visiting slum kitchens in Whitechapel shortly before the third murder, and had actually spoken to the victim, Elizabeth Stride. The case also occurred at the height of the fashion for settlements and slumming, when parts of the East End seemed overrun with philanthropists and purity campaigners, so it is hardly surprising that some of these (including Samuel Barnett) also emerged as suspects.[41] Some, indeed—like the director of the Bank of England, who disguised himself as a laborer—applied slumming techniques in an attempt to solve the case; at least one of these, "a medical man, who had acted as a sort of amateur detective," had his bluff called by local residents, who had him arrested on suspicion of being the Ripper. More often, though, wealthy West Enders occupied the familiar position of spectators, hundreds of whom queued up daily to pay a penny and see the murder sites first-hand.[42]

Entrenched prejudices and patterns of distrust remained. As Walkowitz notes,

> despite the theories about upper-class perverts and maniacal reformers, the police still arrested the same collection of motley East End down-and-outers. . . . They conducted a house-to-house search of Whitechapel, but not of the areas where the Ripper, if he were a "toff" (that is, a gentleman) would be lodging. Long-standing patterns of deference and assumptions of bourgeois respectability ultimately prevailed over speculations about bourgeois criminality circulating in the press.[43]

The case also inflamed long-standing tensions about law enforcement, and perceptions of a double standard in policing tactics motivated residents to form autonomous vigilance groups in order to supplement the official patrols. Filtered through a retroactive reading of Dr. Jekyll as the archetypal privileged offender, public speculations about a "respectable" Ripper also helped to solidify a counter-discourse on the Left, which held West End capitalists and speculators to be more fundamentally at fault for crime in the city. *Justice,* the newspaper of the Social Democratic Federation (which had played a leading role in the recent Hyde Park demonstrations) commented, for example, that "[w]hoever may be the wretch who committed these sanguinary outrages, the real criminal is the vicious bourgeois system which, based on class injustice, condemns thousands to poverty, vice and crime, manufactures criminals, and then punishes them!" At the same time, George Bernard Shaw wrote to the *Star* with incisive irony that

> if the habits of duchesses only admitted of their being decoyed into Whitechapel back-yards, a single experiment in slaughter-house anatomy on an aristocratic victim might fetch in round half a million and save the necessity of sacrificing four women of

the people. Such is the stark-naked reality of these abominable bastard Utopias of genteel charity, in which the poor are first to be robbed and then pauperized by way of compensation, in order that the rich man may combine the idle luxury of the protected thief with the unctuous self-satisfaction of the pious philanthropist.[44]

In this way, crime found a new political context in the late eighties, when the relative offenses of rich and poor were seriously contemplated for the first time since the 1840s. By publicizing what Martin Wiener terms "the criminal within respectability," the Left found a powerful vehicle for exposing the economic system which was responsible for poverty in the capital, as well as the forms of philanthropic benevolence which aimed to ameliorate its effects.[45] Charity was now targeted by free-marketeers on the Right and also the socialist Left, as either doing too much to alter the habits of the working class in London, or too little to change the conditions in which they lived.

### Oscar Wilde and the Politics of Crime

In "The Soul of Man under Socialism" (1891), Oscar Wilde argues that the proper course for dealing with poverty is *"to try and reconstruct society on such a basis that poverty will be impossible."*[46] Part of the current problem, he adds, lies with those same forms of fashionable altruism, which "have really prevented the carrying out of this aim"; like kindly slave-owners in the earlier part of the century, whose actions and attitudes delayed a recognition of the systematic basis of slavery, "the people who do most harm are the people who try to do most good." In recent years, he noted, "we have had the spectacle of men who have really studied the problem and know the life—educated men who live in the East-end—coming forward and imploring the community to restrain its altruistic impulses of charity, benevolence, and the like. They do so on the ground that such charity degrades and demoralizes. They are perfectly right. Charity creates a multitude of sins" (256).

Instead of placing the onus back on the poor and demanding from them a more thrifty attitude toward household economics (as many of the Christian philanthropists and the neo-Benthamites of the C.O.S. would do), Wilde concludes that labor is as inherently unpleasant as poverty, that the goal of life is individual fulfillment, especially through a cultivation of art and the aesthetic, and that society must therefore be reconstructed on the basis of socialist cooperation. One important step in this process, moreover, entails a recognition that crimes are committed out of "starvation, and not sin." Indeed, punishing criminals is counterproductive, and the mark of a debased society: "*a community is infinitely more brutalised by the habitual employment of punishment, than it is by the occasional occurrence of crime. . . . The less punishment, the less crime*" (267; emphasis in original). Echoing the radical thesis of greater guilt outlined by William Morris, Wilde goes on to argue that since most crimes arise out of economic hardship, and are therefore mainly directed against property (which the legal system has correspondingly been developed to protect), they should largely wither away under socialism: "When there is no punishment, crime will either cease to exist, or if it occurs, will be treated by physicians as a very distressing form of dementia, to be cured by care and kindness." [47]

As I have tried to suggest, Wilde's views here are broadly consistent with a Leftist critique of social policies toward the poor, which was forcefully articulated at the time of the Ripper murders by H. M. Hyndman and the Social Democratic Federation, as well as by commentators like Shaw and Morris. Given our dominant image of Wilde, however, as an inveterate socialite and West End clubman, the critique might seem to arise from an unsuspected source. Around this same time, Wilde was engaged in furnishing a grand home in Chelsea, and he seems to have wanted to put into immediate practice the utopian principles outlined in "The Soul of Man." Adrian Hope reported, after his first visit to the house in Tite Street, with its white high-gloss paint, Japaned lacquer work, and elaborate furnishings, that one room at the back (Wilde's study) incorporated a Turkish motif, but unfortunately looked out onto a slum, so its windows were "covered with a wooden grating on the inside copied from a Cairo pattern which considerably reduced the little light there was." [48] The gesture would seem an impatient one, wanting to abolish poverty in the here and now by simply hiding it from view, although a more generous reading might suggest that Wilde instead wanted the home to serve an exemplary function as a show-house for the new aesthetic movement; in this sense the Tite Street house, the contents of which were ultimately auctioned to pay off Wilde's legal costs, might be seen as embodying the principles of pleasurable self-realization which he outlined as the utopian aim in "The Soul of Man."

In the mid-eighties, Wilde met the novelist Olive Schreiner, one of a loose network of "New Women" who found a liberatory potential in charity work in East London, and asked why she lived in the East End; on hearing her say "Because the people there don't wear masks," he supposedly replied, "And I live in the West End because the people there do."[49] Again, such a statement might be seen as registering a simple preference for artifice and triviality at the expense of human misery or the sincere effort toward its amelioration; alternatively, it offers a critique of Schreiner's assumption that she could know a transparent "truth" about the East End, either through a transferential identification or the voluntary divestment of social privilege. It is fair to say, of course, that Wilde's critiques do little in the way of offering an alternative to the charitable philanthropy which dominated the liberal agenda of the 1880s and '90s, besides vague gestures toward science or revolution as the ultimate solution and the more fundamental insistence that the poor need to help themselves. To his credit, though, there is also considerable evidence that he was committed to basic principles of social justice, both before and after his imprisonment in 1895. In his biography, for example, Richard Ellmann reports that Wilde signed a petition circulated by Shaw against the Haymarket massacres, and attended a Hyde Park demonstration with his wife in support of the dock strike of 1889, two years prior to "The Soul of Man" essay, and just one year before *The Picture of Dorian Gray*.[50]

It is perhaps more disturbing to see the critique of charity being advanced by the character of Lord Henry Wotton in that novel, as apparently no more than a convenient reason why Dorian should spend more time with him, instead of engaging to play duets in Whitechapel with his Aunt Agatha. On being asked, for example, what should be done instead to solve the "very important problem" of the East End, Wotton replies with witty evasion that "I don't desire to change anything in England except the weather," and later that "[h]umanity takes itself too seriously" with talk of social responsibilities and sympathies (36–37). Wotton, of course, is not Wilde, although it is a mark of how the text was read after his prosecution four years later that the resemblance now seems to be such a compelling one.[51] Like *Dr. Jekyll and Mr. Hyde,* the novel underwent a dramatic reinterpretation in light of subsequent events, to the extent that discussions from the trials onwards have largely consisted of identifying a model of pernicious influence in the text, which might correlate with Wilde's supposed corruption of Lord Alfred Douglas and a network of lower-class rent boys. At the first aborted trial—brought by Wilde himself for libel against Douglas's father, the Marquis of Queensbury—defense counsel repeatedly cross-examined Wilde about whether a novel might be "immoral" or "perverted," holding the same kind of influence over impressionable readers that an unnamed French novel (modeled after Huysmans's *A Rebours*) is shown to have over Dorian. Since that text is given to him by Lord Henry, the alignment of Wotton/Wilde and Dorian/Douglas seems clear. Even though Wilde would not meet Douglas until the year after the book was published, he so strongly resembled Gray that Neil Bartlett has described the real-life lover as "a fiction," a figure who "already existed in [Wilde's] books."[52]

This is the sense in which Alan Sinfield has suggested that a text like *Dorian Gray* helped "to constitute just those terms in which we might wish, subsequently, to read it."[53] Like those of Jekyll before him, the precise nature of Gray's crimes is deliberately unspecified in the text, yet a common consensus emerged after Wilde's trials about the story's apparent homosexual subtext. On its first appearance, however, only the *Scots Observer* seems to have hinted at this, in an oblique reference to the Cleveland Street scandal of 1886, in which the seduction of a young telegraph delivery boy led to the discovery of a gay brothel, frequented by illustrious clients like Lord Arthur Somerset. Its reviewer claimed that *Dorian Gray* was fit only for the C.I.D., and had been written for "none but outlawed noblemen and perverted telegraph-boys"; Wilde's indignant response argued that "to keep this atmosphere [of 'moral corruption'] vague and indeterminate and wonderful was the aim of the artist. . . . What Dorian Gray's sins are no one knows. He who finds them has brought them."[54] But this review was another uncanny foreshadowing of Wilde's own trial, in which he would play the part of the "outlawed nobleman," engaged in the seduction of working-class boys supplied to him by Alfred Taylor; indeed, even the question of location seems appropriate, since the geo-social significance of Cleveland Street (on the fashionable edge of Regent's Park) was picked up in Wilde's trial, with constant references to Taylor's rooms in Little College Street, "near the Houses of Parliament" or "close to Westminster Abbey."[55] Again, the details refuse to neatly cohere. If Wilde's transgressions were homosexual and cut across class lines, the same clearly cannot be said either for Dorian's relationship with Sibyl Vane or the few hints the text offers about his dangerous influence over other aristocratic youth like Sir Henry Ashton, Adrian Singleton, and Lord Kent's only son.

His relationship with Sibyl does, however, give a sense of Dorian's attitudes toward the poor, which seem very different from those outlined in "The Soul of Man under Socialism." He first discovers Sibyl while on a ramble about town: "One evening about seven o'clock," he later recalls, "I determined to go out in search of some adventure. I felt that this grey, monstrous London of ours, with its myriads of people, its sordid sinners, and its splendid sins . . . must have something in store for me" (42). Already, we might cast him in the role of a flâneur, or perhaps an investigative journalist modeling himself after Dickens or Mayhew. Sibyl (from Euston Road, we are told, to clarify her lower-class / North London background) is performing in a shabby theater, whose patrons he later describes as "common, rough people, with their coarse faces and brutal gestures" (66). The audience is humanized only when Sibyl acts Shakespeare for them, and this performance is also what enables Dorian to maintain a slummer's fantasy of love between the classes; as soon as she stops acting, he loses interest and leaves her to commit suicide over her departed "Prince Charming." Later in the novel, he uses this same alias on nocturnal trips to the opium dens of the East End docklands, one of which is described in some detail. Dorian hails a cab late one night in Bond Street, and lies back in the seat, "his hat pulled over his forehead"; in imagery which is familiar from the period's obsessive investigations of East London, the journey takes him through "streets like the web of some sprawling spider," past monotonous brickfields and along "rough-paven streets" which are home to "monstrous marionettes," who only remind Dorian in turn of how much "[h]e hated them" (142–43).

From passages like this, it is easy to imagine Dorian—contemptuous of the people around him, in disguise, and out for immediate gratification—as another Doctor Jekyll, or even a possible Ripper suspect; elsewhere, for example, the litany of his sins include "brawling with foreign sailors in a low den in the distant parts of Whitechapel," as if to solidify the connection to the recent murders.[56] In a fascinating attempt to think through Wilde's politics in dialogue with a modern gay sensibility, Neil

Bartlett accuses the author of hypocrisy on the basis of scenes like this, which rely heavily on similar exposés of the opium dens by James Greenwood and others: Wilde, he argues,

> was involved in the daily, ordinary realm of "other" (homosexual, criminal) London in 1891, so for him discovering the truth, the secret life of the city, was a pleasure rather than a missionary or journalistic employment. His researches, though, were not made public; he kept his personal account of the lower depths a secret until it was forced out of him in 1895 [at trial]. In print all he did was to repeat the clichés of the descent into London's underworld in one of its most hackneyed locales.[57]

In Wilde's defense, it should be noted that he never claimed first-hand knowledge of the East End, having once proclaimed that "[a] gentleman never goes east of Temple Bar."[58] As we have seen, his own subcultural escapades took him only as far as the symbolic center of London, and it is unlikely that he would have considered himself any kind of underworld figure or sexual outlaw at this time. In fact, the slide Bartlett makes from the homosexual to the criminal is one that seems largely conditioned by Wilde's own prosecution: afterwards, he proudly accepted his criminal self-identity, by suggesting that "The Ballad of Reading Gaol" be offered for publication to *Reynolds's Magazine,* which "circulates widely amongst the criminal classes, to which I now belong, so I shall be read by my peers."[59]

Statements like these have again tended to shape a retroactive interpretation of *Dorian Gray,* in which crime is thought to have been elevated to an art form, on a par with the those successive hobbies—like the study of perfumes, music, jewels, and embroidery—by which Dorian is shown to entertain himself under the influence of Lord Henry's "poisonous book."[60] There is some historical justification for this view. Cultural critics, in explaining what Leslie Stephen termed the "perceptible decline" in the style of murder, had recently returned to the views expounded by de Quincey in "On Murder, Considered as One of the Fine Arts" (1827). Echoing the same theme, the *Spectator* had predicted in 1882 a more prosaic era in the history of crime, "in which evil is stolid, and careful, and prudent, and obtuse," although clearly, no one could have foreseen the Ripper murders six years later.[61] In such a context, it seems very plausible to imagine Wilde as engaged in a public attempt to elevate crime to a new level of aesthetics, using Dorian Gray as his figurehead: he is, after all, the blueprint for what Lord Henry terms a "new Hedonism," the man who would "live out his life fully and completely, . . . give form to every feeling, expression to every thought, reality to every dream" without fear of conscience, the law, or public censure (20–23).

But if Dorian has some success embodying the goals and attitudes of the aesthetic movement, he is a major disappointment as a criminal. Dorian's criminal centerpiece, the murder of the painter Basil Hallward, is particularly poor, and undertaken for the most pedestrian of motives. Having confronted Dorian with a list of his rumored indiscretions, Hallward wonders about the quality of his friend's soul, at which point he is invited to view the picture and see it for himself; but Dorian suddenly feels an intense hatred toward the painter for having set the process in motion, and kills him out of resentment, before hastening to cover up his crime. Commenting on this incident, Alan Sinfield concludes that it arises "from sentimental self-indulgence and want of intelligence and self-control, not from aestheticism and amorality. . . . Dorian arrives at disaster not because he abjures conventional moral principles but because he remains under their sway."[62] As we shall see, this is a judgment with which Wilde himself would reluctantly concur.

Dorian's crime does not sound very elevated and artistic because—like the portrait itself—it needs to remain hidden from the public. This is presumably Lord Henry Wotton's point, when he tells his protégé that "murder is always a mistake. One should never do anything that one cannot talk about after dinner." Behind the familiar rhetoric of inversion that underpins the epigram, though, Lord Henry has another reason for disbelieving Gray's hypothetical confession: "I would say," he replies,

> that you were posing for a character that doesn't suit you. All crime is vulgar, just as all vulgarity is crime. It is not in you, Dorian, to commit a murder. I am sorry if I hurt your vanity by saying so, but I assure you it is true. Crime belongs exclusively to the lower orders. I don't blame them in the smallest degree. I should fancy that crime was to them what art is to us, simply a method of procuring extraordinary sensations. (162)

That last line can mislead us into thinking that Wilde is offering up his usual blend of rhetorical insouciance and imagining a world in which only "extraordinary sensations" count. But there's a more serious point here, which he expresses in "The Soul of Man under Socialism": given the harshness of working-class life and the constant search for the means of subsistence rather than pleasure, Wilde felt that the poor criminal was entirely exonerated. But for someone like Dorian to commit murder is ultimately to borrow a form of justification which is unwarranted in his case, and which cannot be secured by simply renaming murder as an art form: since he has the necessary wealth, leisure, and cultural training for finding enjoyment in the aesthetic realm, an aristocrat really has no business committing crimes, which can be supported only as a response to material need and suffering. Rather than endorsing the notion of an aesthetics of crime, then, Wilde seems instead to offer here a powerful critique of the tendency to flatten out the differences between crime and culture. By acting out the role of the privileged offender, Dorian is simply taking to extremes a process of slumming which Wilde consistently attacked in political terms, because it effectively enabled and justified an ongoing exploitation of the real miseries of East End life. Like the kindly slave-owners, slummers effectively insisted that East End poverty remain what it was, a spectacle of suffering to be gradually ameliorated but never actually abolished.

My understanding of *Dorian Gray* has been aided by a remarkable reinterpretation by Regenia Gagnier of Wilde's 1889 essay on Thomas Wainewright, "Pen Pencil and Poison." This essay has customarily been considered as an updating of de Quincey's thesis, given Wilde's emphasis on the overlapping of the various aspects of Wainewright's celebrity as "a poet and a painter, an art-critic, an antiquarian, and a writer of prose, an amateur of beautiful things, and a dilettante of things delightful, but also a forger of no mean or ordinary capabilities, and as a subtle and secret poisoner almost without rival in this or any age."[63] The essay goes on to detail some of his literary and art criticism, his friendships with Hazlitt, Lamb, and others around the *London Magazine,* in addition to his early successes on the social scene, before stating quite bluntly that "if we set aside his achievements in the sphere of poison, what he has left to us hardly justifies his reputation" (324). As Gagnier argues, Wilde's flippant tone has led most critics to miss the sense of irony, and thus either to misinterpret statements like this or to take them at face value; Richard Ellmann, for instance, suggests that "forgery was a crime which perhaps seems closest to Wilde's social presentation of himself," and concludes that this essay demonstrates that "Wainewright's criminal craft revealed a true artist."[64] The key point, though, is not that he might be more appropriately considered to be an artist in the particular sphere of poisoning, but rather that there is no basis for considering him an artist at all; thus, while "[t]he fact of a man being a poisoner is nothing against his prose" (339), we might equally say that it says nothing in its favor.

Wilde, moreover, is equally critical of claims which have been made concerning Wainewright's status as a master-criminal, and of his celebrity among the intelligentsia of the romantic era. His cell at Newgate, the essay notes, "was for some time a kind of fashionable lounge," yet Wainewright himself felt isolated from those around him. He apparently told visitors that "I have been determined through life to hold the position of a gentleman. I have always done so. I do so still. It is the custom of this place that each of the inmates of a cell shall take his morning's turn of sweeping it out. I occupy a cell with a bricklayer and a sweep, but they never once offer me the broom!" On leaving Newgate, he was transported to Van Diemen's Land, and felt a similar sense of superiority over the "country bumpkins" on board, so different from the "poets and artists" with whom he was used to associating when he was still a celebrity criminal. Commenting on this last quote, Wilde repeats his dictum from "The Soul of Man under Socialism" in order to explain Wainewright's sense of alienation from his fellow criminals: "The phrase that he applies to his companions need not surprise us," he notes, since "[c]rime in England is rarely the result of sin. It is nearly always the result of starvation" (337–38). Despite his pretensions to culture and celebrity status, then, the artist/poisoner ultimately emerges from this essay as a rather sad anomaly, whose claim to fame rests on his combining disparate qualities rather than his abilities at anything in particular. Wainewright might well stand in this respect as a prototype for Dorian Gray, who aims for a similar accommodation of crime and culture. But their conjunction tells us little about either one: crime, Wilde seems to be saying, is best left to those with purpose and motive, while the cultural kudos which comes from a criminal reputation cannot compensate for a lack of artistic talent.

Far from endorsing a view of murder as an art form, then, "Pen Pencil and Poison" criticizes the cultural reflex to accord to crime the alibi of the aesthetic. To be sure, Wilde argues that "[t]here is no essential incongruity between crime and culture" (339), but this is only because the canons of Western culture are so permeated with the activities of criminals. Wainewright is too close to the time of writing to enable a final judgment to be made on him—just as the poisoner himself (in his alter ego as a mediocre art critic) never felt "quite at his ease in his criticisms of contemporary work" (327)—but the same cannot be said for figures of the past: "had the man worn a costume and spoken a language different from our own, had he lived in imperial Rome, or at the time of the Italian Renaissance, or in Spain in the seventeenth century, or in any land or any century but this century and this land, we would be quite able to arrive at a perfectly unprejudiced estimate of his position and his value." Here, as Gagnier notes, Wilde offers an insightful indictment of the disinterested formalism of art criticism, and its tendencies to mystify the past by disengaging historical figures from their social context: "Nobody with the true historical sense," he concludes with a heavy dose of irony, "ever dreams of blaming Nero, or scolding Tiberius or censuring Caesar Borgia. These personages have become like the puppets of a play. They may fill us with terror, or horror, or wonder, but they do not harm us. They are not in immediate relation to us. We have nothing to fear from them. They have passed into the sphere of art and science, and neither art nor science knows anything of moral approval or disapproval" (339–40).

Passages like this, when read in the context of the particular interpretation of *Dorian Gray* which I outlined above, have led critics to assume that Wilde was engaged in a simple promotion of cultural relativism, of "art for art's sake," and that he adopted the romantic stance of the outlaw in the period which preceded his own criminalization in 1895. As Ellmann rightly notes, however, Wilde had been moving for some time toward a more critical position in relation to the aesthetic movement, which he parodied in "The Decay of Lying" (1889) through the figure of the Tired Hedonists club. That same essay discusses the influence which crime stories about Jack Sheppard and Dick Turpin have held over the imagination of impressionable youths in order to illustrate the thesis that life can sometimes imitate art, although this is saying something very different from the clichéd sentiment that the aesthetic is entirely divorced from the realm of morality.[65] In defending *Dorian Gray* to the press, moreover, Wilde reluctantly admitted that the novel had a moral, namely that "all excess, as well as all renunciation, brings its own punishment": Basil Hallward, he notes, dies because of his excessive investment in beauty, "by the hand of one in whose soul he has created a monstrous and absurd vanity." Dorian Gray later suffers from a flawed attempt to "kill conscience," by living "a life of mere sensation and pleasure," while even Lord Henry finds it hard to maintain the absolute separation of his actions from their effects, finding it impossible to remain "merely the spectator of life."[66] His repudiation of responsibility for events in the story involves much the same kind of mystification which enabled criminals to be read in purely aesthetic terms, but is finally insupportable, as Wotton ends up suffering collateral damage from events which he helped to set in motion. Far from representing a celebration of a crime as one of the fine arts, these statements suggest its opposite. Like Thomas Wainewright, Dorian is denied the cover of art and culture, which might otherwise have excused him, and is held to account for his crimes by something as uncharacteristic of Wilde as a "conscience."

Read alongside "Pen Pencil and Poison," *The Picture of Dorian Gray* is shown to have a distinctively critical edge. Like Wainewright, its hero is revealed as entirely unsuited to the task of founding a "new Hedonism," and even that project itself seems uncertain given the moral condemnation of aestheticism that Wilde admitted to having written into his novel. But if aesthetic detachment seems an inappropriate cultural stance for the 1890s, Wilde is also skeptical of its main rival, a politically committed form of literary naturalism which grew out of the settlement movement of the 1880s and sought to expose the sordid realities of life in the East End. As I have already suggested, the impulse for such a cultural stance originated in investigative journalism, which had a long-standing tradition of undercover examinations of "how the other half lived." The forms of impersonation developed by James Greenwood and George Sims now became filtered through the experience of the settlement movement, to emerge as a fully fledged literary style in the hands of Walter Besant, Rudyard Kipling, Margaret Harkness, and others. This style largely consisted of a new form of ventriloquism, in which working-class characters usually took center stage and spoke in a dialect style which would be recognizable as "East End cockney." Problems arose, however, when middle-class authors tried to convey a local consciousness, based on their more detached observances of the external characteristics of East End life. Some, like Besant, adopted a romanticized vision of how East Enders might think in different circumstances, but found this difficult to square with the people they saw; while the majority followed an alternative trajectory outlined by Kipling, which consisted of depicting a life of unremitting violence, squalor, and crime.

In chapter 5, I will argue that the naturalist movement shared a common impulse with the texts that I have examined here. The archetype of the privileged offender—as glimpsed in literary characters like Neville St. Clair and Henry Jekyll, as well as in the speculations about the Ripper's identity—depends upon a similar reduction of East End life to its most degraded characteristics. The crimes committed by these characters are predicated upon a prior criminalization of the area as a whole, which can then function as a playground for the idle rich. In this sense, the shift of agency away from the residents themselves did very little to alter the image of the region. Indeed, a range of illicit pleasures—which are often left vague, but might have included opium and prostitution— appear in these texts as the natural resources of East London, and are made available to disguised and cynical slummers like Mr. Hyde and Dorian Gray. Each, as I have suggested, adopted a different position in relation to charity, which was simultaneously under attack for exacerbating the economic problems of the region; but they also effectively exploited the political space which these arguments opened up, in order to satisfy their personal ambitions and appetites.

# 5  INTO DARKEST LONDON, AND BACK AGAIN

AT THE END of the last chapter, I suggested that Wilde's critical writings dealt as harshly with the new school of British naturalism which flourished under the influence of Zola as it did with the fashion for the privileged offender. Perhaps the clearest statement he makes on the new literary movement appears in "The Decay of Lying," in which he caricatures it as the *"genre ennuyeux . . .* that great and daily increasing school of novelists for whom the sun always rises in the East-end," and for whom "the only thing that can be said about them is that they find life crude, and leave it raw."[1] We have already seen how this critique of naturalism relates to the attacks on charity which he outlined in "The Soul of Man under Socialism," because each focuses on life as it is in the absence of strategies for changing it: in this sense, the naturalist impulse to (once again) expose the conditions of life in darkest London can be read as continuous with philanthropic efforts "to disarm the just rancour of the criminal classes" with improving conversation. This last quote, from Gilbert in "The Critic as Artist," captures both the sympathy which Wilde felt for the dispossessed and also the disdain with which he treated the idle rich, who (he notes elsewhere in the same essay) are bound by a form of self-congratulatory egoism, and so can hardly be expected to furnish a disinterested judgment about either the social conditions they encounter or what should be done to alleviate them. Their attempts to stave off political crises "by means of doles and alms" will inevitably fail, according to Gilbert, with the result that "when the revolution or crisis arrives, we shall be powerless because we shall know nothing."[2]

This knowledge is, of course, what novelists, settlement workers, amateur sociologists, and journalists all aimed to furnish, and it is to Wilde's considerable credit that he could recognize the limits and contradictions of sympathetic identification, which worked to undermine their ambitions, as well as the evasion of class politics which they encouraged. But I do not mean to hold him up as a shining example here, for the simple reason that these criticisms did not easily translate into an active political commitment on Wilde's part. His position seems to be an abstentionist one, which ultimately reifies the separation of spheres outlined in *Dorian Gray,* with crime and politics as the appropriate vehicles for working-class activity while the leisured classes focus on the cultivation of art and beauty. The fault of naturalism, for Wilde, is to confuse the two, to the extent that modern novelists are prone to "raging and roaring over the abuses of contemporary life like a common pamphleteer or a sensational journalist. . . . [We] spend our days in the sordid streets and hideous suburbs of our vile cities when we should be out on the hillside with Apollo."[3] Where earlier in the century progressive opinion invariably looked for inter-class connection and common interests, we now find a principled case being made *for* separation, not (as with earlier urban planning schemes) in order to check the impulse to revolution but to advance it.

This seems an appropriate place to reconsider the connections which Wilde perceived between politics and the aesthetic, as a way of framing this chapter's discussion of how they overlapped in a variety of social and cultural enterprises in the 1880s and '90s. My immediate focus here is on a fascinating institution and example of failed social engineering, the People's Palace, which Queen Victoria opened in 1887. Located on the Mile End Road, less than a mile from the sites of the Jack the Ripper murders a year later, this was conceived as a grand center of learning, culture, and recreation for the East End poor. Unique among institutions of Victorian social reform, the Palace originated in a novel, *All Sorts and Conditions of Men,* published by Walter Besant in 1881, and so offers an instructive case study of what happens when imaginative projects are actualized in a real-world economy. Two years after the novel's appearance, a charitable fund called the Beaumont Trust launched its own appeal to build a real-life Palace in the East End, envisaging a dual strategy whereby "bricks-and-mortar" reform might furnish an appropriate setting within which the poor would be encouraged to "improve themselves from the inside." In practice, this meant a complex undertaking which elaborated on Besant's fictional designs: in addition to the concert halls, library, recreation facilities, and gymnasium envisaged in the novel, the plans also called for swimming baths and schoolrooms for technical instruction. Two years later, however, only half of the budgeted £100,000 had been raised, and it became clear that the Trust needed to petition wealthy Londoners for donations.[4] I stress these issues of funding as an index of how the project was perceived in the centers of power in London, and also to show the ways in which the fate of the Palace was tied to external events like the West End riots of 1886–87 or the Ripper murders of 1888. Contributions began to dry up in the mid-eighties, and the Palace which eventually opened bore little resemblance to Besant's original designs. Its orientation was increasingly toward a middle-class clientele, while its appeal to local people was more as a site of education than of recreation. In 1890, control was assumed by a major contributor called the Draper's Company, which consolidated this new shift in emphasis, and it seems entirely fitting that the site was eventually transformed wholesale into a place of technical instruction, which it remains today.[5]

Besant's novel traces out a blossoming romance between Angela Messenger, the Cambridge-educated heiress to a Stepney brewery who is living in the East End disguised as a dressmaker, and Harry Goslett, who has been brought up a gentleman but decides, on hearing of his true Whitechapel ancestry, to make an honest living as a cabinetmaker. Together they plan a Palace of Delight—a name by which the People's Palace was often referred in its early years—with the idea that what East Enders crucially needed was "a little more of the pleasures and graces of life."[6] This sounds like Wilde's own celebrations of the function of the aesthetic in everyday life, except that his public persona of aristocratic decadence and triviality provides one of the clearest examples of what this privileged couple must renounce in order to perform worthwhile work in the East End: Angela first compares Harry to the men of

Cambridge, concluding that he is "as quick as the most thorough-going Society man who had access to studios, literary circles, musical people and aesthetes; and as careless as any Bertie or Algie of the whole set" (72); even more bluntly, when he later vacillates over his decision, she confronts him with the image of Wilde as a counterexample to their noble sacrifice, asking "Would you really like to become one of those poor creatures who thinks they lead lives devoted to art? Would you like to grow silly over blue china, to quarrel about colour, to worship Form in poetry, to judge everything by the narrow rules of the latest pedantic fashion?" (164).

Considering the force of these casual attacks, it is certainly easy to understand Wilde's own evident hostility to middle-class altruists, and to see him as gladly occupying the demonized position held out for him. And yet what are we to make of a letter from Wilde asking to be considered for the position of secretary to the Beaumont Trust? In it, he claims to be "very anxious to be connected officially with the People's Palace, as I have devoted myself entirely to the spreading of art-culture among the people," and to "have had, both in America and in this country, many opportunities of studying the possibilities of a Wider Technical Education than modern systems afford."[7] Of course, we need not necessarily take Wilde at his word here: his public reputation seems to have been enough to rule him out of consideration for the position, and he may simply have imagined it as a convenient means of paying the rent at his lavish new Chelsea home. He did, however, cherish a long-term ambition of becoming an inspector of schools, and had certainly thought at some length about the potential overlap between aesthetics and instruction.[8] His maxims and aphorisms, for example, repeatedly extol the virtues of culture, especially at the expense of formal schooling, while the successful lecture series he delivered in the United States similarly circled around the educative and practical functions of art in the modern world.[9]

If Wilde and Besant seem unlikely allies, the connection is rooted in their shared belief that art and culture should form a basis for a future civilized society, which is envisaged by the former in "The Soul of Man under Socialism" and by the latter as a possible consequence of institutions like the People's Palace. In an article written at the height of his involvement in the project, Besant predicted that its lasting effects would be felt by the East End youth, rather than by those "whom long years of labour and want of cultivation have rendered stiff of finger, slow of ear and of eye, impenetrable of brain." For those whose shorter working lives promised greater mental and physical health, Besant foresaw a brighter future through the application of "skill, patience, discipline, drill, and obedience to law." This last attribute was key, of course, since this new generation would help the East End to renounce the criminal reputation which the Ripper case had recently solidified, and exemplify instead the deferential respect which would be acquired through cultural enrichment. In prophetic mode, Besant concluded that "[t]hose who master any one of the Arts, the practice of which constitute true recreation, have left once and for ever the ranks of disorder: they belong by virtue of their aptitude and their education—say, by virtue of their Election—to the army of Law and Order." [10]

In the political context of the 1880s, though, Besant's Arnoldian schemes for cultural enlightenment appear short-sighted and doomed to failure precisely because they tried to ignore what was happening outside the Palace walls, and promoted instead an increasingly narrow and tendentious vision of "respectable" East End life. Given the ambitions outlined above, it is easy to see why he felt disappointed at the results, especially in the sphere of cultural development. Besant used his regular column as editor of the in-house *Palace Journal* to urge the development of an autonomous popular culture, and charged its supporters to "never be content until our own bands play our own music: our own singers sing our own songs: our own Journal prints our own literature: our own novelists lie upon our tables: our own critics pronounce our judgments: our own artists paint the pictures for our own exhibitions." The excessive use of plural pronouns already indicates a sense of problems to come, as well as Besant's anxiety to divest himself of the cultural capital which marked him as different, not "one of us." As his *Autobiography* confirms, the Palace literary club, which he had vigorously promoted through his dual role as journal editor and honorary society president, "proved a dead failure; not a soul, when I was connected with the Palace, showed the least literary ability or ambition." [11]

As I shall suggest later in this chapter, this assessment is bitterly ironic, since the Palace did aid in the development of a novelist of considerable talent, Arthur Morrison, who worked under Besant as subeditor of the

*Palace Journal* for about a year in 1889–90. Morrison went to great lengths to disguise his own East End background, which may have confused the issue somewhat; but he was accordingly well placed to evaluate the Palace, its impact on the surrounding area, and the cultural ambitions which inspired it. In this context, it seems appropriate that such a contradictory and utopian project should produce a writer who took British naturalism to a new level in its ambition to portray the sordid realities of East End life, and who crafted scathing indictments of middle-class philanthropy in novels like *A Child of the Jago* (1895). In what follows, I want first to outline the brief history of the People's Palace by looking at a set of internal debates about its proper function, especially in light of important external events like the West End riots or the dock strike of 1888. I will then contrast the romantic idealism of *All Sorts and Conditions of Men* with a harsher style of literary realism, as developed by Kipling, Margaret Harkness, and Morrison, before briefly considering some of the ways in which the East End poor have been imaginatively transformed and repackaged in the twentieth century.

### Aesthetic Education for the Masses: The People's Palace

For someone whose main contribution to the celebrated "Art of Fiction" debates (which he initiated with a lecture in 1884) was to declare that novelists must write only from "personal experience and observation,"[12] Besant gave an odd subtitle to his novel of two years earlier: *All Sorts and Conditions of Men: An Impossible Story.* His reason for doing so is explained in the preface, which states that "I have been told by certain friendly advisers that this story is impossible. I have, therefore, stated the fact on the title-page, so that no one may complain of being taken in." But what he concedes here he takes away with the next sentence, concluding the preface with a strong statement of faith: "But I have never been able to understand why it is impossible" (x). In one sense, of course, the opening of the People's Palace six years later provides convincing evidence that it *was* possible. But it was presumably the means by which the fictional prototype was planned and funded which Besant's advisers had in mind, and which provide the most striking contrasts between the two "palaces."

In the novel, as I have suggested, the Palace of Delight exists at first as the whim of two wealthy "slummers," and as a counter in their games of mutual deception: having heard Harry declare that such a palace is what East Enders most urgently require, the millionairess Angela asks him supposedly hypothetical questions about what it should contain and how it should be presented, while secretly building the institution itself. But while the covert existence of the Palace is somehow kept concealed, the fictional identities that Angela and Harry project only fool each other. There are pressing political motives at stake here. Maintaining these open secrets enables them to continue to pose—however unconvincingly—as "real" East Enders, and even to comment disparagingly on other wealthy "do-gooders" and philanthropists: Angela is thus able to appear as a local benefactor, while Harry ultimately assumes the leadership of a new League of Working Men that seeks to substitute for class struggle a more pragmatic politics of need. The resulting ambiguity is best illustrated when Angela finally shows her dressmakers the building: in the role of "Miss Kennedy," she declares that

> we shall not be like a troop of revellers, thinking of nothing but dance and song and feasting. We shall learn something every day; we shall all belong to some class. Those of us who already know will teach the rest. . . . And if anybody is paid anything, it will be at the rate of a working man's wage—no more. For this is our Palace, the club of working people. . . . All this is provided in the deed of trust by which Miss Messenger hands over the building to the people. (409)

This shows how the disguise operates, by splitting into two distinct subjects "Miss Kennedy" (who is able to speak the collective first-person pronouns: "*our* Palace") and the benevolent Miss Messenger, who has provided the actual building for "the people."

The confusion is intensified in scenes involving Dick Coppin, Harry's ambitious cousin, who aims to be a true representative of the people. Both Harry and Angela lecture him about what political issues to address, preferring a bread-and-butter politics of wages and conditions to an exhausted language of class conflict associated with the specter of Chartism.[13] Harry, for example, tells him to forget about abolishing the House of Lords or disestablishing the church, and to concentrate instead on forms of local action that could deliver healthy food, better houses, schooling, holidays and (above all else) "Pleasure," while Angela makes a similar pitch for self-determination, telling Dick and his friends from the Stepney Advanced Club to

> Be your own police, and make your streets clean. Do you ever go into the courts and places where dock labourers sleep? Have a committee for every one such street or court, and make them decent. When a gang of roughs make the pavement intolerable, you decent men step off and leave them to the policeman, if he dares interfere. Put down the roughs yourselves with a strong hand. Clear out the thieves' dens and the drinking shops; make rogues and vagabonds go elsewhere. I am always about among the people; they are full of sufferings which need not be; there are a great many workers—ladies, priests, clergymen—among them, trying to remove some of the suffering. But why do you not do this for yourselves? (317)

This sounds like bourgeois slum clearance in the guise of autonomous working-class activism, and was the kind of careful compromise position adopted by local organizations like the East London Defence Alliance, which amplified the contemporary critique of charity by suggesting that do-gooders like Besant "had no care for the respectable characters of the East End," and "seemed to vie with each other in decrying the East End, but they grew fat upon it, and cared no more for the poor than the man in the moon." Life in the East End was no worse than elsewhere in London, they asserted, whereas constant press coverage of attention to its worst aspects had the effect of further "depreciating the value of property, and driving capital away."[14] But Angela Messenger can only outline her belief in grassroots improvement through an implicit critique of her own intervention, which has the effect of obscuring class distinctions, while also binding the East Enders to an increasing dependency on West End generosity; indeed, if there is a political moral here, it is that drawn by a former Chartist and colleague of Dick, who concludes that "the working man's best friends would be the swells, if they could be got hold of" (313).

In a sense, Angela's status in the novel as *deus ex machina* simply hypostatizes a more general characteristic of late-Victorian charity, which posed a magical form of resolution for a range of concrete social problems while simultaneously eliding their economic and political basis. Issues of class politics and economics were more pointed in the debates which preceded the founding of the real-life People's Palace, and which turned in various ways on the relationship between West End wealth and East End need. The case was put positively by sections of the London press like the *Weekly Echo,* which declared on 30 May 1885 that "[i]f those from the West-end who recently earned for themselves the designation of 'slummers' have any real sympathy with the London poor, and are genuinely anxious to introduce into their lives a little sweetness and light, they have now an unusually fine opportunity of giving proof of their goodness." Local papers like the *East London Advertiser* took the same line, pointing out on the same day that since "the people in the West End of London are never tired of dwelling upon the hard, cheerless lives lived by the poor of East London . . . an opportunity now offers of giving practical sympathy in the shape of money towards helping the Beaumont Trust provide the winter garden, the cheap concerts, and other attractive items in the programme put forth." Meanwhile, the *Pall Mall Gazette* editorialized that "the People's Palace might be a big concern or it will be nothing; it must either find a millionaire or get a hold of a bit of several, or it will die." In a follow-up editorial a month later, the newspaper began to question the direction of the project: "we cannot help thinking," it declared,

> that the walls of the palace would rise much more quickly if the promoters were to explain more precisely what is to be erected inside. . . . [O]ne fails a little to see any necessary connection between a gymnasium, a swimming-bath, and a winter garden on the one side, and a technical school on the other. A Palace of Delight and a Palace of Industry might no doubt be one and the same thing; and if the technical schools are to be devoted to decoration and design, they are entirely germane to the rest of the scheme. But then one wants to be authoritatively told whether this is to be the case or not; whether, in a word, the object is to be to teach people how to enjoy life or . . . to "succeed in life"—which is a very different thing.[15]

This reflects some of the same frustrations that Besant later admitted to feeling, when he complained in his 1892 *Autobiography* that the Palace suffered from an increasing stress on technical instruction, fostered by the Draper's Company: "Unfortunately a polytechnic was tacked on to it," he noted, so that "the original idea of a palace of recreation was mixed up with a place of education." Aesthetic and instructive ambitions were becoming intermingled, but for Besant it was the emphasis on the former that separated his project from others in London, like the nearby Toynbee Hall or the efforts of the university settlement movement, in which the stress was always on working-class improvement through the imitation of outside role models; to focus on leisure and culture was, in theory at least, a means of encouraging patterns of local self-determination. The sheer scope of the scheme, though, effectively mortgaged it to a very different vision of East End life, with the class on which it was forced to rely for funding concerned to disrupt expressions of working-class consciousness and autonomy, especially in the context of the socialist and union agitation of the late eighties. The Trust's success can be gauged by responses to a request for subscriptions in excess of £5, which guaranteed a seat at the royal grand opening in May 1887. Not surprisingly, given the level of financial commitment demanded, most replies are from North and West London and the outlying suburbs, including the gentlemen's clubs of Westminster and Pall Mall, the fashionable West End of Sloane Square and Kensington Gardens, the Stock Exchange, and the Conservative Club. One handwritten response and half-guinea subscription gives a clear index of bourgeois concerns:

> The Women of England would be much more willing to subscribe to your proposed Establishment if it were for the purpose of educating the poorer classes for the state of life they will be expected to fill—viz: teach the women Reading, Writing, Arithmetic, all Household duties and to sew, so as to fit them for servants, and when they marry that they may be able to cook properly and make their homes comfortable for their husbands—the men to be taught all trades. Of course, where any shows a particular talent, let that be cultivated properly. But the accomplished way in which they are to be taught, will never permit them to become servants afterwards, and where, pray, are we to get servants! Why, many respectable families cannot afford to educate their children in the way the lower classes are now

being educated. It will be the Ruin of the Country, for there must be a distinction of classes.

Beneath the apocalyptic tone, however, what is perhaps most notable here is that the "Ladies of England" took out a subscription nonetheless.[16]

Once the Palace opened, it quickly developed a middle-class orientation, and resistance mainly took the form of rejection, as local attendance dwindled: in his study of its activities during 1888, William J. Fishman notes that dog shows, poultry exhibits, and flower shows all tended to attract both their exhibitors and their audience from a distance, so that a reporter for the *East London Advertiser* was incited to ask whether "it would not be well for the management to make an effort to obtain more *local* entries" (312−15). The *Daily News* warned of the dangers in January 1886, when it predicted that "[a]ll well meaning people who would never venture to suggest the notion of ethical improvement in connection with middle-class relaxation think that no workman ought to be allowed to unbend his mind without it."[17] This caution proved accurate, as the following months saw the Palace consumed by arguments about Sunday opening and the sale of alcohol on the premises, and the article went on to deliver a further critique of charitable "do-gooding" with a well-considered contrast which combined geographical specificity with a larger sense of class relations:

> Nothing is said about amateur theatricals, but this surely ought to be remembered with dancing, and we hope to see a good café and smoking room to which the men may go for the evening pipe, without feeling that they are doing anything wrong, or without being expected to listen to a discourse on the topography of the Holy Land. . . . Most of the existing institutions are unfortunately fettered with some condition of this kind. The man who feels that his time for learning is gone by is out of place in them, and may wander from class-room to class-room without finding a mate. We shall never do much for the East-end, or for any similar quarter, until all this is changed. Think of a Pall Mall club with a compulsory hour and a-half in Greek as a "pass" for the billiard-room!

The force of this opposition between Pall Mall and the Palace—like the larger polarity of West and East Ends which it condensed—was dramatically voiced in a letter to the *East London Advertiser* in September, stating that "the inheritance bequeathed by the dead, and presented by the living, to those whose existence is one long, ceaseless, sunless, hopeless round of chattel-slavery, has been usurped by mainly a horde of giggling, bread-and-butter creatures in bustles, accompanied by a mathematically equivalent number of sniggering, invertebrate, vacuum-skulled prigs in trousers." [18] This criticism hinges on a deliberate deployment of class difference as distinct from more abstract notions of "the people," claiming that the building was originally envisaged as "the *poor* People's Palace" and had thus been usurped by interlopers from another social class, whose lack of any moral entitlement to its benefits was matched by their insistence on maintaining veto power over its activities. Besant was compelled to reply to these charges in his position as editor of the *Palace Journal,* and gave a revealing account of how the term "people" was intended to cover over important class distinctions:

> Some one wrote a most foolish letter to a paper the other day, asking scornfully whether the Palace attracted the "class for which it was intended." The "class"? What class? What is the attitude of this man's mind towards the People's Palace? Of course there is no such thing with us as class. When one speaks of the People, one means all the people, from the Queen to—let us not be invidious by naming anybody. We all belong to the people, and the Palace belongs for all.

This projection of a *déclassé* citizenry quickly unravels, however, and Besant's hesitation to fix a lower limit to contrast with the Queen quickly becomes understandable as he feels compelled to qualify his assertion: "We can," he continues, "only recognise 'class' in one sense. There is in every town a 'class'—that is to say, a certain proportion of people who are unable to take any delight in anything but in the lowest vices: if there is any 'class' for which the Palace is not founded it is for this class." [19]

This reply reveals two features of the ideological discourse of the Palace, each of which suggests an affinity with current forms of populist rhetoric. First, his reluctance to even use the term "class," and indeed to place it within scare-quotes, suggests the extent of the struggle to excise the specter of radical politics from the Palace, as well as a tangible fear of any sign of the repressed's return. "People," in this sense, is intended to signify a brave new world beyond class difference, in which Queen and pauper might share equally in the benefits of study and recreation. The final point Besant makes, however, is clearly intended to mark a distinction which was familiar to late-Victorian reform movements, between the honest working class and a lumpen, criminal "residuum" which remained unreformable. We have already seen such tactics at work in the statements of the East London Defence Alliance, who presumed to speak for the "respectable" East Enders and to distinguish them from criminal elements who got all the press headlines. If the emphasis placed on the "*poor* People's Palace" in the *Advertiser* letter threatened to undermine the fiction of an abstracted "people," it also nicely revealed how that fiction had sought to operate in the first place, by displacing economics onto the sphere of morality and rearticulating class to an ethics of self-reliance and upward mobility. The Palace's ultimate fate eloquently speaks to these submerged ambitions, and also to their ultimate failure.

## Life beyond the Palace Walls

The problem is that the reforming and culturalist aspirations on which the People's Palace was erected were better suited to the relative prosperity of the 1870s, when West End philanthropy flourished and there was little industrial unrest in the capital. The following decade, conversely, saw economic depression, chronic housing shortages and poverty in the East End, anarchist bombings, and a nascent socialist movement which sought to organize and agitate among the unemployed. In these circumstances, the People's Palace was founded on the repression of two key aspects of London life: first, a long-standing radical tradition which periodically erupted in strikes and riots, centered in particular on East London; and second, that region's image as the site of a generalized criminality, the home of a demoralized underclass who threatened to corrupt the social strata above them. The fusion of these two forces that had occurred in the 1840s still acted fifty years later as a cautionary warning, so reformers like Besant were careful to simultaneously bracket criminality and class politics from their accounts of a newly moralized East End working class. Thus, *All Sorts and Conditions of Men* characterizes a

politics of confrontation as anachronistic, embodied in the regressive organization of the Stepney Advanced Club. The novel is similarly dismissive about the place of Whitechapel in the public imaginary, conceding
the criminal notoriety of the Mile End Road only to assert that "the road
is not worthy of this reputation: it has of late years become orderly; its
present condition is dull and law-abiding" (80). In another remarkable
passage, Besant seems to acknowledge the selectivity of his description,
by introducing a lame and weeping dressmaker before confessing that she
can have no place in his narrative: "Why she wept," he writes, "and how
Angela followed her home, and what that home was like . . . belongs to
another story, concerned with the wretchedness and misery which are
found at Whitechapel and Stepney, as well as in Soho and Marylebone
and the back of Regent Street. I shall not write many chapters of that
story, for my own part" (118).

Besant's defensiveness about the class composition of the Palace
membership is also clear from a promotional article he published in 1888
in the *North American Review*. While boasting about the initial scale of local applications for membership, he offers this evaluation: "As to the social standing of these members, they belong, with the exception of a few
clerks, absolutely to the working classes. They are not of the lowest class;
that has been thrown in our teeth; if they were they would not stay in so
orderly and civilized a place; but they are 'respectable.' . . . They are
mostly lads in steady work, and they have a trade; they belong to the
'better class' of labor." [20] Here again, we see the same concerns: to chart
a trajectory of collective self-improvement; to distinguish "respectable"
workers from the disorderly residuum; and to attempt to entirely bracket
the latter from consideration, only to see them return as the repressed
Other, "thrown in our teeth" by skeptical commentators. In *Outcast London,* Gareth Stedman Jones offers a useful summary of the new social
contract being envisaged here, and how far the labor movement was itself co-opted by the strategy of liberal reformists, who sought to rephrase
its demands within a context of moral reform and class interdependence:
"Even independent working-class institutions," he writes,

> which had once served to divide class from class, now fulfilled
> the elevated function of inculcating thrift, self-help, mobility
> of labour, and class harmony. Advanced liberals vied with each

other in heaping praise on the principles of co-operation, and the change of front was even more pronounced in the case of trade unions. . . . As in the case of Malthusianism, the idea of trade unionism as a conductor of class conflict was relegated to a more primitive stage of human development.

Arnold Toynbee, he notes, one of the inspirations behind the university settlement movement, went so far as to envisage this as an earlier "feudal" stage, now in the process of being superseded by "the citizen stage" in which class antagonism was replaced by "the gospel of duty."[21]

In this context, it is not surprising that Besant's "Notes of the Week" in the *Palace Journal* kept clear of controversial topics, especially concerning East End criminality and working-class radicalism. When his columns do address politics, they generally encourage forms of cooperation between capital and labor. On 24 July 1889, for example, Besant editorializes against "a so-called International Congress of 'Workers'" for designating themselves "citizens" in the manner of revolutionary France: the appellation threatens again to oppose a narrow sectional interest to populist constructions of "the people," so Besant offers a more inclusive definition of a citizen as "the inhabitant of a city." The same commentary supports demands for an abolition of night work and child labor, technical education, and equal pay for men and women, but opposes more controversial demands for a minimum wage and the eight-hour day. The reason for this is supplied two months later (18 Sept. 1889), in an editorial on the Dock Strike which speaks of an ideal partnership between the classes, under the formula "Capital, with a fair return: an interest taken out of the profits: labour, which will take all the rest." The column is strangely quiet about the success of the East End dock workers, hoping only "that the men were justified, and that the victory . . . was worth the struggle." This is certainly faint praise, especially considering that this had been a uniquely popular strike, building on the support which was generated a year earlier when East End match-girls had paraded through the city center to demand better working conditions. Besant's reluctance to join in the celebrations is perhaps testimony to the powerful specter of socialist agitation, which explicitly rejected moral distinctions among the working class and thereby threatened to undermine the paternalistic fantasies according to which projects like the People's Palace were governed.

A more overt antagonism was displayed in the events of 1886–87, leading up to the repressive action of "Bloody Sunday," when a demonstration demanding "not charity, but work" was forcibly prevented from entering Trafalgar Square by mounted police. In February 1886, a mass rally of the unemployed in Trafalgar Square had been taken over by the Social Democratic Federation (S.D.F.), which sought to lead marchers into Hyde Park. En route, the crowds passed through fashionable Pall Mall and Piccadilly, and threw stones at the windows of West End clubs. The demonstration quickly degenerated into a riot of destruction and looting, in which carriages were overturned and their passengers robbed of money and jewelry. The targets of these actions seem to have been well-chosen, as representing the most noticeable signs of West End privilege, and mass hysteria settled over the capital in the following days as rumors circulated of tens of thousands preparing to march from South and East London. Encouraged by these rumors, a crowd of 2,000 unemployed laborers assembled south of the river to meet the marchers, while a similar number later gathered for a socialist meeting in North London, and were dispersed only after running battles with the police. These events raised the possibility of an alliance between the artisans of the Left, who traditionally constituted the aristocracy of the London working class as well as its radicalized vanguard, and the unemployed workers who were considered its lowest "residuum."

A measure of the impact of these events can be seen in the immediate evaporation of donations to the Palace fund. The connection was noted by the conservative London *Standard,* which wrote of the project that "[w]e have heard so much within the past few days of Socialism in its destructive form that it is pleasant to come across a Socialistic idea whose immediate purpose is not destruction but construction" (19 Feb. 1886), and also by the more liberal *Daily News,* which reported on 2 June 1886 about the problems of generating support in an atmosphere of suspicion and class antagonism. According to a representative of the Beaumont Trust, fundraising had been going well until the West End riots, after which contributions "fell abruptly, 'and . . . we have never touched three figures since.' Of course," the paper commented, "if all the possible subscribers to a fund of this sort were philosophers, and took a philosophical view of the subject, they would see in an outbreak of turbulent violence not a reason for withholding subscriptions from a great scheme for humanising and elevating the masses, but an excellent reason for pushing it on with all speed." These accounts suggest that the People's Palace was intended to act as a sort of pressure valve, which could contain working-class resentment and redirect its energies in a more "constructive" manner. This was argued in its most cynical form by Shaw in a letter to the *Star* during the Ripper murders of 1888, which I alluded to in chapter 4. Any recent change in West End attitudes, he suggested, was solely attributable to the Ripper, who "by simply murdering and disembowelling four women, converted the proprietary press to an inept sort of communism." Referring back to the spectacle of "Bloody Sunday," he wrote that "[l]ess than a year ago the West-End press, headed by the *St. James's Gazette, The Times,* and the *Saturday Review,* were literally clamoring for the blood of the people . . . behaving, in short, as the proprietary class always does behave when the workers throw it into a frenzy of terror by venturing to show their teeth." Shaw's claim was that only direct threats of violence—and not orderly protests or educational campaigns—galvanized the consciences of the bourgeoisie: "The riots of 1886," he noted in passing, "brought in £78,000 and a People's Palace: it remains to be seen how much [the Ripper] murders may prove to be worth to the East-end in *panem et circenses.*"[22]

As we have seen, Shaw's analysis of the relationship between the Palace and the riots was misjudged, but it is nearer the mark in ascribing the general motivation for such philanthropic concerns to a sublimated fear of class conflict, which manifested itself in grandiose schemes for the cultural containment of the poor. The connection is made more forcefully by Margaret Harkness, in her 1888 novel *Out of Work* (first published under the pseudonym of "John Law"). Originally trained as a nurse, Harkness devoted a great deal of the 1880s to publicizing East End life, while veering between the twin influences of Salvation Army evangelism and the socialism of the S.D.F. Although friendly with a network of "New Woman" activists and Octavia Hill volunteers (including Beatrice Potter Webb, Olive Schreiner, and Eleanor Marx), her first novel, *A City Girl* (1887) had dramatized the seduction of a young Whitechapel woman by a middle-class slummer, and *Out of Work* similarly voices a discomfort with philanthropic benevolence.[23] When the protagonist Jos Conley is introduced, for instance, the narrative lingers over his cropped hair, before commenting that "One does not see this sort of hair dressing in the fashionable parts of London, but it is not unbecoming; so no doubt one of the gentlemen at aesthetic Toynbee Hall, or ascetic Oxford House, will adopt it, and set the fashion in the West End."[24] Later, Jos passes "a Toynbeeite" in the streets, who "hurried past him with a bran-new scheme for raising the masses bulging from the pocket of a short black jacket," but the master-plan does nothing to arrest Jos's slide into poverty and alcoholic despair (230).

Many of Harkness's recurring themes—about upper-class callousness, the hypocrisies of fashionable slumming, and the culpability of the media for the widening gap between the classes—can be seen in *Out of Work*'s fictional account of the Palace opening. In the language first of the popular press, we read that "Whitechapel was gay with flags. Mile End had coloured banners, and festoons of red, yellow, green and blue paper flowers 'all along the line.'" Immediately, though, the perspective shifts to reveal the political interests that underwrite just such accounts, noting how

> [r]eporters were busy at work concocting stories of the royal progress through the East End for the Monday papers; artists were preparing for the illustrated weekly papers pictures of Whitechapel as it may possibly look in the Millenium. No one would speak about the hisses which the denizens of the slums had mingled with faint applause as Her Majesty neared her destination; no one would hint that the crowd about the Palace of Delight had had a sullen, ugly look which may a year or so hence prove dangerous. (1–2)

For Harkness, this media blindness reinforced and enabled larger patterns of upper-class ignorance about the real conditions of the East End. Indeed, its reporting of events like the Palace opening provided a cover under which such ignorance was able to continue unchecked, and thus provided the impetus for yet another "discovery" of slum life. In a remarkable indictment that echoes the cynical attitudes of some local residents, the narrative concludes as follows:

> The ladies on their way back to the Queen's Hall, who had leant languidly in their carriages, heedless of ragged men, hungry women, and little dirty children, the *blasé* frequenters of Hyde Park and the clubs, who had glanced carelessly at the people as they accompanied their wives and daughters to the People's Palace, would be quoted by reporters as philanthropic

persons intent on ministering to the poor by the unction of their presence, and represented by the artists as so many unselfish ladies and gentlemen, who had given up an afternoon's pleasure-hunting to gratify the eyes of under-paid men and over-worked women by their shining hats and charming bonnets. (2)

As a professional journalist and author, Harkness seems especially interested in the role of the press and mass media, as an amplifying mechanism which represents public events, helps to shape popular perceptions, and thereby influences the long-term judgments of history. Her description of the Palace opening focuses less on the events themselves than on how they are manipulated in order to secure a favorable press coverage: the "hisses" and sullen looks of the Whitechapel locals are bound to go unreported, as media attention is drawn instead to a more comforting picture of West End sacrifice, in which colored flags and flowers momentarily blot out the intense squalor of the region.[25]

Later in the novel, a labor agitator argues a radical response on Mile End Waste in which he suggests that "the Queen's nothing but a selfish old woman, what doesn't care if we all starve," but finds a hostile audience among Whitechapel locals, who only seem grateful for good weather and a public holiday (55). In such a context, what is at stake in Harkness's presentation of the 1887 riots is how they should be interpreted, first by the various social classes of the time and secondarily by future generations. At its most hopeful, the novel speculates that

> [y]ears hence, when children read in lesson-books about the Age of Competition, the docks will be given as an illustration of the competitive system after it reached a climax. Boys and girls will read that thousands of Englishmen fought daily at the dock gates for tickets; that starving men behind pressed so hard on starving men in front, that the latter were nearly cut in two by the iron railings which kept them from work; that contractors were mauled by hungry men; that brick-bats were hurled at labour-masters by men whose families were starving. (162)

But this optimism—predicting how the 1888 dock strike would be received—is countered by events in the novel, and especially the riots themselves. Harkness presents "Bloody Sunday" as a clear case of police provocation and brutality, but is acutely aware that the public record will say otherwise: Jos Conley is thrown against a policeman when the soldiers charge the Square, but is arrested and sentenced to four days in prison for assault, despite eye-witness testimony in his favor. In such a context, the ability to control how history is perceived lies entirely on the side of capital, which is consistently able to represent peaceful protest as incendiary rebellion, and unemployed workers as criminal agitators. When the unemployed first begin camping out in Trafalgar Square in the lead-up to the riots of "Bloody Sunday," for instance, a couple arrive in a carriage to observe them. The man is convinced that "[t]here must be some scum in a large place like London" and remains untouched by the spectacle, while his female companion is clearly troubled:

> "I wish I had courage to give up all this luxury and laziness; I am so wrapt in wealth that nothing real ever seems to come near me. Yet I know that thousands of people are starving, men and women I could help if I cut myself off from fashion and prejudice. You need not laugh," she continued, seeing a smile playing upon the face of her companion. "I am in earnest. Shall I always bury my conscience?"

The question hangs unanswered, dismissed by her companion as "absurd nonsense" gleaned from socialist books, and liable to "bring disgrace upon us" (176–77). The woman is clearly in a class above Harkness, but both the crisis of conscience which she faces and the misogyny with which she is greeted presumably are drawn from the novelist's own experience. Even less promising is the perspective of those who look down from the windows of West End clubs overlooking Trafalgar Square, asking "Was it true that the agitators were 'ungry,' or was it false? Did the genuine unemployed come to these daily demonstrations, or were the demonstrators loafers who would not work, vagrants who wanted to play on the sympathies of the public, scum that must be allowed to die like dogs in the streets by order of Political Economists?" (197). Given the mediating role of the press, it seems entirely likely that these observers will come to the latter conclusion, and share in the judgment which the law courts pass on Jos.

An alternative model of social interaction is shown when a laborer comes to visit those occupying Trafalgar Square, to find out for himself: "I've come down 'ere," he announces, on account of all I've read in the papers. Now I don't pay much attention to 'em, for I know they're written by folks as never 'ad a wife ill from want of food, and children starving. If I stood 'ere and told you 'ow folks live up in Jupiter, you'd say "None of your rubbish." It's just so with the folks as write in the papers, the chaps in Parliament, and the upper classes. They don't know what they're talking about. . . . One chap tells us 'ow 'e set three men to work for 'im, and 'ow they went off to a public-'ouse. Another chap says he sent a shoulder of mutton to a family what said they were starving, and they asked for onion sauce to give it a relish. Says I to myself, "None of your rubbish." Now becos the papers tell lies like this, I've come down 'ere, mates, in my dinner hour, to show 'em I'm a legitimate British labourer, like thousands of men who're now tramping the streets with empty pockets. (192)

The passage ends with a gesture of solidarity, but Harkness's point is more about the necessity for direct corroboration, as a way of challenging how the poor are represented in the newspapers and history books. Where Toynbee Hall and the People's Palace preached immediate—and often condescending—forms of ameliorative action, Harkness argues instead for a sympathetic observation and understanding which is bounded by specified limits. When Jos is in jail she notes that the scene "needs a Zola to do justice to it," and this seems to be the role she has set herself, as a publicist who is prepared to amplify the demands of the poor but is uncomfortable acting or speaking for them. What is ultimately both fascinating and discomforting about Harkness's work, though, is its intense focus on the dilemma of being a bourgeois socialist, caught up in inter-class networks of guilt and suspicion. An enormous range of obstacles are placed in the way of middle-class social activism, ranging from the disapprobation and mockery of the privileged classes to perceptions of Toynbee Hall faddism and self-importance. Given these barriers of mutual mistrust, *Out of Work* is understandably pessimistic about the possibilities of cross-class alliance, and dwells instead on the limits of sympathetic identification.

Recognizing the dangers of journalistic ventriloquism, which we encountered in chapter 4 in the examples of Greenwood, Masterman, and

Jack London, Harkness is prepared to take a more passive role, even at the risk that her working-class characters remain opaque. Jos Conley and his partner (nicknamed "the Squirrel") are convincingly—yet also frustratingly—inarticulate participants in important historical events in the nation, lacking the typological status which might earn them praise from Hegelian-Lukácsian schools of literary criticism. The difficulty becomes all too clear when Harkness finally decides to invest their respective deaths with religious significance, in scenes which recall the sentimentalized departure of "poor Jo" in *Bleak House*. Following a brief and entirely externalized description of her life, the Squirrel decides to drown herself, after first thinking she hears a voice from the Thames calling out "all things the same, only in different shapes. Nothing immutable, everything changing place. To put off this mortal coil means cessation of consciousness," and an implausibly pathetic rendering of "My God! My God! Why hast Thou forsaken me?" (267–68). Similarly, Jos's death is accompanied by a poignant cry to the heavens, which reminds us of how Harkness's socialist beliefs continued to coexist uneasily with a Salvation Army evangelism.

*A City Girl* is no more successful, as the generic quality indicated by the title is consistently contradicted by evidence of Nelly Ambrose's exceptional qualities: nicknamed "the masher" because (according to local Whitechapel wisdom) "'er mother was a lady's maid. . . . That's why she fancies 'erself," Nelly dreams of "[a] life of complete idleness, with plenty of smart clothes, and good things to eat."[26] The predictable elements of a sentimental romance are here, as she rejects the devoted caretaker George for the advances of the middle-class—and married—Arthur Grant of Kensington; just as predictable is the tragedy of her pregnancy, followed by the death of the infant child, although an unlikely happy ending is achieved when Grant happens to meet her carrying the dead child, and feels guilty enough to pay for its burial and her climactic marriage to George. Grant's transformation occurs through the influence of a Salvation Army captain, but he is not converted to Christianity, and the role of the evangelists remains strangely muted. While they take in the pregnant and destitute Nelly, Harkness is enough of a realist to admit that their larger message is rejected by the targeted population: Captain Lode acknowledges that they often need police protection, and two unnamed locals respond to his farewell address by "[thinking] the whole thing a

, and [making] inquiries about the state of one another's souls between the verses." [27]

I do not mean to belittle Harkness's efforts here, but rather to underscore a constitutive tension in turn-of-the-century depictions of the
East End poor, which veered from Besant's patronizing romanticism to
harsher forms of naturalism in which working-class consciousness was
abandoned in favor of a strictly externalized rendering of action. In a
sense, her novels combine the best and worst of both schools: from
the former, Harkness draws the ability to place her characters in a larger
historical framework, and to use them to comment on contemporary
events, but also the sentimentalism which comes from over-investing
meaning in inarticulate figures; while she also shares the naturalists' suspicion of such benevolent gestures, their insistence on revealing the un-
romantic aspects of East End life (like hunger, domestic violence, and al-
coholism), and—in *Out of Work,* at least—their necessarily pessimistic
conclusions.

### Into Darkest London (and Out Again)

This harsher form of naturalist writing develops out of a very different
tradition of journalistic reportage, which starkly contrasts with the opti-
mism of Besant's future-centered romance. Besides the exposés of East
End life already alluded to, the major influence on Arthur Morrison and
others was probably the massive sociological survey begun by Charles
Booth in 1889. Originally undertaken in order to contest the claim by
H. M. Hyndman of the S.D.F. that a quarter of Londoners lived under
conditions of extreme poverty, Booth's seventeen volumes on *Life and
Labour of the People of London* (beginning, quite predictably, with *East
London*) more than confirmed Hyndman's assessment. Breaking the population down into socioeconomic categories, Booth's statistics suggested
that close to half of London's workers lived above the poverty line (nom-
inated as category E), while a quarter were more accurately described as
irregular wage-earners (categories C and D); beneath them, smaller classifications denoted those incapable of work, or living a hand-to-mouth
existence as casual laborers (B, constituting 7.5% of the total, but 11%
of East Londoners), and an even smaller hard core of the vicious and
semi-criminal (A, 1.2%), so that the total living below the poverty line
(i.e., A through D) amounted to closer to 35%. Booth's categories are

notoriously slippery, even when represented visually on shaded maps of
the city, but they did help give weight to the claims of the S.D.F. and
to draw attention to the extreme distress of areas like Whitechapel and
Bethnal Green, where those below the poverty line climbed up to half
of the population. On the other hand, the relatively small concentrations
of people in the lowest categories also helped to substantiate theories of
a criminal residuum, and enabled a more sharply moralistic interpretation to gain force: thus, instead of the poverty line, a more common
marker was placed between B and C, to denote where the underclass
ended and the respectable working class began.

In order to safeguard the latter from contaminating influences, Booth
and others proposed moving the residuum out of London, and resettling
them in labor colonies, where they might be supplied with the necessi-
ties of life but kept separate from the general population. Different versions of this scheme were supported by Samuel Barnett of Toynbee Hall,
the *Pall Mall Gazette,* the Salvation Army, and eventually by novelists like
Morrison and Harkness (after her break with the S.D.F.). In a modified
form, it served as the foundation for what Gareth Stedman Jones terms
"social-imperialist" solutions, which operated according to rigorously
xenophobic and eugenic theories of degeneration. Since London stood
at the center of the empire as well as the nation, it attracted supposedly-
inferior surplus populations who would increasingly overwhelm the
respectable working class and undermine its productive capabilities;
correspondingly, however, the casual labor force of the capital (which
often originated from rural areas of Britain) might be encouraged—or
coerced—into emigrating to the colonies, where those unwanted at
home could presumably still be counted on to hold sway over the natives. This seems if anything to be an exaggeration of the health of the
London poor. As John L. Kijinski notes, army recruitment was a continuing problem during the Boer War, when "an alarming number of
working-class recruits were found to be unfit for service," leading to the
formation of an Interdepartmental Committee on Physical Deteriora-
tion in 1904.[28]

At their most integrated, then, these schemes aimed to solve a range
of problems at once: that proposed by General William Booth of the Salvation Army, for example, involved resettling the residuum of the capital ("the submerged tenth") first in city colonies, where they would be

given moral instruction, then in farm colonies, where this would be supplemented by agricultural training, and then finally in the overseas colonies. General Booth's *In Darkest England and the Way Out* (1890) specifically set itself against the strain of political economy which decried charitable philanthropy, and called for public donations to set the scheme in motion. As Victor Bailey has detailed, the book sold very well (115,000 copies in the first few months), and the money was soon raised, but there were serious problems when it came to be implemented: the farms lost substantial sums of money, while the city colonies also ran into trouble as a result of charges that they were undercutting union wages in other trades, an accusation that Bailey contends to have been false. As a result, the project received mixed reactions from the labor movement, finding some support among Liberals and Fabian socialists (most notably Beatrice Webb) but a hostile reception from Hyndman, the S.D.F., and William Morris, who argued in *Commonweal* that it constituted a "Workhouse Socialism . . . which casts about for devices at once to get [the workers] better rations and to lower the cost of keeping them to the capitalists."[29]

The planned colonial settlements entirely failed to find administrative support, even though they helped to shape the dominant rhetorical framework within which the East End poor were cast by literary naturalists and Christian philanthropists. The most obvious reference point for describing this rhetoric is Edward Said's influential discussion of Orientalism, a mode of discourse in which the ostensible subject of the East comes to define in negative the preferred self-image of Western colonial powers. In such a framework, it hardly matters whether an "accurate" picture of the Orient is produced, since an overriding concern is that it act as an imaginative counter-image to the West, so that "European culture gained in strength and identity by setting itself off against the Orient as a sort of surrogate and even underground self."[30] There is, for example, something strikingly consistent in the ways that descriptions of colonial dependents and of the East End poor hesitate over the question of whether "the natives" can be attributed full subjectivity. In the case of colonial dependents, Terry Eagleton has pointed to a central paradox in imperial discourse, which vacillates between seeing "them" as essentially the same as "us" (sharing in a fundamental and common humanity) or as ontologically Other (and thus irredeemable). His account encapsulates much of the ambivalence that I am highlighting in this chapter, although its constitutive tension between sameness and difference runs all the way back to the early chapters on romantic attitudes toward the city and its inhabitants:

> Genuine savages could not be governed, since they would lack all concept of authority and subjugation. The fact that you can conquer another society suggests that you shouldn't, since for this to be possible the natives must be sufficiently like us to render it morally dubious. If, on the other hand, they are incapable of our own level of civility, you can use this fact to justify exploiting them, but will be forced to give up trying to rationalise that exploitation as part of a civilising process.[31]

I am hesitant to apply the concept of Orientalism in relation to the East End because that would seem to exemplify precisely the move that Said and others have underlined. By shifting from an international to a domestic sense of difference—and indeed, to the internal differentiation between parts of a single city—it would appear that the East itself recedes even further from view, functioning in effect as a rhetorical trope at two stages removed.

Proposed programs like General Booth's farm colonies do, however, make clear that there is more than a simple etymological connection between the colonies of the Far East and the population of London's East End. Said's focus is on Orientalism as a discourse of Enlightenment which developed its own "supporting institutions, vocabulary, scholarship, imagery, doctrines," and methods of bureaucratic management from the late eighteenth century through the twentieth—during the same period, in other words, when the "problem" of the East End was consistently being posed, publicized, confronted, and evaded. It is perhaps with Mayhew that we can begin to see a more direct connection with the institutional discourses of Orientalism, as articulated through the language and ideology of the social sciences. As Deborah Epstein Nord has argued, what separates Mayhew from his predecessors is his—admittedly clumsy—attempt to develop an ethnography of contemporary urban life.[32] It is a project which General Booth implicitly followed by invoking the metaphor of "darkest England," as an echo of Stanley's discovery of the "dark continent" of Africa: "The lot of the Negress in the Equatorial Forest is not, perhaps, a very happy one," Booth argued, "but is it so very much worse than that of many a pretty orphan girl in our Christian capital?"[33] Similarly, John Kijinski has encapsulated the assumptions of colonial ethnographers in terms which immediately suggest a parallel at home: "What marked a people as degraded," he writes, "was the acceptance of 'criminal' or deviant behavior as normal. Ethnographers such as Tylor and Lubbock argued the fact that what is seen as aberrant or criminal behavior in civilized nations is promoted as the norm in 'savage' societies offers convincing evidence for the existence of *moral*— as well as material—evolution among European peoples."[34]

Within such a Darwinian model of progress, it made perfect sense to treat the East End like a backwater of empire, and to work through the same ameliorative strategies that had proven successful abroad: settlement by Christian evangelists, the attempted cultivation of aesthetic appreciation, limited technological instruction, and so on, all of which would ultimately be underwritten by the threat of violence or supplanted by harsher schemes of enforced emigration. In a sense, then, what underlies Booth's plan is the assumption that East Enders would *fail* the test of citizenship and remain alien in much the same way that colonial subjects did. Speaking as the voice of Victorian science, and echoing sentiments voiced earlier in the century by Mayhew, Dickens, and others, T. H. Huxley remarked that the Polynesian savage "in his most primitive condition" was "not half so savage, so unclean, so *irreclaimable* as the tenant of a tenement in an East London slum."[35] It is this sense of "irreclaimability" which characterizes the work of 1890s naturalism. Rejecting the utopian romanticism of Walter Besant or the political ambivalence of Margaret Harkness, a writer like Arthur Morrison set out to establish the unreformable, unimprovable life of the underclass at the center of his work. Ironically, one of his major literary influences was Rudyard Kipling, whose stories of army life did much to restore public confidence in the colonial forces. After the success of *Soldiers Three* (1888), and especially the Cockney figure of Private Tommy Atkins, Kipling returned to England in 1890 thinking about what London soldiers in particular might be coming home to.

Continuing the experiments with dialect begun with his tales of barracks life, he published "The Ballad of Badalia Herodsfoot," about a coster girl who volunteers to keep accounts for a local clergyman-philanthropist, the Reverend Eustace Hanna. One day, though, her husband Tom—who has abandoned her at the opening of the story—decides to move back, after having been thrown out by his mistress, Jenny: "He would return to Badalia his wife. Probably she would have been doing something wrong while he was away, and he could then vindicate his authority as a husband. Certainly she would have money. Single women always seemed to possess the pence that God and the government denied to hard-working men."[36] The language of interior monologue here stands in marked—and uneasy—contrast with Kipling's uses of reported speech: "'Oo's she took up while I bin gone?" for example, or "I don't want none o' your kissin's and slaverin's. I'm sick of 'em" (Tom's first words to Badalia on his return). The net effect, as Raymond Williams has noted, is that "the 'commentary' is now completely incorporated; it is part of a whole way of seeing, at a 'sociological' distance. The confident, winning ways of these late Victorian and Edwardian storytellers depend . . . on that descriptive, representative, carefully-observed naturalism, from which the problems of consciousness and the problems of explicit and controversial ideas have been set aside."[37] In this sense, the characters fulfill a precise expectation, acting out their lives in a mechanical sequence: Tom demands money for beer, Badalia expresses a defiance rooted in her loyalty to (and barely suppressed love for) the Reverend Hanna, Tom beats and kicks her to death, then takes up with Jenny again. Before her death, Badalia makes a halting speech to exonerate Tom, blaming

> "Man from outside. Never seed 'im no more'n Adam. Drunk, I s'pose. S'elp me Gawd that's truth! . . . Allus 'avin' kids, these people. I 'adn't oughter talk, for *my* 'usband 'e never come a-nigh me these two years, or I'd a-bin as bad as the rest . . . The book's in the drawer, Mister 'Anna, an' it's all right an' I never guv up a copper o' the trust money—not a copper. You look under the chist o' drawers—all wot isn't spent this week is there . . ." and so on. (27; emphasis in original)

Arthur Morrison had begun developing a similar style of dialect speech while employed as subeditor on the *Palace Journal*. One entry from the "Notes of the Week" column (written while substituting for Besant) opens as follows: "'DROP of beer. Said something to other fellow. Got together. Knocked him down. Drunk, I s'pose, same as I was.'" Considering these paratactic phrases, uttered by a laborer at Marlborough Street Police Court, Morrison comments how "[o]ne hesitates whether or not to award these sentences higher distinction on account of their straightforward ingenuousness than on account of their admirable brevity and force. Could anything be put with more clearness and truth?"[38] It is this emphasis on dialect and realism as a *style* which most separates Morrison from Kipling, whom he otherwise seems to have followed very closely.[39] In a passage like this, he seems relatively untroubled by the privileged editorial position and the implied commentary that this involves. There are fascinating issues concerning the precise cultural position from which Morrison is writing here, which I will address in a moment. First, though, I want to note how the naturalist style develops in Morrison alongside a close critical attention to the cultural practices and attitudes which others adopted in their attempts to understand the East End, including presumably those which underwrote the People's Palace project. In the first of three sketches published in the *Palace Journal* under the heading of "Cockney Corners," he noted two prevalent and intersecting approaches to Whitechapel: first, as a "horrible black labyrinth . . . its every wall, its every object, slimy with the indigenous ooze of the place; swarming with human vermin whose trade is robbery, and whose recreation is murder"; or alternatively, "in a pitiful aspect. Outcast London. Black and nasty still, a wilderness of crazy dens into which pallid wastrels crawl to die; where several families lie in each fetid room, and fathers, mothers, and children watch each other starve." Residents are pathologized by the first approach, and condescended to by the second. But Morrison's point is not Besant's, that such scenes should not be reported and may not actually occur. Rather, it is that they are unrepresentative of Whitechapel as a whole. Such distinctions cannot be made by do-gooders and casual slummers, however, whose clichéd assumptions are mocked later in this essay:

> Nowadays, we fear we must reluctantly confess the most enthusiastic slummer could scarcely achieve the memorable and once proverbial feat of entering Petticoat Lane with his pocket

handkerchief safely in its appointed place, and half-way through, observing it gracefully fluttering from the door-post of a clothes shop, with its marking neatly picked out, because, even if, with patience and perseverance, he succeeded in getting it stolen, there isn't a shop where handkerchiefs of any kind hang at the door in Petticoat Lane.

This is no cause for blind optimism either, for the essay ends by identifying "a numerous and equally hopeless race" in the worse parts of Whitechapel, where "the inmates may ruin the character of a house, but no house can alter the character of its inmates."[40] But what is key for Morrison is the local and historical knowledge that enables the observer to make these distinctions.

Morrison's own sense of authority was based on a carefully produced autobiography, which meant that he could present himself as an external observer of East End life while also criticizing "outsiders" for their own distance from local problems. An indication of this delicate balance can be seen in the defensive statements he produced to counter negative criticisms of A Child of the Jago, especially from H. D. Traill who had accused him of a sham realism and an exaggeration of the violence and squalor of slum life.[41] Arguing that such critics produced evaluative criteria themselves, "inspired by the completest ignorance of the life of which I have written," Morrison claimed a familiarity with his subjects: "For a good few years I have lived in the East End of London, and have been, not an occasional visitor, but a familiar and equal friend in the house of the East-Ender in all his degrees." But this is offset in the same essay by a countervailing emphasis on his own authorial distance, which meant that he approached "the Jago" itself (a small square modeled on the Old Nichol area of Shoreditch) as an outsider: "It was my fate," he wrote, "to encounter a place in Shoreditch, where children were born and reared in circumstances that gave those children no reasonable chance of living decent lives: where they were born fore-damned to a criminal or semi-criminal career. It was my experience to learn the ways of this place, to know its inhabitants, to talk with them, eat, drink, and work with them."[42] As I shall suggest, these two lines of argument are not contradictory, but need to be seen as more situational and strategic in their assessment of Morrison's own audience; together, they suggest an image of the author as what contemporary sociology would term a "participant observer," who straddles but also thereby draws attention to the conventional boundaries separating a study's subjects from external (and supposedly "objective") researchers.

Some of the same ambivalence is evident in Morrison's own autobiographical statements, which were only challenged by Peter Keating's meticulous research as recently as the 1960s. Morrison had claimed to have been born in Kent and educated at private schools, and to be the son of a "professional man," while his position with the People's Palace was originally glossed as a "civil servant" or "secretary of an old Charity Trust." In reality, Keating revealed, he was the son of an engine fitter from Poplar, although it is likely that the family soon moved away.[43] A couple of points could be made here. First, that there is a perversity about Morrison's concealment here, especially in relation to his employment at the Palace, where the cultural authority which accompanies a sense of local knowledge would have been an obvious benefit—recall Besant's self-critical lament that "not a soul, when I was connected with the Palace, showed the least literary ability or ambition." In effect, Morrison was *posing* as a slummer during this period, and Keating has noted the double irony that "while he was the only person to respond to Besant's advice" concerning the development of an autonomous cultural practice, "no one seems to have been aware of his East End working-class background."[44] My second point is that this background would place Morrison squarely within the "respectable" working class targeted by the Palace rather than the "residuum" which he wrote about, so that it is not entirely accurate to characterize his fiction as motivated by shame and self-loathing, as Pamela Fox has recently suggested.[45]

The distinction is worth holding onto precisely because Morrison's work is *about* making distinctions, and under what circumstances they hold or collapse. *A Child of the Jago* cannot be read simply as a disguised autobiography because its central figure, Dicky Perrott, belongs to a family who have already slipped into the underclass. His father Josh had been trained as plasterer, and "[i]n moments of pride he declared himself the only member of his family who had ever learned a trade, and worked at it. It was a long relinquished habit, but while it lasted he had married a decent boilermaker's daughter, who had known nothing of the Jago in those days" (58). That familiarity marks a decisive shift in the family's sense of identity, however. Josh has already shifted to "cosh-carrying"—a form of mugging described as "the major industry of the Jago"—when the book opens, and this clearly outweighs Hannah Perrott's desires for respectability: among the strikes against her, the novel lists the fact that "she was never drunk, she never quarrelled, she did not gossip freely"; that "her husband beat her but rarely, and then not with a chair nor a poker"; and that she had been married in church (66–67). If the novel can be imagined as a contest for the future of Dicky, then Hannah's residual values are clearly losing the battle, at least initially: "you must alwis be respectable and straight," she tells him, but Dicky's idols are the gentlemen-criminals of the High Mob, and he shares in the Jago's judgment of a new family, the Ropers, that "they're mighty per-tickler. Fancy themselves too good for their neighbours" (50–51).

The Ropers manage to succeed where Hannah Perrott failed. First, they excite the hatred of the entire area, briefly uniting the warring factions of Ranns and Learys, by complaining that they have been robbed, thus breaking the sole Jago commandment that "Thou shalt not nark!":

> For nothing was so dangerous in the Jago as to impugn its honesty. To rob another was reasonable and legitimate, and to avoid being robbed, as far as might be, was natural and proper. But to accuse anybody of theft was unsportsmanlike, a foul outrage, a shameful abuse, a thing unpardonable. You might rob a man, bash a man, even kill a man; but to "take away his character"—even when he had none—was to draw the execrations of the whole Jago. (93)

More importantly, the Ropers eventually manage to escape the area entirely, under the protection of the mysterious Father Sturt, who had earlier defended them by declaring to an assembled mob that "[t]his is a sort of thing I will *not* tolerate in my parish" (82; emphasis in original). Father Sturt is one of the more opaque characters in the novel, around whom much of its political ambivalence centers. Modeled after Morrison's friend and guide through the real-life Jago of the Old Nichol, the Reverend Arthur Osborne Jay (to whom *Jago* is dedicated), Father Sturt seems in many ways to be a positive representation of the settlement movement. Whereas his predecessor confined his attentions to a "less savage district" of the parish, Sturt practices a hands-on ministry, builds a church in the area, and even gets Josh Perrott inside it on one occasion. He later encourages dreams of respectability in Dicky, speaking "in the approving voice that a Jago would do almost anything—except turn honest—to hear" (128). The parenthesis is interesting here: it is not clear if it should simply be read as a joke or as a serious statement that is designed to undercut Father Sturt's authority. Dicky succumbs to its call nonetheless, when given a chance to work as a shop boy, and he daydreams of himself as "a tradesman, with a shop of his own and the name 'R. Perrott,' with a gold flourish, over the door. He would employ a boy himself then; and there would be a parlour, with stuff-bottomed chairs and a shade of flowers, and [sister] Em grown up and playing on the piano. Truly Father Sturt was right: the hooks were fools, and the straight game was the better" (131). But this most conventional of petit bourgeois dreams comes to nothing when Dicky is wrongly accused of theft, as if confirming a sentence of "guilty unless proven innocent" which has retroactively been passed on all Jago residents: "he was of the Jago," Dicky concluded, "and he must prey on the outer world, as all the Jago did; not stray foolishly off the regular track in chase of visions, and fall headlong. Father Sturt was a creature of another mould. Who was he, Dicky Perrott, that he should break away from the Jago habit, and strain after another nature? What could come of it but defeat and bitterness?" (140).

If we make an exception for the Roper family, and two long-time residents that Father Sturt marries (but in secret), it is difficult to argue with this assessment. Dicky falls back into petty crime, sees his father imprisoned and finally hung for murder, ands comes to a predictable end himself. Stabbed in the course of a local feud, having inexplicably shouted encouragement for the Jago to "hold tight! . . . Come on, Father Sturt's boys," Dicky's dying words are to "Tell Mist' Beveridge there's 'nother way out—better," but his meaning is obscure (202–3). These last words refer back to an earlier conversation with Beveridge (a kind of local philosopher) who had told Dicky to look up to the High Mob as role models: "There it is—that's your aim in life—there's your pattern. Learn to read and write, learn all you can, learn cunning, spare nobody and stop at nothing, and perhaps— . . . It's the best the world has for you, for the Jago's got you, and that's the only way out, except gaol and the gallows" (95). This is presumably not Dicky's "better" way, but the novel leaves unclear what that might be (besides death) or how it is connected to the exertions of Father Sturt. This is because its more hopeful prospects are repeatedly countered by a pessimistic defeatism, voiced by Dicky just before his death as he thinks that "[i]t would be a comfortable thing for himself if he could die quietly then and there" (201); it is expressed more generally by the narrator, who notes that "albeit the Jago death-rate ruled full four times that of all London beyond, still the Jago rats bred and bred their kind unhindered, multiplying apace and infecting the world" (113). This is the language of the residuum and social Darwinism, echoing (as many commentators have argued) the rhetoric of colonial relations.[46] It is surprising, however, that its clearest articulation is offered by Father Sturt, in a diagnosis which Morrison presumably endorsed. In a notorious passage, a doctor calls to help deliver a new brother for Dicky, and wonders out loud whether the child would not be better off dead. In a moment of candor, Father Sturt agrees with him, merely wondering "who'll listen if you shout it from the housetops? I might try to proclaim it myself, if I had time and energy to waste. But I have none—I must work, and so must you. The burden grows day by day, as you say. The thing's hopeless, perhaps, but that is not for me to discuss. I have my duty" (171).

The inference, of course, is that his "duty" has taken him in other directions, and perhaps to futile efforts at reform and local management. In reality, however, his intervention into the Jago largely takes the form of a slum clearance scheme, the only difference being that it is supported by local knowledge and a face-to-face ministry. The new church is built, for example, over the demolished houses of Jago Court. Residents respond to the news with a resigned fatalism: having heard that the condemned houses will be offered at reduced rents, they all try to move in, and the lucky ones spend their savings on drink. Finally evicted, they demand alternative lodgings from Father Sturt (with some justification, considering the role he has played), then set about developing a new Jago in adjacent areas, as if to thwart the dreams of extermination which had grounded Sturt's plans all along. Later, after the County Council has begun redevelopment of the original streets, we learn that

> [t]he dispossessed Jagos had gone to infect the neighbourhoods across the border, and to crowd the people a little closer. They

did not return to live in the new barracks-buildings; which was a strange thing, for the County Council was charging very little more than double the rents which the landlords of the old Jago had charged. And so another Jago, teeming and villainous as the one displaced, was slowly growing, in the form of a ring, round the great yellow houses. (179)

As we have seen, this was the predictable result of slum clearances dating back to the demolition of St. Giles for New Oxford Street during the 1840s. The only surprise is that Morrison seems to want to offer credit to Father Sturt for actions which he would have condemned if they had been initiated by the Council, whose rackrenting practices are noted in the passage above, or by a philanthropic agency like the Peabody Trust.

Elsewhere, as I have shown, Morrison was precise in his criticisms of such agencies, based in part on his unhappy experience with the People's Palace, which he—even more than Besant—felt was misguided in its orientation toward a middle-class clientele.[47] In an early chapter of *A Child of the Jago,* for example, he satirizes "the East End Elevation Mission and Pansophical Institute" in a scene which presumably recalls his days at the Palace. In a late echo of Dickens's critique of telescopic philanthropy, we are told that it is appreciated most by those who knew less of East London than Asia Minor, and who therefore fail to recognize that its patrons consist primarily of "tradesmen's sons, small shopkeepers and their families, and neat clerks," those "respectable" workers for whom Besant had held out such hope. In a speech which accurately mimics the optimistic pronouncements of Victorian philanthropists, the bishop opens a new wing by blindly declaring himself pleased

> to find himself in the midst of so admirably typical an assem-blage—so representative, if he might say so, of that great East End of London, thirsting and crying out for—for Elevation: for that—ah—Elevation which the fortunately circumstanced denizens of—of other places, had so munificently—laid on. The people of the East End had been so badly misrepresented— in popular periodicals and in—in other ways. The East End, he was convinced, was not so black as it was painted. (Applause.) He had but to look about him. *Etcetera, etcetera.* He questioned

whether so well-conducted, morally-given, and respectable a gathering could be brought together in any West End parish with which he was acquainted. (56)

Morrison's burlesque of speaking to the converted finds an appropriate response from Dicky Perrott, who "had learnt to hold in serene contempt" any well-dressed people whom he encountered. Lured to the Institute by the promise of cake, he infiltrates a gathering which is nominally arranged for people like him and steals the bishop's gold watch.

As I have tried to indicate, the trouble with Morrison is that it is difficult to square this highly effective critique of the bishop of London with his fulsome praise of Father Sturt. In the previous chapter, I suggested that the settlement movement, out of which a figure like Sturt or the real-life Reverend Jay emerges, was designed to redress the more casual attitude toward East End poverty that we see here in the bishop's speech, and it might be argued that Morrison is making a similar point by focusing so much attention on Sturt's more practical hands-on approach. But the novelist had also witnessed the debacle of the People's Palace, and knew that simply taking up residence in the region was no guarantee of a better understanding of its people or its problems. I would argue that the explanation for Father Sturt lies elsewhere, in Morrison's basic acceptance of a conventional rhetoric for describing the poor which borrowed from eugenic race theories and rested on the concept of the residuum, as it had been developed as a descriptive category by Charles Booth and as a moral category by General Booth and the Salvation Army. As I suggested earlier, this is the sense in which Morrison was writing as an outsider, having "encountered" and observed the alien inhabitants of Jay's parish in Shoreditch. What is distinctive is his use of the concept of the residuum not to describe a category of population—like Charles Booth's "category A" or the General's "submerged tenth"—but a tightly circumscribed region, the Jago itself. The implication is that a neighborhood can be demolished and its population dispersed without resorting to more drastic ideas of expatriation, although Morrison also came out in support of the Salvation Army's home colonies plan.

This is why it is difficult to draw a coherent political position from *A Child of the Jago,* which ultimately borders on a kind of apocalyptic

nihilism that might even be considered proto-modernist—thinking of
the dystopian visions of London life in Eliot's *The Waste Land,* for
example. As H. G. Wells noted in a review of the novel, its particularity
is both its main strength and its weakness: "It is as if Mr. Morrison had
determined to write of the Jago and nothing but the Jago. It is the Jago
without relativity. . . . But the origin of the Jago, the place of the Jago in
the general scheme of things, the trend of change in it, its probable destiny—such matters are not in his mind."[48] Despite its more melodramatic suggestions that the Jago infected nearby areas and might ultimately resurrect itself, the novel presents its inhabitants as purely residual
and reactionary in their outlook, a throwback to earlier models of the urban criminal subculture like the Wapping Mint or St. Giles, but hopelessly anachronistic in an era of council housing, urban regeneration, and
socialist parties. Dick Hebdige's celebrated study of subculture, for instance, tellingly misdates the novel, arguing that it offers "a fascinating if
depressing account of life in a mid-century slum," and discusses it in the
context of Mayhew and Dickens.[49]

What has changed is partly ascribable to the extraordinary power
of Darwinian thinking, which condemns the Jago to its eventual fate.
When Mayhew had used the language of tribal affiliation fifty years earlier to describe the "nomadic" London costermongers, the term res-
onated with a wider romantic fetishization of the freedom of movement.
Dickens had also applied the language of race in a text like *Bleak House,*
but in order to condemn ways of thinking that would equate Tom-all-
Alone's with the outposts of empire. Such metaphors harden into beliefs
in the 1890s: the people Morrison is describing are, in every way but national identity, "savages," who cannot be moved on far enough in order
to purge their areas of residence. In the sense that nineteenth-century
thinkers inherited a racial philosophy of history from Hegel, the Jago-
ites are outside of history entirely, occupying a prehistoric and primor-
dial black hole that is both chronologically and geographically anterior
to Western modernity. Such peoples could find no place, either, in the
reinvigorated British State that begins to take shape in the early years of
the twentieth century, one which presumes minimal requirements for
subjectivity and citizenship. In many respects, it is a legislative philosophy that took its cue from Charles Booth's studies, drawing the line
of working-class respectability above the hardened criminals and casual

laborers in categories A and B. Simultaneously, as we shall see from the brief conclusion that follows, new cultural representations of the London poor, now fully disentangled from radical class politics and articulating instead a fierce loyalty to crown and country, were being produced on the stages of the capital's music halls.

# CONCLUSION

THE HISTORY I HAVE been tracing through the preceding chapters bears little resemblance to the influential account of the cultural representation of crime offered first by Michel Foucault. In *Discipline and Punish,* despite his cautions elsewhere about the dangers of viewing history as a teleology, Foucault figures progress as unidirectional and irreversible. In place of an older broadsheet tradition of criminal biography, he identifies a distinctively new cultural practice emerging in the nineteenth century, echoing the epistemic shift to a more insidious and dispersed form of power. "We are now," he argues, "far removed from those accounts of the life and misdeeds of the criminal in which he admitted his crimes, and which recounted in detail the tortures of his execution: we have moved from the exposition of facts or the confession to the slow process of discovery; from the execution to the investigation; from the physical confrontation to the intellectual struggle between criminal and investigation."[1] In essence, we have witnessed the birth of a new fictional genre: the detective story.

My own account sees each of those earlier aspects as having an afterlife that is inexplicable according to the logic of Panopticism. Thus, if there is a core element that accounts for the success and also the controversies that were set in motion by the Newgate novels of the 1830s and

'40s, it was surely that they, too, encouraged an immediate readerly identification with crime. Later, Gothic-inflected novels like *Jekyll and Hyde*
or *Dorian Gray* take the resemblance further, being more obviously con-
fessional narratives in which the agencies of investigation and detection
play little part. Finally, the shift from the physical to the mental plane,
while certainly evident in Conan Doyle and (to a lesser extent) Stevenson and Wilde, finds itself challenged by the appearance of a hard-edged
naturalism in the 1890s. This is not to argue, however, that nothing
changes in the nineteenth century; just that the cultural representations
of the police and the private detective are far less triumphant, and far
more conflicted, than Foucault and his followers would allow. The "dialectical somersault" described by Ernest Mandel—whereby "[y]ester-
day's bandit hero has become today's villain, and yesterday's villainous
representative of authority today's hero"[2]—also needs nuancing. It is not
simply that the roles get reversed, with the reader's allegiance decisively
shifting from a sympathy with crime to an unquestioning endorsement
of law and order; such unidirectional shifts are complicated as soon as we
register the return of the privileged offender in the second half of the
century. Unlike the earlier "good bandits" that Mandel is discussing,
these figures are explicitly unsympathetic, in part because they reverse
the traditional image of Robin Hood through their cynical exploitation
of the poor.

Contemporary cultural studies sometimes seeks to lionize poor
criminals, as expressing a subcultural resistance to dominant ideology or
a largely symbolic alternative to capitalist property rights. Such an approach would find some support from the 1840s, and in particular from
the ways that the popular and critical reception of Newgate novels insistently foregrounded links to the political struggles of Chartism. It is impossible to adopt the same attitude toward the East End naturalist novels
of the last decades of the nineteenth century, however, and it is important to consider why. After all, Morrison's Jago seems roughly consistent
with the lower-class areas described by Dickens, even if its representative
figures are deliberately drawn as more "lifelike" (and thus, less sympathetic to middle-class readers) than Nancy or the Artful Dodger. The political, social, and moral problems posed by the continued existence of
such areas are broadly the same for Morrison as they were for the later
Dickens, who created "poor Jo" as a kind of litmus test for the legislative

and philanthropic ideas of the 1850s; indeed, in many respects Morrison's notorious fatalism is simply an updating of the death of Jo, and both fall victim to similar institutional shortcomings and prejudices. Again, it is the issue of sympathy that separates the two. *Bleak House* presumes that we at least try to feel as Jo does, and places that effort at the center of whatever hopes it holds out for amelioration. In *A Child of the Jago,* by contrast, we find the imagery of exterminating rats, and no "better way" except in death. The readiness of many progressive thinkers to embrace the Salvation Army's colonial settllement scheme illustrates just how widespread the bankruptcy of ideas had become, partly under the influence of social Darwinist and imperialist modes of thought.

And yet, what is immediately striking about the early years of the twentieth century is the rapid emergence of new legislation designed to improve the life of the poor, including unemployment and health insurance, labor exchanges, and old-age pensions. Many of these innovations were inspired by the writings of sociologists like Charles Booth and Beatrice and Sidney Webb, and were enacted by the so-called "New Liberal" government that came to power in 1908 and included young politicians like C. F. G. Masterman, who had gained first-hand experience through the university settlements.[3] The thinking behind such legislative efforts was not entirely devoid of the moralism and social Darwinism of the 1890s: Booth thought that those in his categories A and B (hardened criminals, casual earners) should be taken out of the job market and placed under the care of the State, while William Beveridge—later to become the architect of the postwar welfare state—argued that disenfranchisement was "part of the 'stigma' of pauperism."[4] What is different, however, is the distinctive emphasis on the role of the State as the guarantor of basic human and social rights to all but those in "the residuum," with the implication that extermination or forced emigration really do represent the only options for the children of the Jago.

In their historical analyses of the historical roots of Thatcherism, Stuart Hall and others have found close parallels in the early years of this century. If, as they suggest, a broad Victorian consensus would have seen the Liberals as the "natural" party of the bourgeoisie and the enfranchised lower classes, and the Tories as representing the interests of the rural gentry, then the loosening of such allegiances opened up a space for new political formations: alongside the Fabian Socialists and the New Liberalism of Lloyd George, Masterman, and others, Stuart Hall and Bill Schwarz identify a new form of conservatism they term "social-imperialist," which "worked energetically to enlist a populist movement in the country" in support of domestic social reforms that were allied to aggressive imperialist expansion.[5] As we have seen in the case of the Salvation Army's home colonies scheme, such an appeal might well have spoken to rising sections of the working class who would otherwise be lumped in with the urban residuum.

As Conservatives attempted to build their own constituencies beyond the traditional "squirearchy," it is not surprising that they might make overtures (however opportunistic) to a self-defined "respectable" working class in the cities, on the basis of immediate issues like licensing laws and anti-immigration, thereby casting the Liberal Party as the friend of foreigners and the enemy of innocent pleasures. In a fascinating oral account of the life of a real "Jago rat," Arthur Harding (who was born in 1886 in the Old Nichol) describes his family as having been staunchly Conservative in its politics, even if the basis for their allegiance may seem trivial: Harding claims to have been a Tory by birth, partly because "[t]he Conservatives stood for beer" and a tax on imports, while "[t]he other side, the Liberals, were more for the foreigner—Free Trade—" and "against the pubs."[6]

What is fascinating is the way that Harding's political sympathies were deepened rather than challenged by the Party's image as the national champions of law and order. His childhood was not all that different from that of the fictional Dicky Perrott, as Harding quickly learned how to rob local shops and mobile vans, then the art of begging, before graduating into petty theft and armed robbery. What enabled his uneasy marriage of criminality and conservatism was an unquestioning sense of loyalty, pledged at different moments to the local community or subculture (and thus, in opposition to the police and judiciary) and also to a more abstract entity like the nation or the royal family—the chief ornaments he remembers from growing up, for instance, were pictures of the Crucifixion and Queen Victoria. Perhaps his most telling comment concerns the West End riots of 1886 (the year Harding was born), "when the unemployed smashed up the jeweller's shops, trying to impress the people up west with their condition, they marched back to the East End singing 'Rule Britannia.' Now what more patriotic, more conservative song can you play than that?" (277).

Harding's memoirs also provide a useful retrospective of nineteenth-century crime fiction, describing in particular his encounters with Dickens. *Oliver Twist* is a novel he reads for the first time in Borstal, and he claims to have "learnt about pickpocketing just like the Artful Dodger" (75). At the same time, however, he considered that Oliver "could never have existed because he wasn't able to help himself," whereas a local child of eight or nine would already know to beg or thieve in order to survive. If Harding's childhood is closer to that described by Morrison, though, he also allows us to see the elements of the new East End image in formation. In twentieth-century popular culture, various styles of petty crime—ranging from small-time gangsterism to tax evasion—have formed part of a new image of London's East End, intersecting seamlessly with its presumed patriotism, its distrust of central government, and a commitment to traditional family values.[7] The BBC's long-running soap opera, *East Enders,* for instance, centers the fictional community of Walford around the twin sites of the local pub (the patriotically named "Queen Victoria") and a street market which encourages the sale of stolen goods, where traders go to great lengths to avoid government taxes, and where the Jago commandment "thou shalt not nark" is still in force.

In a landmark essay, Gareth Stedman Jones has argued that the London working class was transformed during the 1890s, although not exactly in the preferred image of liberal or Christian crusaders. He begins his account with the Mafeking Night celebrations of 1900, in which East End met West in public celebrations of imperial victory in South Africa, and ends with the Victorian music halls which had increasingly supplanted workmen's clubs as places for proletarian relaxation. These were places where the working class mixed with aristocratic "bloods" like the Prince of Wales or a young Winston Churchill, the descendants of the "slummers" of Pierce Egan who had by now cast off the uneasy associations with criminal deviance fostered by Doctor Jekyll and the Ripper murders. Music hall's rhetoric, according to Stedman Jones, was "both escapist *and yet* strongly rooted in the realities of working-class life."[8] Its repertoire of songs could encompass support for the dock strike of 1889, a recognition of class differences (as in the well-known lyric, "it's the rich what gets the pleasure / It's the poor what gets the blame"), as well as patriotic enthusiasm during the Boer War—although in the latter case, sympathy was mainly reserved for the working-class soldiers fighting in Africa, just as they served as a focus for Kipling's popular depictions of military life.[9]

It is dangerous to take too literally the projections of a new cross-class alliance of those at the top and bottom of society against the middle ground of late-Victorian liberalism, but it is nonetheless evident that such ideological re-alignments were routinely imagined during the early years of the twentieth century.[10] Walter Besant's political fantasy of class cooperation—the consoling myth that "the working man's best friends would be the swells, if they could be got hold of"—resurfaces in the period, and testifies to the partial incorporation of the working class within a ruling hegemonic bloc. This does not mean that the social and cultural antagonisms I have traced through the nineteenth century ever entirely dissipated, or that the police have ever fully secured popular consent for their actions, especially among poor and immigrant communities. As I have tried to indicate, though, a form of political accommodation was clearly reached early in the twentieth century, which signaled important shifts in the cultural representations of crime within a dramatically re-configured political landscape.

# Notes

## Introduction

1. Judith Walkowitz, *City of Dreadful Delight: Narratives of Sexual Danger in Late Victorian London* (London: Virago, 1992); Deborah Epstein Nord, *Walking the Victorian Streets: Women, Representation, and the City* (Ithaca: Cornell University Press, 1995); Julian Wolfreys, *Writing London: The Trace of the Urban Text from Blake to Dickens* (New York: St. Martin's Press, 1998); Lynda Nead, *Victorian Babylon: People, Streets, and Images in Nineteenth-Century London* (New Haven: Yale University Press, 2000).

2. Franco Moretti, *Atlas of the European Novel, 1800–1900* (London: Verso, 1998).

3. Kevin Lynch, *The Image of the City* (Cambridge: M.I.T. Press, 1960), 10.

4. See Fredric Jameson, "Cognitive Mapping," in *Marxism and the Interpretation of Culture,* ed. Cary Nelson and Lawrence Grossberg (Urbana: University of Illinois Press, 1988), 347–57.

5. In 1841, the population of the capital was around a million and a half, or close to a tenth of the total population of England. In the rest of Europe, by contrast, only Paris reached a total of a million by 1850. By itself, this growth rate is not especially striking. The number of inhabitants in Manchester doubled between 1801 and 1831, and almost doubled again in the decade that followed. To put such figures in perspective, though, it should be noted that Manchester's population in 1841 had only reached 217,000, roughly equivalent to the London population around 1600. These numbers are drawn largely from Raymond Williams's *The Country and the City* (Oxford: Oxford University Press, 1975), 217, and Steven Marcus's "Historical Prologue" to *Engels, Manchester, and the Working Class* (New York: Random House, 1974).

6. Wolfreys, *Writing London,* 129.

7. Moretti, *Atlas,* 115–17.

8. J. B. Harley, "Deconstructing the Map," in *Writing Worlds: Discourse, Text and Metaphor in the Representation of Landscape,* ed. Trevor J. Barnes and James S. Duncan (London: Routledge, 1992), 242–43.

9. Jeremy Black has criticized Harley's work for its inability to theorize conflicts and tensions among competing versions of the world, and for settling instead for a monolithic and conspiratorial idea of Power, which is also recognizable as a particular (and increasingly discredited) reading of Foucault. See Jeremy Black, *Maps and Politics* (Chicago: University of Chicago Press, 1997), chapter 1.

10. Nead, *Victorian Babylon,* 22. Nead is drawing here on the work on Louis Marin.

11. See especially Stuart Hall, "Encoding/Decoding," in *Culture, Media, Language: Working Papers in Cultural Studies, 1972–79,* ed. Stuart Hall, Dorothy Hobson, Andrew Lowe, and Paul Willis (London: Routledge, 1992), 128–38.

12. Colin Mercer, "Entertainment, or the Policing of Virtue," *New Formations* 4 (1986), 52.

13. Mercer, "That's Entertainment: The Resilience of Popular Forms," in *Popular Culture and Social Relations,* ed. Tony Bennett, Colin Mercer, and Janet Woollacott (Milton Keynes: Open University Press, 1986), 186. See also Tony Bennett, "Texts, Readers, Reading Formations," *Literature and History* 9:2 (autumn 1983), 214–27.

14. See especially D. A. Miller, *The Novel and the Police* (Berkeley: University of California Press, 1988).

15. For a detailed analysis of Chartist rhetoric that shows how these links might be made, see Gareth Stedman Jones, "Rethinking Chartism," in *Languages of Class, 1832–1982: Studies in English Working Class History, 1832–1982* (Cambridge: Cambridge University Press, 1983), 90–178.

16. Arthur Morrison is emblematic of the argument I am making here, because his literary output combines naturalist stories of the East End like *Tales of Mean Streets* (1894) and *A Child of the Jago* (1896) with the less successful adventures of "Martin Hewitt, Investigator," a detective in the popular mold of Sherlock Holmes.

17. Cited in Friedrich Engels, *The Condition of the Working-Class in England in 1844,* trans. W. O. Henderson and W. H. Chaloner (Stanford: Stanford University Press, 1968), 35–36.

18. George R. Sims, *How the Poor Live,* cited in *Into Unknown England, 1866–1913: Selections from the Social Explorers,* ed. Peter Keating (Manchester: Manchester University Press, 1976), 65.

19. William Booth, *In Darkest England and the Way Out,* cited in Asa Briggs, *Victorian Cities* (New York: Harper and Row, 1965), 325.

20. Williams, *The Country and the City,* 145.

21. For a fascinating account of Soho's recent history, see Frank Mort, *Cultures of Consumption: Masculinities and Social Space in Twentieth-Century Britain* (London: Routledge, 1996), 149–82.

22. See Joseph McLaughlin, *Writing the Urban Jungle: Reading Empire in London from Doyle to Eliot* (Charlottesville: University Press of Virginia, 2000), 133.

23. The phrase originates in 1910 with the bishop of Kensington, and is cited in McLaughlin, 141.

24. Ronald R. Thomas, *Detective Fiction and the Rise of Forensic Science* (Cambridge: Cambridge University Press, 1999), 284–85.

25. Joseph Conrad, *The Secret Agent* (Harmondsworth: Penguin, 1994), 249.

## 1. Mapping the Capital City

1. For a useful summary of these contrary definitions, see Rita Felski, *The Gender of Modernity* (Cambridge: Harvard University Press, 1995), 11–14.

2. See *The Sociology of Georg Simmel*, trans. Kurt Wolff (New York: Free Press, 1950), 423.

3. William Wordsworth, *The Prelude*, 1805 edition (Oxford: Oxford University Press, 1970), 109–10.

4. Wordsworth, "Preface to *Lyrical Ballads*," in *The Selected Poetry and Prose of Wordsworth*, ed. Geoffrey Hartman (New York: Meridian, 1980), 414.

5. Dana Brand, *The Spectator and the City in Nineteenth-Century American Literature* (Cambridge: Cambridge University Press, 1991), 3–4.

6. Simmel, "The Metropolis and Mental Life," in *The Sociology of Georg Simmel*, 409–24.

7. For a more developed version of this argument, see Marilyn Butler, *Romantics, Rebels, and Reactionaries: English Literature and Its Background, 1760–1830* (Oxford: Oxford University Press, 1981), 113–17, and Jon Klancher, *The Making of English Reading Audiences, 1790–1832* (Madison: University of Wisconsin Press, 1987).

8. Martha Woodmansee, *The Author, Art, and the Market: Rereading the History of Aesthetics* (New York: Columbia University Press), 118.

9. Walter Benjamin, *Charles Baudelaire: A Lyric Poet in an Era of High Capitalism*, trans. Harry Zohn (London: Verso, 1983), 40; 120.

10. Karl Marx and Friedrich Engels, *Manifesto of the Communist Party* (New York: International Publishers, 1948), 21.

11. Raymond Williams, *The Country and the City*, 302–6. For a version of this attitude, see Charles Kingsley's 1850 novel *Alton Locke* (London: Macmillan and Co., 1890). When asked if the country (i.e., the nation) will join a proposed Chartist uprising in 1848, organizer John Crossthwaite responds "The cities will; never mind the country. They are too weak to resist their own tyrants—and they are too weak to resist us." To this Locke replies "It is the cities . . . where the light dawns first— where man meets man, and spirit quickens spirit, and intercourse breeds knowledge, and knowledge sympathy, and sympathy enthusiasm, combination, power irresistible; while the agriculturists remain ignorant, selfish, weak, because they are isolated from each other" (238–39).

12. For a discussion of this dialectic, and of some of its unintended consequences in Marx, see Marshall Berman, *All That Is Solid Melts into Air: The Experience of Modernity* (New York: Simon and Schuster, 1982), especially part 2.

13. Engels, *The Condition of the Working-Class in England in 1844*, trans. W. O. Henderson and W. H. Chaloner (Stanford: Stanford University Press, 1968), 30.

14. Alexis de Tocqueville's *Journeys to England and Ireland* offers an earlier version of this dialectic, from an 1835 visit to Manchester: "From this foul drain the greatest stream of human industry flows out to fertilize the whole world. From this filthy sewer pure gold flows. Here humanity attains its most complete development and its most brutish; here civilization works its miracles, and civilized man is turned back almost into a savage." Cited in Steven Marcus, *Engels, Manchester, and the Working Class* (New York: Random House, 1974), 66.

15. Engels's response here is, as Walter Benjamin argues, primarily a moral and aesthetic reaction to an unsettling experience of the crowd. See *Charles Baudelaire*, 121–22.

16. Thomas de Quincey, "The Nation of London," in *Autobiographic Sketches* (Boston: Ticknor, Reed, and Fields, 1853), 204–43.

17. For a discussion of early uses of these metaphors of the social body of England, see Max Byrd, *London Transformed: Images of the City in the Eighteenth Century* (New Haven: Yale University Press, 1978), 13–17, and Marcus, 57–60. James Winter notes a similar preponderance of medical metaphors, which increasingly define the dysfunctioning of the Victorian city in terms of clogged arteries and poor circulation. See his *London's Teeming Streets, 1830–1914* (London: Routledge, 1993), 2–4.

18. Josiah Tucker, "Four Letters . . . to the Earl of Shelburne," cited in Byrd, 15. Raymond Williams also notes the link between this passage and William Cobbett's denunciations of the "Great Wen" of London in *The Country and the City*, 146.

19. Cited in Byrd, 114.

20. Charles Lamb, "The Londoner. To the Editor of the Reflector," in *Poems, Plays and Miscellaneous Essays* (London: The Chesterfield Society, n.d.), 2:248–51.

21. "Prospectus of the London Magazine," *London Magazine* 1 (1820), iv–v.

22. "Historical and Critical Summary of Public Events," *London Magazine* 1:100–102. For a useful account of Peterloo, its aftermath, and its significance in the British radical tradition, see E. P. Thompson, *The Making of the English Working Class* (New York: Vintage, 1966), 669–710.

23. John Fisher Murray, *The World of London* (1843), cited in Brand, *The Spectator and the City*, 42–44.

24. Leigh Hunt, "A Human Being and a Crowd," in *The Seer; or Common-Places Refreshed* (Boston: Roberts Brothers, 1865), 1:329–31.

25. The passage occurs toward the end of Lewis's novel, in volume 3, chapter 3. De Sade wrote in 1800 that *The Monk* was "the inevitable product of the revolutionary shocks with which the whole of Europe resounded." For a useful discussion of the ways in which this novel and the wider Gothic tradition represented events in France for English audiences, see Ronald Paulson, "Gothic Fiction and the French Revolution," *ELH* 48 (1981), 532–54.

26. "Life in London," *New Monthly Magazine* 11 (1824), 226–30.

27. "Life in London," *Mirror of Literature* 74 (March 1824), 173–74. The proliferation of articles bearing this title presumably stems from the enormous success of Pierce Egan's 1821 novel of the same name.

28. F. S. Schwarzbach, *Dickens and the City* (London: Athlone Press, 1979), 126.

29. Jonathan Dollimore, *Sexual Dissidence: Augustine to Wilde, Freud to Foucault* (Oxford: Clarendon, 1991), 33; emphasis in original.

30. Lynda Nead notes a parallel instance from Henry Mayhew's *London Labour and the London Poor,* in which the narrator observes the pickpocketing of a well-dressed lady in Cheapside: as Nead comments, "Identities in the city, based on appearance rather than personal knowledge, could never be certain. They could be accurate indices of social status, or they could be assumed for deception. The sights of the city invited preoccupation; but the physical proximity of the streets could transform absorption into violation." See Nead, *Victorian Babylon: People, Streets, and Images in Nineteenth-Century London* (New Haven: Yale University Press, 2000), 72.

31. Engels, *The Condition of the Working-Class in England in 1844,* 33–34.

32. *Times* (12 October 1843), cited in Engels, 39. The ultra-Chartist weekly *The Red Republican* cited a similar editorial during the run-up to the Great Exhibition of 1851:

under the sarcastic heading of "Proofs of Prosperity," editor Julian Harney noted that "The *Times* of September 28th, giving an account of the progress of the works in Hyde Park, in connection with the forthcoming monster exhibition, states that between 250 and 300 workmen are employed in preparing the 'palace of iron and glass.' The *Times* adds: 'At the main entrance *crowds of labourers are collected in the hope of employment!*' Poor fellows, they are likely to experience the force of the sad truth that 'hope deferred makes the heart sick.'" In *The Red Republican,* October 12, 1850 (reprinted in facsimile, New York: Barnes and Noble, 1966), 133; emphasis in original.

33. Kevin Lynch, *The Image of the City* (Cambridge: M.I.T. Press, 1960), 4.

34. De Quincey, "The Nation of London," 210–14.

35. Charles Dickens, preface to *Oliver Twist* (Harmondsworth: Penguin, 1985), 33.

36. Illustration by John Leech, in *Punch,* volume 19 (1850), 167.

37. "The Police System of London," *Edinburgh Review* (July 1852), 5.

38. Kellow Chesney, *Victorian Underworld* (London: Penguin, 1972), 127–28.

39. Henry Mayhew, "A Visit to the Rookery of St. Giles and Its Neighbourhood," in *London's Underworld,* ed. Peter Quennell (London: William Kimber, 1950), 175–88.

40. Cited in Sheila M. Smith, "'Savages and Martyrs': Images of the Urban Poor in Victorian Literature and Art," in *Victorian Artists and the City: A Collection of Critical Essays,* ed. Ira Bruce Nadel and F. S. Schwarzbach (New York: Pergamon Press, 1980) 14–29.

41. "The Police System of London," 9.

42. Cited in John Butt and Kathleen Tillotson, *Dickens at Work* (London: Methuen, 1957), 191. Pierce Egan's *Life in London* develops a similar contrast, punning on a popular slang term for gin ("max"). In this account of two West End swells on their "Rambles and Sprees through the Metropolis," Jerry Hawthorn and Corinthian Tom, are encouraged to visit an East End gin shop, with the boast that "as you have your 'Highflyers' at ALMACK's, at the West End, we also have some 'choice creatures' at our ALL MAX in the East" (London: John Camden Hotten, 1869), 318–19.

43. Douglas Jerrold, *St. Giles and St. James* (London: Bradbury and Evans, 1851), 17–18.

44. See Robert A. Colby, "Oliver's Progeny: Some Unfortunate Foundlings," in *Dickens Quarterly* 4:2 (June 1987), 109–21.

45. *Baker's Chronicle* of 1665, for example, speaks of "[t]hat part of the Suburbs of London commonly called Covent Garden"; while Defoe's 1727 *Tour of Great Britain* remarks that "This Street is call'd the Cannon-Gate, . . . which Part, tho' a Suburb, is a kind of Corporation by itself, as Westminster to London."

46. The classic study of nineteenth-century suburbia is H. J. Dyos's *Victorian Suburb* (Edinburgh: Leicester University Press, 1961), a study of Camberwell in south London. See also Donald J. Olsen, *The Growth of Victorian London* (New York: Holmes and Meier, 1976), chapter 5.

47. "Beppo," lxvi, in *The Poetical Works of Lord Byron* (London: Oxford University Press, 1945), 631.

48. Lewis Mumford, *The Culture of Cities* (New York: Harcourt, Brace and Company, 1938), 215.

49. For more on the impact of gas lighting, see Lynda Nead, *Victorian Babylon,* part 2. Nead interestingly writes of a "poetics of gas" during this time; much as I argue in relation to "The Man of the Crowd," she notes that "[c]ities are defined by temporal as well as by spatial geographies," so that "mid-Victorian London was seen to have

a distinctive character by day and by night. Gas bore witness to night scenes, to aspects of the city that were hidden by day" (83).

50. Edgar Allan Poe, "The Man of the Crowd," in *Tales of Mystery and Imagination* (London: Everyman, 1984), 108–9.
51. Benjamin, *Charles Baudelaire,* 48–54.
52. Edward Mayhew, "Midnight Mishaps," in *Bentley's Miscellany* 1:8 (1837), 197–206.
53. Donald J. Olsen, "Victorian London: Specialization, Segregation, and Privacy," *Victorian Studies* 17 (March 1974), 277–78.
54. Peter Stallybrass and Allon White, *The Politics and Poetics of Transgression* (Ithaca: Cornell University Press, 1986), 135.
55. "Boz," prologue to volume 1 of *Bentley's Miscellany* (January 1837), 5.

## 2. Reading Run Riot

1. Tony Bennett, "Texts, Readers, Reading Formations," *Literature and History* 9:2 (autumn 1983), 220.
2. See Tony Bennett and Janet Woollacott, *Bond and Beyond: The Political Career of a Popular Hero* (London: Macmillan, 1987). They specifically designate this reading formation as "inter-textual," but define that term, in opposition to its more common use in critical practice (without the hyphen), as "the social organisation of the relations between texts within specific conditions of reading" (44–45).
3. Deborah Vlock has similarly suggested that we attend to the "imaginary text" of Dickens, a comparable amalgam of "novels and their specific adaptations, as well as the entire theatrical and literary repertoires, works of social criticism, politics, journalism—all of the written and performance-based genres which played the same figures and voices—the same social stereotypes—against a backdrop of normalcy, of standard speech, dress, behavior." In *Dickens, Novel Reading, and the Victorian Popular Theatre* (Cambridge: Cambridge University Press, 1998), 29–30.
4. Barbara Herrnstein Smith, *Contingencies of Value* (Cambridge: Harvard University Press, 1988), 13.
5. Indeed, the play premiered on November 19, just ten days after Sikes's death had appeared in print. It ran through February 1839, making it easily the most popular of many theatrical adaptations of the story. Others—like one by Gilbert à Beckett which opened in March, when the novel was only half-completed—had little success, and closed almost immediately.
6. John Hollingshead, *My Lifetime* (1895), cited in Philip Collins, *Dickens and Crime* (Bloomington: Indiana University Press, 1968), 265–66. Forster records Dickens's own response to these theatrical stagings: having tried unsuccessfully to have some control over proposed productions by Frederick Yates and William Macready, he went to see Almar's in 1838, lay down on the floor of his box during the opening scene, and remained there until the end of the play! See John Forster, *The Life of Charles Dickens* (London: J. M. Dent, 1966), 1:100.
7. See Keith Hollingsworth, *The Newgate Novel, 1830–1847* (Detroit: Wayne State University Press, 1963), 139–40.
8. Cited in *William Harrison Ainsworth and His Friends,* ed. S. M. Ellis (London: John Lane, 1911), 1:376.
9. Cited in Ellis, 1:366.

10. Their friendship ended, in fact, because of a misunderstanding over Forster's role in negotiations with the magazine, which Dickens sought to leave after completing *Oliver Twist*. The details of this dispute, and a letter from Dickens to Ainsworth, are contained in Ellis, 1:383–89.

11. By 1840, Dickens was himself seeking this distance, writing in a letter to R. H. Horne in February that "I am by some jolter-headed enemies most unjustly and untruly charged with having written a book after Mr. Ainsworth's fashion." He even imagines writing his own text on the life of Sheppard, but considers that such an effort would "seem an unmanly way of disavowing any sympathy with that school, and a means of shielding myself." Madeline House and Graham Storey, eds., *The Letters of Charles Dickens* (Oxford: Clarendon, 1969), 2:20–21. Philip Cox notes a similar attempt at distinguishing himself from Egan's *Life in London,* arguing that Dickens was consistently troubled by his likeness to "popular" authors, including those (like George Almar or William Moncrieff) whom he felt made a parasitic living off of his own texts. See Cox, *Reading Adaptations: Novel and Verse Narratives on the Stage, 1790–1840* (Manchester: Manchester University Press, 2000), 124–39.

12. From "The Three Literary Graces" by Buller, Sen., *Bentley's Miscellany* 5:5 (May 1839), 559–62.

13. In a similar sense, Lynda Nead writes of the Victorian subgenre of "night-walk fiction," best personified by Dickens's early depiction of "The Streets—Night" in *Sketches by Boz:* "The basic tenet of night-walk fiction," she notes, "is that the reader is safe and warm at home, while the author assumes the mantle of outsider and wanderer." See Nead, *Victorian Babylon: People, Streets, and Images in Nineteenth-Century London* (New Haven: Yale University Press, 2000), 102.

14. *Monthly Review* (January 1839), reprinted in *The Dickensian* 1 (1905), 35–40; my emphasis.

15. *Quarterly Review* 64 (July 1839), 90–91.

16. (February 1840), 240. This essay has generally been attributed to Thackeray, who routinely used *Fraser's* as his preferred vehicle to campaign against the Newgate novelists, and Bulwer Lytton in particular. See Hollingsworth, *The Newgate Novel,* 148–65.

17. William Makepeace Thackeray, "Horae Catnachianae," in *Fraser's Magazine* 19 (April 1839), 407–8; emphasis in original. Dickens replied to these charges in a new preface in 1850, cited in chapter 1, in which he wrote "I have yet to learn that a lesson of the purest good may not be drawn from the vilest evil. . . . I saw no reason, when I wrote this book, why the very dregs of life, so long as their speech did not offend the ear, should not serve the purpose of a moral, at least as well as its froth and cream. . . . I did not," he added, " . . . abate one hole in the Dodger's coat, or one scrap of curl-paper in the girl's dishevelled hair" for the sake of his genteel readers. "It is wonderful," he declares in an acid phrase directed at Thackeray, "how Virtue turns from dirty stockings." *Oliver Twist* (Harmondsworth: Penguin, 1985), 33–37.

18. Thackeray, "Fielding's Works," in *Catherine, A Shabby Genteel Story, The Second Funeral of Napoleon, and Miscellanies, 1840–1* (London: Oxford University Press, n.d.), 385.

19. *Quarterly Review* 64 (July 1839), 96–97; emphasis in original. Earlier, the reviewer explicitly remarks that while "it is perfectly natural that Oliver Twist . . . should

be the joy of the ten-pounders: it is another affair why the ten thousand and ten-thousand-a-year men should join in this universal suffrage" (87). This comment directly acknowledges a diverse range of reading interests and practices, in addition to making a connection with the politics of electoral reform which I develop in this chapter.

20. Dorothy Thompson, *The Chartists: Popular Politics in the Industrial Revolution* (Aldershot: Wildwood House, 1986), 295.

21. "The Chartists and Universal Suffrage," *Blackwood's Edinburgh Magazine* 46:287 (September 1839), 290.

22. This is the sense in which Habermas cites Chartism as one of the central sites of an emergent "plebeian public sphere" during this time, which helped to foreground conflicting demands and interests between classes which had previously been outlawed from public discussion. See Jürgen Habermas, *The Structural Transformation of the Public Sphere,* trans. Thomas Burger and Frederick Lawrence (Cambridge: M.I.T. Press, 1989), xviii and 168.

23. See Patrick Brantlinger, *The Spirit of Reform: British Literature and Politics, 1832–1867* (Cambridge: Harvard University Press, 1977), chapter 4.

24. Gareth Stedman Jones, "Rethinking Chartism," in *Languages of Class,* 122 (emphasis in original) and 174; citations from William Thompson, "One of the Idle Classes" (1827) and *The Northern Star* (1839).

25. *Quarterly Review* 64 (July 1839), 92.

26. This substitution has further consequences, however, since it is Charley who gives up Sikes in the novel, before choosing to forgo his young life of crime and settle down as a farmer. Having the Dodger betray the whereabouts of Sikes—as he does in both the Almar version and the David Lean film—implicitly holds out the promise that he too might be rehabilitated, even if the motivation behind the change is presumably to allow him more time on stage.

27. *Oliver Twist. A Serio-Comic Burletta* by George Almar, Comedian. As performed at the Winter Garden (New York: Samuel French and Son, 1864), act 1, scene 4.

28. "Writings of Charles Dickens," *North British Review* 3 (1845), 82; 69. The *Athenaeum,* in a lengthy review of *Jack Sheppard* which approaches the Newgate novel as a sociological phenomenon, more typically seeks to distance Dickens from the critique it levels at Ainsworth and others: "In thus introducing Mr. Dickens's name," it insists, "we are far from classing him with his imitators, or ranging his works with the Factory Boys and the Jack Sheppards,—in external appearance so similar." The review goes on to align Dickens with the more respectable forefathers of the genre, Gay and Fielding. No. 626 (26 October 1839), 803.

29. Deborah Epstein Nord, *Walking the Victorian Streets: Women, Representation, and the City* (Ithaca: Cornell University Press, 1995), 51.

30. See Franco Moretti, *Atlas of the European Novel, 1800–1900* (London: Verso, 1998), 86.

31. D. A. Miller, *The Novel and the Police* (Berkeley: University of California Press, 1988), 5–6.

32. As I shall elaborate in chapter 3, the most advanced form of this denial of responsibility, or even of simple *fact,* can be found in London alderman Sir Peter Laurie's response to *Oliver Twist,* in which he publicly questioned the existence of the rookery of Jacob's Island where Bill Sikes is finally hunted down and killed.

33. Early advertisements for Grose's volume testified to its authenticity—as having been "printed from a *Copy taken on one of their Gang, in the late Scuffle between the Watchmen and a Party of them on Clerkenwell Green*"—and also suggested its potential uses: it was, the ad proclaims, "A Book very useful and necessary (to be known, but not practised) for all People." Reprinted in the *1811 Dictionary of the Vulgar Tongue* (Chicago: Follett Publishing Company, 1971).

34. See Allon White, "'The Dismal Sacred Word': Academic Language and the Social Reproduction of Seriousness," in *Carnival, Hysteria, and Writing* (Oxford: Clarendon Press, 1993), 130.

35. Aside from those already mentioned, the main examples of this work would be the essays collected in *Resistance through Rituals: Youth Subcultures in Postwar Britain,* ed. Stuart Hall and Tony Jefferson (London: Hutchinson, 1976), and Dick Hebdige's *Subculture: The Meaning of Style* (London: Methuen, 1979).

36. *Oliver Twist,* 390. Luckily for Charley, the Dodger turns in a memorable performance, by refusing to address himself to the judge or witnesses, on the basis that "this ain't the shop for justice; beside which, my attorney is a-breakfasting this morning with the Wice-President of the House of Commons." Finally, on being committed for transportation, he declares to the judges in a fine piece of parodic inversion: "*You'll* pay for this, my fine fellers. I wouldn't be you for something! I wouldn't go free, now, if you was to fall down on your knees and ask me. Here, carry me off to prison!" (394–96; emphasis in original).

37. See Richard Maxwell, *The Mysteries of Paris and London* (Charlottesville: University Press of Virginia, 1992), 80–84.

38. Interestingly, Ainsworth exploited this connection in his earlier crime novel *Rookwood* (1834), which placed the story of highwayman Dick Turpin in the setting of an itinerant gypsy camp. This is also where the popular "flash" song "Nix My Dolly, Pals, Fake Away" first appeared, to underscore the linguistic connections between Romani cant and underworld slang. For a fascinating discussion of how gypsies have been represented in Enlightenment culture, see Katie Trumpener's "The Time of the Gypsies: a 'People without History' in the Narratives of the West," *Critical Inquiry* 18:4 (summer 1992), 843–84.

39. I am borrowing the term "accented" from Michael Denning's *Mechanic Accents: Dime Novels and Working-Class Culture in America* (London: Verso, 1986), 73–74. Denning, in turn, is drawing on V. N. Volosinov's *Marxism and the Philosophy of Language,* (trans. Ladislav Matejka and I. R. Titunik; Cambridge: Harvard University Press, 1986), which argues that linguistic signs are inherently dialectical and thus open to appropriation and accenting by different classes and social groups.

40. For more information on theatrical adaptations of Dickens, see H. Philip Bolton, *Dickens Dramatized* (London: Mansell, 1987) and Cox, *Reading Adaptations,* chapter 4.

41. The line actually appeared in the original *Bentley's* serialization, but was deleted in the published novel, perhaps because Dickens later revised his opinions about the new police in London. See chapter 3 for more on his attitudes toward them.

42. Louis James, *Fiction for the Working Man, 1830–1850* (London: Oxford University Press, 1963), chapter 4. Among the more memorable titles which he records are *The Penny Pickwick* (Bos); *Current American Notes* (Buz); *Master Timothy's Bookcase* by G. M. W. Reynolds; and *Nickollberry Nikollas, Barnaby Fudge,* and *Martin Puzzlewhit,* published by Edward Lloyd.

43. See "Bos," *The Life and Adventures of Oliver Twiss, the Workhouse Boy* (London: E. Lloyd, 1839), 443–44. By giving him this name of "Solomons," Bos suggests one of the likely sources for Fagin's character, the real-life Jewish fence Ikey Solomon.

44. See the essays in Douglas Hay, Peter Linebaugh, John Rule, E. P. Thompson, and Cal Winslow, *Albion's Fatal Tree: Crime and Society in Eighteenth-Century England* (Harmondsworth: Penguin, 1977), and the companion volume by Thompson, *Whigs and Hunters: The Origin of the Black Act* (Harmondsworth: Penguin, 1977).

45. Cox, *Reading Adaptations*, 154–55.

46. "Poetical Epistle from Father Prout to Boz," *Bentley's Miscellany* 3:1 (January 1838), 71.

47. Steven Marcus, *Dickens from Pickwick to Dombey* (New York: Clarion, 1965), chapter 2. Michael Denning presumably had a similar process in mind when he characterized working-class reading practices as "allegorical" in *Mechanic Accents*, 73–74, although the example of Father Prout suggests that the same tactics might also extend to middle-class readers.

48. Patrick Brantlinger, "How Oliver Twist Learned to Read, and What He Read," in *Culture and Education in Victorian England,* ed. Patrick Scott and Pauline Fletcher (Lewisburg: Bucknell University Press, 1990), 59–81. Mayhew made a similar argument in articles attacking the "ragged schools" for the poor, in which he quoted a policeman as arguing that improved literacy only made for better criminals: its main result, he claimed, was that "We are teaching the thieves to prig the articles marked at the highest figures." Cited in E. P. Thompson, "Mayhew and the *Morning Chronicle*," in *The Unknown Mayhew,* ed. Eileen Yeo and E. P. Thompson (New York: Pantheon, 1971), 33.

49. Miller, *The Novel and the Police,* 59.

50. Michel Foucault, ed., *I, Pierre Rivière, having slaughtered my mother, my sister, and my brother . . .* (Harmondsworth: Penguin, 1978), 40. This is perhaps the appropriate place to mention Dickens's own murderous identification with Sikes during his energetic performances of the death of Nancy, which some critics have offered as one of the reasons for the author's own death the following year. For a useful discussion of these arguments, see Collins, *Dickens and Crime,* 265–72. Dickens experienced a similar identification with the Newgate rioters while writing *Barnaby Rudge* (which generally warns of the dangers of mob action), boasting in letters of having "just burnt into Newgate" and that "as to the riot, I am going to try if I can't make a better one than [Gordon] did." See House and Storey, eds., *The Letters of Charles Dickens,* 2:377 (to Forster) and 2:296 (to Ollier) respectively.

51. William Harrison Ainsworth, *Jack Sheppard* (London: Gibbing and Company, 1902), 1:81.

52. For the legal history of the Mint, see Luke Owen Pike, *A History of Crime in England* (Montclair, N.J.: Patterson Smith, 1968), 2:252–55, and Leon Radzinowicz, *A History of English Criminal Law* (London: Stevens and Stevens, 1948), 1:622–23.

53. Baptist Kettleby, indeed, stands perfectly within a critical tradition of thinking about utopia, which would include Fredric Jameson's influential argument that popular culture always contains a utopian/critical component which is structurally uncontainable, and Michel De Certeau's notion of a utopian space within resistance movements, which can only gesture toward a realm of "miraculous" possibility.

See Jameson, "Reification and Utopia in Mass Culture," in *Signatures of the Visible* (London: Routledge, 1990), 9–34, and De Certeau, *The Practice of Everday Life,* trans. Steven Rendall (Berkeley: University of California Press, 1984), 16–18.

54. Hollingsworth, *The Newgate Novel,* 141. Interestingly, the novels themselves often foreground this sense of historical distance: *Rookwood,* for example, laments Dick Turpin as the last of a noble race of highwaymen, while Ainsworth similarly ends a lengthy description of conditions inside the old Newgate prison in *Jack Sheppard* with the following acknowledgment of the work of prison reformer John Howard: "It is a cheering reflection, that in the present prison, with its clean, well-whitewashed, and well-ventilated wards, its airy courts, its infirmary, its improved regulations, and its humane and intelligent officers, many of the miseries of the old gaol are removed. For these beneficial changes society is mainly indebted to the unremitting exertions of the philanthropic HOWARD" (2:89).

55. Jeremy Bentham, "Panopticon, or the Prison-House," in *The Works of Jeremy Bentham,* ed. John Bowring (New York: Russell and Russell, 1962), volume 4:39.

56. *Athenaeum* 626 (26 October 1839), 803–5.

57. *Monthly Magazine* (March 1840; emphasis in original), cited in Kathryn Chittick, *Dickens and the 1830s* (Cambridge: Cambridge University Press, 1990), 157–58.

58. Friedrich Engels, *The Condition of the Working-Class in England in 1844,* trans. W. O. Henderson and W. H. Chaloner (Stanford: Stanford University Press, 1968), 127; Henry Mayhew, *London Labour and the London Poor* (London: Frank Cass and Co., 1967) 4:221.

59. J. B. Buckstone, *Jack Sheppard: A Drama* (New York: Samuel French, n.d.) in *English and American Drama of the Nineteenth Century,* ed. Allardyce Nicoll and George Freedley (New York: Readex Microprint, 1965–1971).

60. Cited in Hollingsworth, *The Newgate Novel,* 139–40. Almost a half-century later, Oscar Wilde used the same example to illustrate the thesis that life imitates art: "The most obvious and the vulgarest form in which this is shown is in the case of the silly boys who, after reading the adventures of Jack Sheppard or Dick Turpin, pillage the stalls of unfortunate apple-women, break into sweet-shops at night, and alarm old gentlemen who are returning home from the city by leaping out on them in suburban lanes, with black masks and unloaded revolvers." See Wilde, "The Decay of Lying," in *The Artist as Critic: Critical Writings of Oscar Wilde,* ed. Richard Ellmann (Chicago: University of Chicago Press, 1969), 308.

61. "Mr. Phillips's Defence of Courvoisier," *Examiner* (28 June 1840).

62. "Going to See a Man Hanged," in *The Works of William Makepeace Thackeray* (New York: P. F. Collier, n.d.), 7:172–80.

63. I am adapting the phrase "domino effect" from Gayle Rubin, who speaks of a "domino theory of sexual peril" in her influential essay "Thinking Sex: Notes for a Radical Theory of the Politics of Sexuality," in *Pleasure and Danger,* ed. Carol Vance (London: Routledge and Kegan Paul, 1984), 282.

64. Thackeray, *Catherine: A Story,* in *Works* 13: 206–7.

65. "The Cruel Murder of old Father Prout by a Barber's Apprentice," *Bentley's Miscellany* 11 (May 1842), 467–71; emphasis in original. Hollingsworth identifies the poem as the work of Francis Mahony.

66. Hollingsworth suggests that *Vanity Fair* (1848) might be taken as Thackeray's final and decisive lunge, in a battle that had been fought out in the public press for much

of the decade. See *The Newgate Novel,* chapter 6, for the details of this final flicker of controversy.

67. Cited in Hollingsworth, 164–65. As Thackeray's attacks on Bulwer in particular begin to mount, it is hard not to feel the sense of an internal struggle, which he is waging against an insufficently-distanciated or repressed impulse of his own.

## 3. Resisting Arrest/Arresting Resistance

1. Cited by Dickens, in his 1850 preface to the First Cheap Edition of *Oliver Twist.*
2. "You see, my friend," remarks Alderman Cute, "there's a great deal of nonsense talked about Want—'hard up,' you know: that's the phrase, isn't it? ha! ha! ha!—and I intend to Put it Down. There's a certain amount of cant in vogue about Starvation, and I mean to Put it Down. . . . And if you attempt, desperately, and ungratefully, and impiously, and fraudulently attempt, to drown yourself, or hang yourself, I'll have no pity on you, for I have made up my mind to Put all suicide Down." Dickens, "The Chimes," in *Christmas Books* (Oxford: Oxford University Press, 1954), 97–99.
3. Dickens, preface to First Cheap Edition.
4. Cited in Gareth Stedman Jones, *Outcast London: A Study in the Relationship between Classes in Victorian Society* (Oxford: Clarendon Press, 1971), 179–80.
5. See Richard Maxwell, *The Mysteries of Paris and London* (Charlottesville: University Press of Virginia, 1992), 341, n. 15.
6. There is some dispute about whether Mayhew originated the idea for the series (as he claimed) or whether the *Morning Chronicle* had already formulated it (as its editors claimed). At any rate, the partnership lasted just over a year, by which point a dispute about editorial policy and censorship led Mayhew to quit, and publish *London Labour* independently. The best source for this background information is Anne Humpherys, *Travels into the Poor Man's Country: The Work of Henry Mayhew* (Athens: University of Georgia Press, 1977).
7. Henry Mayhew, "Jacob's Island" (24 September 1849), reprinted in *Voices of the Poor,* ed. Anne Humpherys (London: Frank Cass and Co., 1971), 3–5.
8. See Humpherys, *Travels,* 31–33.
9. Henry Mayhew, *London Labour and the London Poor* (London: Frank Cass and Co., 1967), 1:2; the distinction between those that will, can't, and won't work was developed as early as the first official article in the *Morning Chronicle* on 19 October 1849, and continued to be used in the title pages of *London Labour* even when it no longer gave an accurate reflection of the volumes' contents. Catherine Gallagher has usefully developed the links between Mayhew and Malthus: see her "The Body versus the Social Body in the Works of Thomas Malthus and Henry Mayhew," in *The Making of the Modern Body: Sexuality and Society in the Nineteenth Century,* ed. Catherine Gallagher and Thomas Laqueur (Berkeley: University of California Press, 1987), 83–106.
10. Gertrude Himmelfarb, "The Culture of Poverty," in *The Victorian City: Images and Realities,* ed. H. J. Dyos and Michael Wolff (London: Routledge and Kegan Paul, 1973), 2:707–36. Interestingly, Himmelfarb finds it difficult to maintain the race/class distinction she sets up here, suggesting later that Mayhew shared with most mid-century reformers the conceptual idea of "a 'class' of paupers, a 'race' of streetfolk, uncivilized and unsocialized" (723).

11. Karl Marx and Friedrich Engels, *Manifesto of the Communist Party* (New York: International Publishers, 1948), 20.

12. See Gertrude Himmelfarb, *The Idea of Poverty: England in the Early Industrial Age* (New York: Alfred A. Knopf, 1984), 351.

13. Himmelfarb, *The Idea of Poverty,* 385–86; emphasis in original. The quote given here is a citation from an 1851 text by Thomas Plint, *Crime in England, Its Relation, Character, and Extent, as Developed from 1801 to 1848.*

14. Mayhew, *London Labour,* 1:22. Paul Q. Hirst, in a useful summary of classical Marxist writing on crime and the law, concludes that Marx and Engels "were far from moralizing with the bourgeoisie about the conditions which produced criminality, which filled the ranks of the criminal classes with recruits. They demonstrated that it was the very capitalist system, which the bourgeoisie put forward as a model of a just and virtuous society, that produced these threats to its own 'order,' 'respectability' and 'property.'" See Hirst, "Marx and Engels on Law, Crime and Morality," in *Critical Criminology,* ed. Ian Taylor, Paul Walton, and Jock Young (London: Routledge and Kegan Paul, 1975), 203–32.

15. The distinction between Left and Right solutions can still be difficult to maintain in practice. The *Red Republican,* an ultra-Chartist newspaper of the period which published the first English translation of *The Communist Manifesto* in November 1850, also ran an article the previous month by Howard Morton on "The Democratic and Social Republic" (12 October 1850), which outlined how the country would be transformed after acceptance of the People's Charter. When Morton writes about the slums of the cities, however, the solution seems momentarily indistinguishable from that of moralizing reformers: as houses in the city are left vacant by an exodus to the countryside, they "will be pulled down; and wide, clean, well-ventilated streets will take the place of the present filthy holes and corners, the fitting habitus for disease and crime" (132).

16. Mayhew organized a tailors' meeting after the *Chronicle* had censored a report noting the connection between free trade and the depression of wages, and afterwards published an article praising the firm of H. J. and D. Nicholl who had exemplified some of the worst practices of the "sweating system" of tailoring. Mayhew's speech to the meeting noted the irony of "conferring civic honours and dignities upon a person whose mode of dealing is a disgrace and an abomination," and proclaimed that "we should learn to look upon these men as the greatest enemies to the country—as the really 'dangerous classes.'" See E. P. Thompson, "Mayhew and the *Morning Chronicle,*" in *The Unknown Mayhew,* ed. Eileen Yeo and E. P. Thompson (New York: Pantheon, 1971),11–50, for an account of these events.

17. See Deborah Epstein Nord, "The Social Explorer as Anthropologist," in *Visions of the Modern City: Essays in History, Art, and Literature,* ed. William Sharpe and Leonard Wallock (Baltimore: Johns Hopkins University Press, 1987), 118–30; and Humpherys, *Travels,* especially chapter 6.

18. Humpherys, *Travels,* 40; 185–86.

19. Mayhew, *London Labour,* 1:43–46; 1:39–40; emphasis in original.

20. Charles Reith, *British Police and the Democratic Ideal* (London: Oxford University Press, 1943), 3; 12

21. Leon Radzinowicz, *A History of English Criminal Law* (London: Stevens and Stevens, 1968), 4:283.

22. See Robert Reiner, *The Politics of the Police* (Brighton: Wheatsheaf Books, 1985), 37.

23. Cited in Randall McGowen, "Getting to Know the Criminal Class in Nineteenth-Century England," *Nineteenth-Century Contexts* 14:1 (1990), 46; emphasis in original.

24. Sir William Mildmay, cited in Clive Emsley, *Policing and Its Context, 1750–1850* (New York: Schocken Books, 1983), 21.

25. Radzinowicz, *English Criminal Law*, 4:164.

26. Emsley, *Policing*, 128.

27. "The Chartists and Universal Suffrage," *Blackwood's Edinburgh Magazine* 46:287 (September 1839), 293.

28. For more on the Popay scandal, see James Winter, *London's Teeming Streets, 1830–1914* (London: Routledge, 1993), 50–52, and Ian Ousby, *Bloodhounds of Heaven: The Detective in English Fiction from Godwin to Doyle* (Cambridge: Harvard University Press, 1976), 63–64.

29. Radzinowicz, *English Criminal Law*, 4:188–89.

30. Stuart Hall, Chas Critcher, Tony Jefferson, John Clarke, and Brian Roberts, *Policing the Crisis: Mugging, the State and Law and Order* (London: Macmillan, 1978), 48. The best empirical account of the police's conflicted role in nineteenth-century Britain is Robert Storch's "The Plague of Blue Locusts: Police Reform and Popular Resistance in Northern England, 1840–57," *International Review of Social History* 20:1 (1975), 61–90.

31. Phil Cohen, "Policing the Working-Class City," in *Crime and Society: Readings in History and Theory,* ed. Mike Fitzgerald, Gregor McLennan, and Jennie Pawson (London: Routledge/Open University, 1981), 125. See Raymond Williams, *Marxism and Literature* (Oxford: Oxford University Press, 1977), 83–89.

32. Cohen, "Policing," 125. Besides the influence of Gramsci, there are clear echoes here of Louis Althusser's famous distinction between "ideological" and "repressive" state apparatuses, in "Ideology and Ideological State Apparatuses (Notes towards an Investigation)." See Althusser, *Lenin and Philosophy,* trans. Ben Brewster (New York: Monthly Review Press, 1971), 127–86.

33. Cohen, "Policing," 126–28.

34. Mayhew, *London Labour* 1:101.

35. See Thomas Carlyle, "Chartism," in *Critical and Miscellaneous Essays* (New York: Scribner's, 1899), 4:118–204. The best discussion of these "condition of England" novels can be found in Catherine Gallagher, *The Industrial Reformation of English Fiction, 1832–1867* (Chicago: University of Chicago Press, 1985), and Joseph W. Childers, *Novel Possibilities: Fiction and the Formation of Early Victorian Culture* (Philadelphia: University of Pennsylvania Press, 1995).

36. In his Introduction to the Penguin *Dombey and Son* (Harmondsworth: Penguin, 1970), Raymond Williams comments on the function of 1848 as a pivot in British fiction, and of this novel as a pivot in Dickens's work. He also usefully characterizes the impulses which underlie the earlier and later phases of that work, noting that the former deploys society as "a background against which the drama of personal virtues and vices in enacted," while in the latter work "society is the creator of virtues and vices; its active relationships and institutions at once generating and controlling, or failing to control, what in the earlier mode of analysis could be seen as faults of the soul" (16).

37. These changing attitudes are elaborated in Philip Collins, *Dickens and Crime* (Bloomington: Indiana University Press, 1968), 220–48.

38. Dickens, *Barnaby Rudge* (Harmondsworth: Penguin, 1986), 453.

39. In that novel, two anonymous officers investigate a case of assault by doing "pretty much what I had heard and read of like authorities doing in such cases. They took up several obviously wrong people, and they ran their heads very hard against wrong ideas, and persisted in trying to fit the circumstances to the ideas, instead of trying to extract ideas from the circumstances. Also, they stood about the door of the Jolly Bargeman . . . and they had a mysterious manner of taking their drink, that was almost as good as taking a culprit. But not quite, for they never did it." Dickens, *Great Expectations* (Harmondsworth: Penguin, 1965), 149.

40. Dickens, "The Detective Police," collected in *The Uncommercial Traveller and Reprinted Pieces* (Oxford: Oxford University Press, 1958), 485; originally in *Household Words*, 27 July 1850.

41. Humphry House, for example, notes Dickens's "most fanatical devotion to the Metropolitan Police," and hypothesizes that it might arise from the novelist's rejection of more individualistic schemes for self-improvement, against which he reacted (like others of the period) by favoring instead a "highly concentrated central power" as the cure for social problems. See *The Dickens World* (Oxford: Oxford University Press, 1960), 201. An alternative account of his relationship with the London detectives, which stresses that any exaggeration of their abilities proceeded from Field rather than Dickens, is offered by William Long in "The 'Singler Stories' of Inspector Field," *The Dickensian* 83:3 (1987) 149–62.

42. Kellow Chesney, *The Victorian Underworld* (London: Penguin, 1972), 124.

43. Dickens directly links journalists and the police in an 1869 essay called "On an Amateur Beat," in which he states that "it is my habit to regard my walk as my beat, and myself as a higher sort of police-constable doing duty on the same." *The Uncommercial Traveller*, 345.

44. See McGowen, "Getting to Know the Criminal Class," 33–54.

45. The above summary is indebted to McGowen, 35–40.

46. See Winter, *London's Teeming Streets*, 62–63. For a useful discussion of the debates over garotting, see Jennifer Davis, "The London Garotting Panic of 1862: A Moral Panic and the Creation of a Criminal Class in Mid-Victorian England," in *Crime and the Law: The Social History of Crime in Western Europe since 1500*, ed. V. A. C. Gatrell et al. (London: Europa, 1980), 190–213.

47. Cited in McGowen, "Getting to Know the Criminal Class," 47.

48. Dickens, "The Ruffian," in *The Uncommercial Traveller*, 302; originally in *All the Year Round*, 10 October 1868. This is the famous essay in which Dickens narrates his dogged insistence on having a young girl prosecuted for using bad language in public; it ends, more ominously, by lamenting that the people have learned not to take the law into their own hands, given the police's "absurd" and "inefficient" attempts to deal with "The Ruffian."

49. For more on this scheme, see F. S. Schwarzbach, *Dickens and the City* (London: Athlone Press, 1979), 128–29. The site they ultimately settled on was in Bermondsey, very close to Jacob's Island, although the project apparently collapsed because they had problems in evicting the principal tenant.

50. Dickens, *Bleak House* (Harmondsworth: Penguin, 1971), 364.

51. D. A. Miller, *The Novel and the Police* (Berkeley: University of California Press, 1988), 76–77; emphasis in original.

52. Fredric Jameson, *The Political Unconscious: Narrative as a Socially Symbolic Act* (Ithaca: Cornell University Press, 1981), 91; emphasis in original.

53. *Illustrated London News* (1853); this and other contemporary reviews are reprinted in *Bleak House: A Casebook*, ed. A. E. Dyson (London: Macmillan, 1969), 49–91.

54. *Eclectic Review*, reprinted in Dyson, 81–86.

55. The theme of contagion is discussed at some length by Jonathan Arac in *Commissioned Spirits: The Shaping of Social Motion in Dickens, Carlyle, Melville, and Hawthorne* (New Brunswick: Rutgers University Press, 1976), chapter 6, and by Deborah Epstein Nord in *Walking the Victorian Streets: Women, Representation, and the City* (Ithaca: Cornell University Press, 1995), 96–111.

56. See John Butt and Kathleen Tillotson, "The Topicality of *Bleak House*," in *Dickens at Work* (London: Methuen, 1957), 177–200.

57. See Schwarzbach, *Dickens and the City*, 125–27.

58. Terry Eagleton, *Criticism and Ideology* (London: Verso, 1978), 129.

59. His job was to clear a passage through the filth for wealthy pedestrians. As such, it is not surprising that "[h]omely filth begrimes him, homely parasites devour him, homely sores are in him, homely rags are on him: native ignorance, the growth of English soil and climate, sinks his immortal nature lower than the beasts that perish" (696).

60. Bruce Robbins, "Telescopic Philanthropy: Professionalism and Responsibility in *Bleak House*," in *Nation and Narration*, ed. Homi Bhabha (London: Routledge, 1990), 222.

61. John Bender, *Imagining the Penitentiary: Fiction and the Architecture of Mind in Eighteenth-Century England* (Chicago: University of Chicago Press, 1979).

62. See Louis Althusser, "Ideology and Ideological State Apparatuses," 127–86.

63. These reviews are reprinted in Dyson, *Casebook*, pages 70, 82, and 79 respectively. It is worth recalling at this point that Dickens's original title for the novel was *Tom-all-Alone's*, after which he experimented with a number of titles involving the phrase "East Wind." For a note on the book's title, see *Bleak House*, 936–37.

64. See Dyson, 88.

65. I am indebted to H. Philip Bolton, "*Bleak House* and the Playhouse," *Dickens Studies Annual* (New York: AMS Press, 1983), 81–116, for the discussion of play versions of the novel in this paragraph.

66. The play script of Lander's *Bleak House; or Poor Jo* (1876) appears in *English and American Drama of the Nineteenth Century*, ed. Allardyce Nicoll and George Freedley (New York: Readex Microprint, 1965–1971).

## 4. "Lords of the Street, and Terrors of the Way"

1. Franco Moretti, *Atlas of the European Novel, 1800–1900* (London: Verso, 1998), 134.

2. Arthur Conan Doyle, "The Man with the Twisted Lip," in *The Penguin Complete Adventures of Sherlock Holmes* (Harmondsworth: Penguin, 1981), 230.

3. In "The Red-Headed League," for example, Holmes suspects John Clay on the basis that he agrees to work as assistant to a pawnbroker at half-wages.

4. See Audrey Jaffe, "Detecting the Beggar: Arthur Conan Doyle, Henry Mayhew, and 'The Man with the Twisted Lip,'" in *Representations* 31 (summer 1990), 97–99.

5. Martin J. Wiener, *Reconstructing the Criminal: Culture, Law and Policy in England, 1830–1914* (Cambridge: Cambridge University Press, 1990), 244.

6. The quoted phrase in the chapter title is drawn from Samuel Johnson, "London: A Poem. In Imitation of the Third Satire of Juvenal" (1738):

> Yet ev'n these Heroes, mischeviously gay,
> Lords of the Street, and Terrors of the Way;
> Flush'd as they are with folly, Youth and Wine,
> Their prudent Insults to the Poor confine.

7. This is not to suggest that there had been no such critiques earlier in the century. As Alexander Welsh shows in *The City of Dickens* (Oxford: Clarendon, 1971), Dickens for one was ambivalent about charity (as opposed to sanitary reform or education) as a way of improving the life of the poor (92–100). But his reservations are advanced in the context of a larger attack on the thinking behind the New Poor Law, of course, whereas the new critiques of the 1870s seem both more uncompromising and also reluctant to imagine alternatives outside of a narrow economism which in many ways replicated the Benthamite strains of the Poor Law.

8. Robert Louis Stevenson, *Doctor Jekyll and Mr. Hyde, and Other Stories* (Harmondsworth: Penguin, 1979), 56.

9. Oscar Wilde, *The Picture of Dorian Gray* (New York: W. W. Norton, 1988), 36.

10. Matthew Arnold, *Culture and Anarchy* (New Haven: Yale University Press, 1994), 52.

11. I have mainly drawn on Gareth Stedman Jones, *Outcast London: A Study in the Relationship between Classes in Victorian Society* (Oxford: Clarendon Press, 1971), chapter 13, for the summary of events described in this paragraph.

12. Brooke Lambert, *East End Pauperism* (1868), cited in Stedman Jones, *Outcast London*, 247.

13. Cited in *Outcast London*, 197; emphasis added. For more on the failure of suburban resettlement programs, see Lewis Mumford, *The Culture of Cities* (New York: Harcourt, Brace and Company, 1938), 176–78.

14. Dickens, "On Duty with Inspector Field," in *The Uncommercial Traveller and Reprinted Pieces* (Oxford: Oxford University Press, 1958), 518.

15. See J. A. Yelling, *Slums and Slum Clearance in Victorian London* (London: Allen and Unwin, 1986), 12–13.

16. George R. Sims, *How the Poor Live* (first published serially in 1883, and as a book in 1889); cited in *Into Unknown England, 1866–1913: Selections from the Social Explorers*, ed. Peter Keating (Manchester: Manchester University Press, 1976), 65.

17. Andrew Mearns, "The Bitter Cry of Outcast London" (first published as an anonymous pamphlet in 1883); cited in Keating, *Into Unknown England*, 92.

18. Judith Walkowitz, *City of Dreadful Delight: Narratives of Sexual Danger in Late Victorian London* (London: Virago, 1992), 11.

19. James Greenwood, "A Night in the Workhouse," in Keating, *Into Unknown England*, 33–54.

20. For insightful discussions of Malvery and London, see Judith Walkowitz, "The Indian Woman, the Flower Girl, and the Jew: Photojournalism in Edwardian London," *Victorian Studies* 42:1 (autumn 1999–2000), 3–46, and Richard Stein, "London's London: Photographing Poverty in *The People of the Abyss*," *Nineteenth-Century Contexts* 22:4 (2001), 587–629.

21. Ernest Mandel, *Delightful Murder: A Social History of the Crime Novel* (London: Pluto Press, 1984), 1 and 8–9.

22. Marie-Christine Leps, *Apprehending the Criminal: The Production of Deviance in Nineteenth-Century Discourse* (Durham: Duke University Press, 1992), 207.

23. In a letter to John Paul Bocock, Stevenson explicitly denied that there was an erotic component to Jekyll's desires or Hyde's crimes: "The harm was in Jekyll," he wrote, "because he was a hypocrite—not because he was fond of women; he says so himself; but people are so filled full of folly and inverted lust, that they can think of nothing but sexuality. The hypocrite let out the beast Hyde—who is no more sensual than another, but who is the essence of cruelty and malice, and selfishness and cowardice." Reprinted in *Robert Louis Stevenson: The Critical Heritage*, ed. Paul Maixner (London: Routledge and Kegan Paul, 1981), 231.

24. Stevenson, *Dr. Jekyll and Mr. Hyde*, 49. Stevenson insisted, in a fascinating exchange of letters with F. W. H. Myers, that Hyde bought the "good picture." Myers had originally written to Stevenson with suggestions for corrections to the text: among these, he felt strongly that Hyde would not have killed Sir Danvers Carew, that Jekyll should commit suicide, and that Hyde should have no knowledge of the arts, and so would not have bought a painting. See Maixner, ed., *The Critical Heritage*, 212–22.

25. Stephen D. Arata, *Fictions of Loss in the Victorian Fin de Siecle* (Cambridge: Cambridge University Press, 1996), 34. For more on "criminal man," see Leps, *Apprehending the Criminal*, chapters 1–3.

26. Max Nordau, *Degeneration* (1893), cited in Alan Sinfield, *The Wilde Century: Effeminacy, Oscar Wilde and the Queer Moment* (New York: Columbia University Press, 1994), 94.

27. Arata, *Fictions of Loss*, 35. He also suggestively notes that the original figure of the murder victim in Stevenson's manuscript—the "anoemically pale" and "incurable cad," Mr. Lemsome—equated more closely to the classical archetype of the decadent aristocrat (38).

28. For a useful analysis of linguistic usage as a problematic guarantor of subjective identity in this text, see Peter K. Garrett, "Cries and Voices: Reading *Jekyll and Hyde*," in *Doctor Jekyll and Mr. Hyde after One Hundred Years*, ed. William Veeder and Gordon Hirsch (Chicago: University of Chicago Press, 1988), 59–72.

29. Stevenson, *Jekyll and Hyde*, 66. The strain of credulity which this theory demands is not lost on Utterson himself, who claims simply that "it is plain and natural, hangs well together and delivers us from all exorbitant alarms." Even after this point, he advances three separate hypotheses: that Hyde has killed Jekyll; that Hyde has killed himself; and that Jekyll has killed Hyde and fled.

30. See Walkowitz, *City of Dreadful Delight*, 196 and 206–7. W. T. Stead's article on "Murder and More to Follow," which appeared in the *Pall Mall Gazette* in September 1888, referred to the Ripper as "a Mr. Hyde of Humanity," as well as a "plebeian Marquis de Sade at large in Whitechapel."

31. *East London Advertiser* (*ELA*), 8 September and 6 October 1888.

32. *Times*, 23 January 1886, cited in Maixner, ed., *The Critical Heritage*, 203–5.

33. See Donald Rumbelow, *The Complete Jack the Ripper* (Harmondsworth: Penguin, 1988), 113.

34. "Notes of the Week," *Palace Journal*, 19 September 1888.

35. Detective Inspector Henry Moore, cited in Martin Howells and Keith Skinner, *The Ripper Legacy: The Life and Death of Jack the Ripper* (London: Sphere Books, 1987), 75.

36. *Times*, 19 September 1888. See Leps, *Apprehending the Criminal*, 122–27, for a useful analysis of this editorial, and other notable examples of the coverage of the murders by the West End press.

37. Jerry White, *Rothschild Buildings* (1980), cited in William J. Fishman, *East End 1888: Life in a London Borough among the Labouring Poor* (Philadelphia: Temple University Press, 1988), 225.

38. *East London Organiser*, 15 September 1888.

39. Cited in Howells and Skinner, *The Ripper Legacy*, 53.

40. *ELA*, 6 October 1888. These suspicions continue to exist today, of course. Among recent conspiracy theories, pride of place has to go to Stephen Knight, who wove an elaborate alliance of politicians, freemasons, and royal doctors engaged in covering up the illicit activities of Prince Albert Victor in his *Jack the Ripper: The Final Solution* (London: Harrap, 1976).

41. According to Christopher Frayling, high-profile suspects included Samuel Barnett, the signwriter for General Booth of the Salvation Army, and trade unionist John Burns, who led the victorious dock strike the year following the Ripper murders. See "The House That Jack Built: Some Stereotypes of the Rapist in Popular Culture," in *Rape*, ed. Sylvia Tomaselli and Roy Porter (Oxford: Basil Blackwell, 1986), 201.

42. Reported in *ELA*, 17 November and 8 and 15 September 1888.

43. Walkowitz, *City of Dreadful Delight*, 212.

44. *Justice*, cited in Fishman, *East End 1888*, 226; Shaw, "Blood Money to Whitechapel," reprinted in *Agitations: Letters to the Press, 1875–1950* (New York: Frederick Ungar, 1985), 10–11.

45. Martin Wiener, *Reconstructing the Criminal*, 244.

46. *The Artist as Critic: Critical Writings of Oscar Wilde*, ed. Richard Ellmann (Chicago: University of Chicago Press, 1969), 256; emphasis in original.

47. This is a position that is shared by the majority of utopian novels of the period, including Edward Bellamy's *Looking Backward* (1889), Morris's *News from Nowhere* (1890), and Charlotte Perkins Gilman's *Herland* (1915).

48. Cited in Philippe Jullian, *Oscar Wilde* (London: Constable, 1969), 145–46.

49. Reported by Richard Ellmann in *Oscar Wilde* (London: Hamish Hamilton, 1987), 243.

50. See Ellmann, *Oscar Wilde*, 273 and 268.

51. Wilde himself thought that he more closely resembled the painter Basil Hallward, although he acknowledged that the world thought of him as Wotton. See Ellman, *Oscar Wilde*, 301.

52. Neil Bartlett, *Who Was That Man? A Present for Mr. Oscar Wilde* (London: Serpent's Tail, 1988), 195–96.

53. Sinfield, *The Wilde Century*, 103.

54. *Scots Observer*, 5 July 1890; Wilde's reply, 9 July. Both are reprinted in the Norton edition of *Dorian Gray* I am using here, 346–47.

55. See H. Montgomery Hyde, *Famous Trials: Oscar Wilde* (Harmondsworth: Penguin, 1962), 203 and 250. In this sense, it seems fitting that the charges against Wilde centrally feature the location of each offense: "Do you find the prisoner at the bar guilty

of an act of gross indecency with Charles Parker at the Savoy Hotel, . . . of a similar offence at St. James's Place, . . . with Alfred Wood at Tite Street?" and so on (269–70).

56. *Dorian Gray,* 110. Sure enough, Colin Wilson reports on a new theory in his introduction to Rumbelow's *Complete Jack the Ripper:* that the Ripper was Wilde's onetime friend and housemate Frank Miles, on whom the character of Dorian was supposedly based; and "that Wilde knew Miles to be Jack the Ripper, and dropped clues about it in the novel—for example, Dorian's murder of the painter Basil Hallward with a knife" (13–14).

57. Bartlett, *Who Was That Man?* 144. He goes on to suggest that Dorian's opium den might be Tiger Bay in Limehouse, which had already been described by Greenwood in the *Daily Telegraph,* and by Richard Rowe in *Found in the Streets* (1880); the implication, of course, is that Wilde had simply "borrowed the details from another book."

58. Cited in Ellmann, *Oscar Wilde,* 243.

59. To Leonard Smithers, 19 October 1897. In *The Letters of Oscar Wilde,* ed. Rupert Hart-Davis (New York: Harcourt, Brace, 1962), 663.

60. These pursuits, modeled after those of Des Esseintes in Huysmans's *A Rebours,* are listed in chapter 11 of the novel, which immediately moves into a catalog of Gray's rumored transgressions.

61. A Cynic [Leslie Stephen], "The Decay of Murder" (1869), and the *Spectator* on "The Fenayrou Trial" (1882); both cited in Martin Wiener, *Reconstructing the Criminal,* 224–25.

62. Alan Sinfield, *The Wilde Century,* 100.

63. Wilde, "Pen Pencil Poison," in Ellmann, ed., *The Artist as Critic,* 321.

64. Regenia Gagnier, *Idylls of the Marketplace: Oscar Wilde and the Victorian Public* (Stanford: Stanford University Press, 1986), 34; Ellmann, *Oscar Wilde,* 282–83.

65. See Wilde, "The Decay of Lying," in Ellmann, ed., *The Artist as Critic,* 293; 308.

66. Wilde to the editor of the *St. James's Gazette* (26 June 1890), in *Dorian Gray,* 339.

## 5. Into Darkest London, and Back Again

1. Oscar Wilde, "The Decay of Lying," in *The Artist as Critic: Critical Writings of Oscar Wilde,* ed. Richard Ellmann (Chicago: University of Chicago Press, 1969), 296.

2. Wilde, "The Critic as Artist," in Ellman, ed., *The Artist as Critic,* 349; 385–86.

3. "The Decay of Lying," 300.

4. My account here is based on *A Brief History of the Beaumont Trust,* ed. W. Spencer Beaumont (London: Charles and Edwin Layton, 1887), 37–43, which reprints the Trust's original appeal from January 1883. Deborah Weiner notes similar appeals addressed to the "Merchants of London," promoting the Palace as an "advantageous investment . . . of most extraordinary and securely profitable description"; see her essay on "The People's Palace: An Image for East London in the 1880s," in *Metropolis London: Histories and Representations since 1800,* ed. David Feldman and Gareth Stedman Jones (London: Routledge, 1989), 40–55.

5. Queen Mary and Westfield College now stands on the site of the original Palace.

6. Walter Besant, *All Sorts and Conditions of Men: An Impossible Story* (London: Chatto and Windus, 1902), 65.

7. Wilde, letter to Sir Edmund Currie, 22 February 1886, in *More Letters of Oscar Wilde,* ed. Rupert Hart-Davis (New York: The Vanguard Press, 1985), 62.

8. Richard Ellmann notes Wilde's ambitions in *Oscar Wilde* (London: Hamish Hamilton, 1987), 104.

9. See, for example, "A Few Maxims for the Instruction of the Over-Educated," in *The Complete Works of Oscar Wilde* (London: Collins, 1948), 1203–4. While touring America, Wilde's lectures routinely concerned the pre-Raphaelite movement in England, as a model of handicraft art which might be encouraged in schools.

10. Besant, writing in the *Contemporary Review,* February 1887.

11. *Palace Journal,* 16 January 1889; *Autobiography of Sir Walter Besant* (New York: Dodd Mead and Co., 1902), 245.

12. Besant, *The Art of Fiction: A Lecture* (London: Chatto and Windus, 1884), 15.

13. The point is driven home through the characterization of the Stepney Advanced Club, to which Dick Coppin belongs: its members "were mostly young men, but there was a sprinkling among them of grizzled beards who remembered '48 and the dreams of Chartism. They had got by this time pretty well all they clamoured for in their bygone days. . . . Nevertheless, the habit of demanding remained, because the reformer is like the daughter of the horse-leech, and still cries for more" (250). Its chairman—who "having been all his life an Irreconcilable, . . . was suspected of being a Socialist, and was certainly a Red Republican"—is converted to Harry's politics of need, and is finally enshrined as one of the trustees of the Palace of Delight.

14. Reported in the *East London Advertiser* (*ELA*), 26 February 1887.

15. *Pall Mall Gazette,* 27 May and 24 June 1885.

16. See *Autobiography of Sir Walter Besant,* 244. The People's Palace subscription replies are in the archives of Queen Mary and Westfield College.

17. *Daily News,* 12 January 1886. Wilde makes much the same point in chapter 1 of *Dorian Gray,* when Lord Henry imagines a luncheon at Aunt Agatha's in which "[e]ach class would have preached the importance of those virtues, for whose exercise there was no necessity in their own lives. The rich would have spoken on the value of thrift, and the idle grown eloquent over the dignity of labour" (16).

18. E. J. C., "The People's Palace Exposure," *ELA,* 29 September 1888.

19. "Notes of the Week," *Palace Journal* 3:58 (19 December 1888).

20. Besant, "The People's Palace," *North American Review* 147 (1888), 59.

21. See Gareth Stedman Jones, *Outcast London: A Study in the Relationship between Classes in Victorian Society* (Oxford: Clarendon Press, 1971), 10.

22. Bernard Shaw, "Blood Money to Whitechapel" (letter to the *Star,* 24 September 1888), reprinted in *Agitations: Letters to the Press, 1875–1950* (New York: Frederick Ungar, 1985), 10–11.

23. The best account of Harkness's life can be found in J. M. Rignall, "Margaret Harkness and the Socialist Novel," in H. Gustav Klaus, *The Socialist Novel in Britain: Towards the Recovery of a Tradition* (New York: St. Martin's Press, 1982), 45–66.

24. "John Law" (Margaret Harkness), *Out of Work* (London: Merlin Press, 1990), 39.

25. This was mainly the orientation of the mainstream press; local papers were somewhat more critical. The *East London Observer,* for example, included among its coverage of the Palace opening a report of an "Alleged Serious Assault by a Police Constable," 17 July and 7 August 1886.

26. Harkness/Law, *A City Girl* (New York: Garland, 1984), 15–17.

27. *A City Girl,* 179. Harkness's own hesitations about the Salvation Army's effective-ness, especially when set against rival socialist influences, seem foregrounded in a re-vealing exchange between the doubting Arthur and Captain Lobe: "How long have you been in the Salvation Army?" asks the former, to which Lobe replies, "Two years. I joined it because I found less hypocrisy in it than in other religions, and I shall leave it directly I find anything better" (174).

28. John L. Kijinski, "Ethnography in the East End: Native Customs and Colonial So-lutions in *A Child of the Jago,*" *English Literature in Transition* 37:4 (1994), 490–501.

29. See Victor Bailey, " 'In Darkest England and the Way Out': The Salvation Army, So-cial Reform and the Labour Movement, 1885–1910," *International Review of Social History* 29: 2 (1984), 133–71.

30. Edward Said, *Orientalism* (New York: Vintage, 1979), 3.

31. Terry Eagleton, "Pretty Much like Ourselves," *London Review of Books,* 4 September 1997, 6–7.

32. See Deborah Epstein Nord, "The Social Explorer as Anthropologist," in Sharpe and Wallock, eds., *Visions of the Modern City,* 118–30.

33. William Booth, *In Darkest England and the Way Out,* cited in Asa Briggs, *Victorian Cities* (New York: Harper and Row, 1965), 325.

34. Kijinski, "Ethnography in the East End," 495; emphasis in original.

35. Cited in Briggs, *Victorian Cities,* 326; emphasis in original.

36. Rudyard Kipling, "The Ballad of Badalia Herodsfoot," in *Working-Class Stories of the 1890s,* ed. P. J. Keating (London: Routledge and Kegan Paul, 1971), 8–28. The best account of Kipling's career during this period is in P. J. Keating, *The Working Classes in Victorian Fiction* (New York: Barnes and Noble, 1971), 139–66.

37. Raymond Williams, *The Country and the City,* 226.

38. (Arthur Morrison), "Notes of the Week," *Palace Journal,* 7 August 1889, 146.

39. One of Morrison's earliest published stories, "Lizerunt," seems for example to be al-most a revision of "Badalia Herodsfoot," containing many of the same themes and incidents.

40. Arthur Morrison, "Whitechapel," *Palace Journal,* 24 April 1889, 1022–23. The other entries in "Cockney Corners" were "On Blackwall Pier" (8 May 1889) and "Christ-mas Eve in the Streets" (25 December 1889).

41. H. D. Traill, "The New Realism," *Fortnightly Review* 67 (January 1897).

42. Arthur Morrison, "What Is a Realist?" *The New Review* 16:94 (March 1897), 326–36. The emphasis on Morrison's authorial distance from his subjects was echoed by a short article in *Academy* on his methods of composition: "Hither, then, Mr. Mor-rison came day after day for more than eighteen months, learning every inch of the half-dozen streets—now improved off the face of the earth—which make up the Jago, haunting the public-houses, sitting with the people in their homes, and even trying in his own person what it feels like to earn a living by making match-boxes." See "The Methods of Mr. Morrison," *Academy* 50 (12 December 1896).

43. P. J. Keating, "Biographical Study," in Arthur Morrison, *A Child of the Jago* (Wood-bridge: Boydell Press, 1982), 11–36.

44. Keating, *Working Classes in Victorian Fiction,* 114.

45. See Pamela Fox, *Class Fictions: Shame and Resistance in the British Working-Class Novel, 1890–1945* (Durham: Duke University Press, 1994), 109–18.

46. See, for example, Kijinski, "Ethnography in the East End"; and Gill Davies, "Foreign Bodies: Images of the London Working-Class at the End of the Nineteenth Century," *Literature and History* 14:1 (spring 1988), 64–79.

47. Morrison resigned in July 1890, as the Draper's Company was assuming control of the Palace. The following year, he published "A Street," in which he depicted the monotonies of life in a typical East London street, and concluded, "Where in the East-end lies this street? Everywhere; our hundred and fifty yards is only a fragment, only a turn in the maze. . . . A Palace of Delight was once set in the midst of this street, but Commissioners brandished their pens over it and it became a Polytechnic Institution, whereat all the young men lodgers might crowd to carry into evening the dock and shipyard work of the day, and learn the more efficiently to fight with each other for the eternally desired bread and beer and boots. There is no delight in this street." Morrison, "A Street," *MacMillan's Magazine* 64 (October 1891), 460–63.

48. (H. G. Wells), "A Slum Novel," *Saturday Review,* 28 November 1896, 573.

49. Dick Hebdige, *Subculture: The Meaning of Style* (London: Methuen, 1979), 154, 75.

## Conclusion

1. Michel Foucault, *Discipline and Punish: The Birth of the Prison,* trans. Alan Sheridan (New York: Vintage, 1977), 69.

2. Ernest Mandel, *Delightful Murder: A Social History of the Crime Novel* (London: Pluto Press, 1984), 1.

3. Masterman's experience of the settlement movement was not entirely positive, which may account in part for his conversion to large-scale government intervention as the best solution for London's social problems. As he wrote in 1901, "The Universities and the cultured classes, as a whole, care little about the matter. The wave of enthusiasm which created the modern settlement has ceased to advance; the buildings remain and a few energetic toilers, and the memory of a great hope. . . . I cannot believe that this is the machinery destined to bridge the ever-widening gulf between class and class, and to initiate the new heavens and the new earth." *The Heart of the Empire: Discussions of Problems of Modern City Life in England* (Brighton: Harvester Press, 1973), 35.

4. William Beveridge, "Unemployment in London" (1905), cited in Standish Meacham, *Toynbee Hall and Social Reform, 1880–1914: The Search for Community* (New Haven: Yale University Press, 1987), 150. I have discussed the origins of Welfare State thinking, and its relationship to late-Victorian debates about poverty and crime, in "Victorian Continuities: Early British Sociology and the Welfare of the State," in *Disciplinarity at the Fin de Siecle,* ed. Amanda Anderson and Joseph Valente (Princeton: Princeton University Press, 2002), 261–80.

5. Stuart Hall and Bill Schwarz, "State and Society, 1880–1930," in Stuart Hall, *The Hard Road to Renewal: Thatcherism and the Crisis of the Left* (London: Verso, 1998), 110.

6. Arthur Harding recounted his life in a series of interviews with Raphael Samuel in the 1970s. See *East End Underworld: Chapters in the Life of Arthur Harding,* ed. Raphael Samuel (London: Routledge and Kegan Paul, 1981), 262–64. This strain of working-class conservatism, and its seemingly arbitrary basis, is also described in Margaret Harkness's *A City Girl* (New York: Garland, 1984), in which the ambitious caretaker George boasts of having "given his vote to a Conservative candidate who

had canvassed the Buildings; for the good reason that a drive to the poll had suited him better than a walk on the day of the election. Which party had 'the rights of it' he did not pretend to know; but the Conservatives had the most money, so it was best not to offend them, he used to say" (32).

7. Iain Sinclair has highlighted the case of the notorious Kray twins, postwar East End mobsters who were also paid-up members of the Bethnal Green Conservative Association; according to Sinclair, their ruthless commitment to free-market capitalism made Ronnie and Reg Kray in effect Thatcherites *avant la lettre*. See his *Lights Out for the Territory: Nine Excursions into the Secret History of London* (London: Granta Books, 1997), 72.

8. Gareth Stedman Jones, "Working-Class Culture and Working-Class Politics in London, 1870–1900: Notes on the Remaking of a Working Class," in *Languages of Class: Studies in English Working Class History, 1832–1982* (Cambridge: Cambridge University Press, 1983), 225; emphasis in original.

9. Arthur Harding, too, recalls popular support for the army during the Boer War, and sees it as contributing to the phenomenon of working-class Toryism, noting that "[t]he Conservatives had a powerful party just before 1900 and for a few years after. They stood for law and order. They were powerful enough to send a vast army to South Africa, and protected the rights of the landowners and the diamond dealers" (263). "Tommy Atkins" and "Rule Britannia" formed part of his busking repertoire as a child during the Boer War (48).

10. One notable early example would be the Bloomsbury Group's use of the low/middle/highbrow classification. As Francis Mulhern argues in the case of Virginia Woolf, her purpose "was to affirm the integrity and mutuality of 'highbrow' and 'lowbrow' as cultural types, in the face of an intruding third type, the 'middlebrow'. . . . Highbrows 'needed' and 'honoured' lowbrows, each group finding in the other the indispensable complement of their own genius." See Mulhern, *Culture/Metaculture* (London: Routledge, 2000), 29.

# Index

# Victorian Literature and Culture Series